# GREAT AMERICAN

# COWBOY STORIES

LYONS PRESS CLASSICS

# GREAT
# AMERICAN
# COWBOY
# STORIES

EDITED BY
## MICHAEL McCOY

LYONS
PRESS

GUILFORD
CONNECTICUT

An imprint of The Rowman & Littlefield Publishing Group, Inc.
4501 Forbes Blvd., Ste. 200
Lanham, MD 20706
www.rowman.com

Distributed by NATIONAL BOOK NETWORK

British Library Cataloguing in Publication Information available

**Library of Congress Cataloging-in-Publication Data available**
ISBN 978-1-4930-4210-4 (paperback)
ISBN 978-1-4930-4212-8 (e-book)

♾™ The paper used in this publication meets the minimum requirements
of American National Standard for Information Sciences—Permanence of
Paper for Printed Library Materials, ANSI/NISO Z39.48-1992.

*To windy, wild Wyoming,*
*breeding ground of cowboys and other independent souls*

# ACKNOWLEDGMENTS

Extremely helpful to me in my initial research for this project was the staff of the American Heritage Center at my alma mater, the University of Wyoming. A big thank you goes out to those folks, as well as to the Teton County Library in Jackson, Wyoming, and the Valley of the Tetons Library in Victor, Idaho. The biggest thank you of all, however, is reserved for the men and women who wrote these stories late in the nineteenth century and early in the twentieth century. *Vayan con Dios, vaqueros.*

# CONTENTS

# INTRODUCTION

I'm a major-league fan of both baseball and apple pie, yet I maintain that there's nothing more American than a good cowboy story. Thanks partly to the true nature of the late-nineteenth-century cowpuncher, and thanks in part to the way we'd like to think he was—an image portrayed and promoted by some of the yarns in this book and elsewhere, and then greatly embellished by Hollywood—cowboys symbolize the American ideal of manhood: taciturn, staunchly independent, and fearless; unforgiving of his enemies but tender with women, children, and animals.

Such are the traits of the lead character in this volume's first tale, taken from Owen Wister's best-seller, *The Virginian: A Horseman of the Plains*. "Em'ly" is the account of how a most unlikely and absurd catalyst—a rooster-hating hen that couldn't, or wouldn't, lay eggs of her own—led to the dissolution of social barriers between a bungling Eastern tenderfoot and a plainsman from Wyoming, by way of Virginia. A mutual concern for the befuddled fowl helped to forge the pair's friendship and enhance their respect for one another.

Originally published in 1902, *The Virginian* is widely credited with molding the future of cowboy novels to come, fashioning a style, theme, and characterization that still influence Western writers a century later. Wister paved the road—make that dusted the trail—for such greats as Zane Grey, Max Brand, *Shane* author Jack Schaefer, and contemporaries like Larry McMurtry, author of the modern classics *Lonesome Dove* and *Streets of Laredo*.

Yet, even writers early on the scene like Wister and his fellow Easterner Alfred Henry Lewis, author of *Wolfville* (1897) and several sequels, would have had plenty of published works to reference when they were crafting their cowpoke tales. Take, for instance, *Live Boys: or Charley and Nacho in Texas*, written in 1878 by Texas attorney Thomas Pilgrim under the pseudonym Arthur Morecamp. It's often held up as the first true-to-life narrative about a cattle drive and the cowboys working it. Although it's not represented in *Classic Cowboy Stories*, other pieces of both fact and fiction written prior to *The Virginian* are.

Following "Em'ly," Wister's ironic and wistful opener, comes a first-person account from none other than Theodore Roosevelt, a friend of Wister's, to whom he dedicated *The Virginian* thusly: "Some of these pages you have seen, some you have praised, one stands new-written because you blamed it; and all, my dear critic, beg leave to remind you of their author's changeless admiration." Like Wister,

Roosevelt was an Easterner who had his eyes and mind pried open by the vast spaces and earthy lifestyles of the West. In Wister's case it was Wyoming; in T. R.'s, the Dakota Territory. Roosevelt, who bought a ranch in the North Dakota badlands in the mid-1880s, wrote "Winter Weather" when he was in his late twenties. In it he provides a dramatic look at the rough living often dished up by the badlands, a character-constructing existence that helped transform a frail young greenhorn into the vigorous man who would become the twenty-sixth president of the United States.

Some of the tales and first-hand accounts in this volume are not cowboy stories in the strictest sense, yet they offer vivid glimpses into the days and ways of the range rider. Take the passage from Isabella L. Bird's *A Lady's Life in the Rocky Mountains*, which contains letters she penned in the fall and early winter of 1873 on her way home to England from the Hawaiian Islands. These first appeared in 1878 in the British weekly *Leisure Hour*. Interestingly, Bird appears free of the "superiority complex" over Americans shared by many of her English countrymen of the day.

A pair of distinct takes on the character of the cowboy are dished up by Bill Nye and Stewart Edward White. In "The Cow-Boy," humorist Nye paints a tongue-in-cheek picture of the legendary cowpoke as, in truth, a blusterous and bravado-filled coward, a boy not long off the farm wearing chaps and a six-shooter. Like the bulk of Nye's material, it comes from the years of 1876 through 1883 when he lived in Wyoming, where he served as a lawyer and as editor of the *Laramie Boomerang* newspaper. More complimentary of the cowpuncher is White, who spent time with the breed in California's Sierra Nevada and in the deserts of Arizona. In "On Cowboys" he writes: " . . . when it comes to a case of real hospitality or helpfulness, your cowboy is there every time."

Of the wild-western cowtown of Abilene, Kansas, and its frontier ilk, Joseph G. McCoy (no relation, as far as I know) once wrote: "No quiet-turned man could or would care to take the office of marshal, which jeopardized his life; hence the necessity of employing a desperado—one who feared nothing and would as soon shoot an offending subject as to look at him." In keeping with this philosophy, after becoming Abilene's first mayor in 1871, McCoy hired as town marshal the intimidating and inimitable "Wild Bill" Hickok. The badman lawman is the subject of a story in this book by Emerson Hough (pronounced *Huff*). A native of Newton, Iowa, who moved to New Mexico initially to practice law, Hough relates the bloody story of Wild Bill's life, estimating that he killed at least eighty-five men, "not counting Indians"—a distinction that speaks volumes about the attitudes of the day.

In contrast, novelist and fellow New Mexican Eugene Manlove Rhodes, whose *Good Men and True* was published in 1910, was relatively free of the prejudices commonly held against Mexicans and other non-Anglos in those days. Born in 1869 in Tecumseh, Nebraska, Rhodes moved in 1881 with his homesteading family to New Mexico, where he gained experience that granted him the ability to write about the cowboy's life from the inside out. The late historian Bernard De Voto praised Rhodes's books, calling them " . . . the only body of fiction devoted to the cattle kingdom which is both true to it and written by an artist in prose."

The work of prolific writer B. M. (Bertha Muzzy) Bower also finds its way into this collection. Her slice of life entitled "Love Finds Its Hour" is taken from the 1906 novel *Chip of the Flying U*. After moving to Montana as a girl, Bower evolved into the best known female crafter of the Western genre, authoring more than five dozen novels, beginning with *Chip*. The book's hero, Chip Bennett, is thought to have been inspired by the legendary western artist, Charles M. Russell, a friend of Bower's who drew the illustrations for *Chip*.

Within these pages you'll read stories by not only the well-known—Wister, Roosevelt, Zane Grey, and others—but also the little known, such as Frank Benton, a Wyoming cowboy with a penchant for penning tall-tales in the same colorful language that he no doubt used for verbal communication. And you'll enjoy a piece of narrative nonfiction by a man far better known as an artist and illustrator than as a writer. Yet the scribblings of Frederic Remington reveal that his keen powers of observation were not turned off simply because he lacked a canvas sitting in front of him.

A gem of a story from Owen Wister's first novel, *Lin McLean*, which predates *The Virginian* by five years, also made its way into these pages. In addition to being a beautiful story, the tale reminds us of this: If the materialism we associate with Christmas is not eternal, then it is at least a hundred years old. And a surprise is "The Caballero's Way" by William Sydney Porter, better known as O. Henry. What is most surprising, perhaps, is not that it was the famous short-story writer who fabricated the Cisco Kid, but that the Kid as he created him was nothing like the good-natured, take-from-the-rich-and-give-to-the-poor personality that baby boomers came to know on television in the early 1950s. Rather, O. Henry's Cisco Kid was a cold-hearted, cold-blooded killer.

The use of the vernacular and overuse of the passive voice lends some of these tales a distant, venerable feel, while a sometimes cold outlook on violence and racial prejudice, whether stated or implied, can insult our modern sensibilities. Yet certain stories also make it clear that some things—like humor—are timeless. Consider, for instance "Cowboy Golf," by Zane Grey, a college baseball star-turned-dentist-turned-writer, who was also a rabid ocean fisherman. Other eternal themes are represented as well, such as an adoration of wild, natural surroundings and a love of circling the campfire at night, watching sparks rise into the black void and listening to the yip-yammering of coyotes echoing in the distance.

So, pull up a chair, set yerself down, and sit a spell—and git ready to gnaw on some right good readin'.

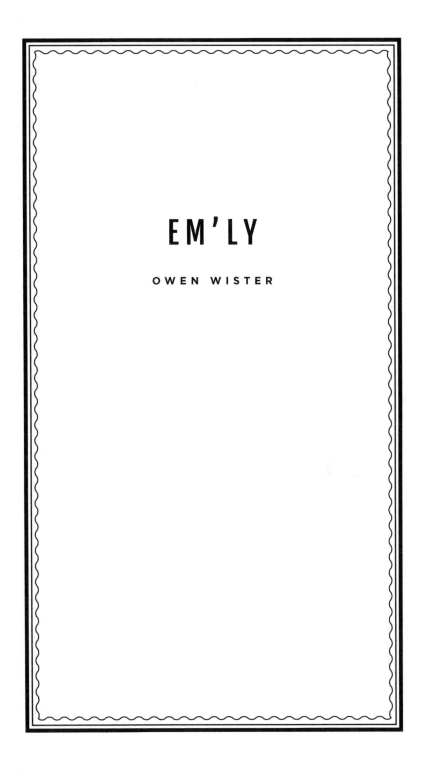

# EM'LY

OWEN WISTER

My personage was a hen, and she lived at the Sunk Creek Ranch.

Judge Henry's ranch was notable for several luxuries. He had milk, for example. In those days his brother ranchmen had thousands of cattle very often, but not a drop of milk, save the condensed variety. Therefore they had no butter. The Judge had plenty. Next rarest to butter and milk in the cattle country were eggs. But my host had chickens. Whether this was because he had followed cock-fighting in his early days, or whether it was due to Mrs. Henry, I cannot say. I only know that when I took a meal elsewhere, I was likely to find nothing but the eternal "sowbelly," beans, and coffee; while at Sunk Creek the omelet and the custard were frequent. The passing traveller was glad to tie his horse to the fence here, and sit down to the Judge's table. For its fame was as wide as Wyoming. It was an oasis in the Territory's desolate bill-of-fare.

The long fences of Judge Henry's home ranch began upon Sunk Creek soon after that stream emerged from its cañon through the Bow Leg. It was a place always well cared for by the owner, even in the days of his bachelorhood. The placid regiments of cattle lay in the cool of the cotton-woods by the water, or slowly moved among the sage-brush, feeding upon the grass that in those forever departed years was plentiful and tall. The steers came fat off his unenclosed range and fattened still more in his large pasture; while his small pasture, a field some eight miles square, was for several seasons given to the Judge's horses, and over this ample space there played and prospered the good colts which he raised from Paladin, his imported stallion. After he married, I have been assured that his wife's influence became visible in and about the house at once. Shade trees were planted, flowers attempted, and to the chickens was added the much more troublesome turkey. I, the visitor, was pressed into service when I arrived, green from the East. I took hold of the farmyard and began building a better chicken house, while the Judge was off creating meadow land in his gray and yellow wilderness. When any cow-boy was unoccupied, he would lounge over to my neighborhood, and silently regard my carpentering.

Those cow-punchers bore names of various denominations. There was Honey Wiggin; there was Nebrasky, and Dollar Bill, and Chalk-eye. And they came from farms and cities, from Maine and from California. But the romance of American adventure had drawn them all alike to this great playground of young men, and in their courage, their generosity, and their amusement at me they bore a close resemblance to each other. Each one would silently observe my achievements with the hammer and the chisel. Then he would retire to the bunk-house, and presently I would overhear laughter. But this was only in the morning. In the afternoon on many days of the summer which I spent at the Sunk Creek Ranch I would go shooting, or ride up toward the entrance of the cañon and watch the men working on the irrigation ditches. Pleasant systems of water running in channels were being led through the soil, and there was a sound of rippling here and there among the yellow grain; the green thick alfalfa grass waved almost, it seemed, of its own accord, for the wind never blew; and when at evening the sun lay against the plain, the rift of the cañon was filled with a violet light, and the Bow Leg Mountains became transfigured with hues of floating and unimaginable color. The sun shone in a sky where never a cloud came, and noon was not too warm nor the dark too cool. And so for two months I went through these pleasant uneventful days, improving the chickens, an object of mirth, living in the open air, and basking in the perfection of content.

I was justly styled a tenderfoot. Mrs. Henry had in the beginning endeavored to shield me from this humiliation; but when she found that I was inveterate in laying my inexperience of Western matters bare to all the world, begging to be enlightened upon rattle-snakes, prairie-dogs, owls, blue and willow grouse, sage-hens, how to rope a horse or tighten the front cinch of my saddle, and that my spirit soared into enthusism at the mere sight of so ordinary an animal as a white-tailed deer, she let me rush about with my firearms, and made no further effort to stave off the ridicule that my blunders perpetually earned from the ranch hands, her own humorous husband, and any chance visitor who stopped for a meal or stayed the night.

I was not called by my name after the first feeble etiquette due to a stranger in his first few hours had died away. I was known simply as "the tenderfoot." I was introduced to the neighborhood (a circle of eighty miles) as "the tenderfoot." It was thus that Balaam, the maltreater of horses, learned to address me when he came a two days' journey to pay a visit. And it was this name and my notorious helplessness that bid fair to end what relations I had with the Virginian. For when Judge Henry ascertained that nothing could prevent me from losing myself, that it was not uncommon for me to saunter out after breakfast with a gun and in thirty minutes cease to know north from south, he arranged for my protection. He detailed an escort for me;

and the escort was once more the trustworthy man! The poor Virginian was taken from his work and his comrades and set to playing nurse for me. And for a while this humiliation ate into his untamed soul. It was his lugubrious lot to accompany me in my rambles, preside over my blunders, and save me from calamitously passing into the next world. He bore it in courteous silence, except when speaking was necessary. He would show me the lower ford, which I could never find for myself, generally mistaking a quicksand for it. He would tie my horse properly. He would recommend me not to shoot my rifle at a white-tailed deer in the particular moment that the outfit wagon was passing behind the animal on the further side of the brush. There was seldom a day that he was not obliged to hasten and save me from sudden death or from ridicule, which is worse. Yet never once did he lose his patience and his gentle, slow voice, and apparently lazy manner remained the same, whether we were sitting at lunch together or up in the mountains during a hunt, or whether he was bringing me back my horse, which had run away because I had again forgotten to throw the reins over his head and let them trail.

"He'll always stand if yu' do that," the Virginian would say. "See how my hawss stays right quiet yondeh."

After such admonition he would say no more to me. But this tame nursery business was assuredly gall to him. For though utterly a man in countenance and in his self-possession and incapacity to be put at a loss, he was still boyishly proud of his wild calling, and wore his leathern chaps and jingled his spurs with obvious pleasure. His tiger limberness and his beauty were rich with unabated youth; and that force which lurked beneath his surface must often have curbed his intolerance of me. In spite of what I knew must be his opinion of me, the tenderfoot, my liking for him grew, and I found his silent company more and more agreeable. That he had spells of talking, I had already learned at Medicine Bow. But his present taciturnity might almost have effaced this impression, had I not happened to pass by the bunk-house one evening after dark, when Honey Wiggin and the rest of the cow-boys were gathered inside it.

That afternoon the Virginian and I had gone duck shooting. We had found several in a beaver dam, and I had killed two as they sat close together; but they floated against the breastwork of sticks out in the water some four feet deep, where the escaping current might carry them down the stream. The Judge's red setter had not accompanied us, because she was expecting a family.

"We don't want her along anyways," the cow-puncher had explained to me. "She runs around mighty irresponsible, and she'll stand a prairie-dog 'bout as often as she'll stand a bird. She's a triflin' animal."

My anxiety to own the ducks caused me to pitch into the water with all my clothes on, and subsequently crawl out a slippery, triumphant, weltering heap. The Virginian's serious eyes had rested upon this spectacle of mud; but he expressed nothing, as usual.

"They ain't overly good eatin'," he observed, tying the birds to his saddle. "They're divers."

"Divers!" I exclaimed. "Why didn't they dive?"

"I reckon they was young ones and hadn't experience."

"Well," I said, crestfallen, but attempting to be humorous, "I did the diving myself."

But the Virginian made no comment. He handed me my double-barrelled English gun, which I was about to leave deserted on the ground behind me, and we rode home in our usual silence, the mean little white-breasted, sharp-billed divers dangling from his saddle.

It was in the bunk-house that he took his revenge. As I passed I heard his gentle voice silently achieving some narrative to an attentive audience, and just as I came by the open window where he sat on his bed in shirt and drawers, his back to me, I heard his concluding words, "And the hat on his haid was the one mark showed yu' he weren't a snappin'-turtle."

The anecdote met with instantaneous success, and I hurried away into the dark.

The next morning I was occupied with the chickens. Two hens were fighting to sit on some eggs that a third was daily laying, and which I did not want hatched, and for the third time I had kicked Em'ly off seven potatoes she had rolled together and was determined to raise I know not what sort of family from. She was shrieking about the hen-house as the Virginian came in to observe (I suspect) what I might be doing now that could be useful for him to mention in the bunk-house.

He stood awhile, and at length said, "We lost our best rooster when Mrs. Henry came to live hyeh."

I paid no attention.

"He was a right elegant Dominicker," he continued.

I felt a little ruffled about the snapping-turtle, and showed no interest in what he was saying, but continued my functions among the hens. This unusual silence of mine seemed to elicit unusual speech from him.

"Yu' see, that rooster he'd always lived round hyeh when the Judge was a bachelor, and he never seen no ladies or any persons wearing female gyarments. You ain't got rheumatism, seh?"

"Me? No."

"I reckoned maybe them little old divers yu' got damp goin' afteh—" He paused.

"Oh, no, not in the least, thank you."

"Yu' seemed sort o' grave this mawnin', and I'm cert'nly glad it ain't them divers."

"Well, the rooster?" I inquired finally.

"Oh, him! He weren't raised where he could see petticoats. Mrs. Henry she come hyeh from the railroad with the Judge afteh dark. Next mawnin' early she walked out to view her new home, and the rooster was a-feedin' by the door, and he seen her. Well, seh, he screeched that awful I run out of the bunk-house; and he jus' went over the fence and took down Sunk Creek shoutin' fire, right along. He has never come back."

"There's a hen over there now that has no judgment," I said, indicating Em'ly. She had got herself outside the house, and was on the bars of a corral, her vociferations reduced to an occasional squawk. I told him about the potatoes.

"I never knowed her name before," said he. "That runaway rooster, he hated her. And she hated him same as she hates 'em all."

"I named her myself," said I, "after I came to notice her particularly. There's an old maid at home who's charitable, and belongs to the Cruelty to Animals, and she never knows whether she had better cross in front of a street car or wait. I named the hen after her. Does she ever lay eggs?"

The Virginian had not "troubled his haid" over the poultry.

"Well, I don't believe she knows how. I think she came near being a rooster."

"She's sure manly-lookin'," said the Virginian. We had walked toward the corral, and he was now scrutinizing Em'ly with interest.

She was an egregious fowl. She was huge and gaunt, with great yellow beak, and she stood straight and alert in the manner of responsible people. There was something wrong with her tail. It slanted far to one side, one feather in it twice as long as the rest. Feathers on her breast there were none. These had been worn entirely off by her habit of sitting upon potatoes and other rough abnormal objects. And this lent to her appearance an air of being décolleté, singularly at variance with her otherwise prudish ensemble. Her eye was remarkably bright, but somehow it had an outraged expression. It was as if she went about the world perpetually scandalized over the doings that fell beneath her notice. Her legs were blue, long, and remarkably stout.

"She'd ought to wear knickerbockers," murmured the Virginian. "She'd look a heap better'n some o' them college students. And she'll set on potatoes, yu' say?"

"She thinks she can hatch out anything. I've found her with onions, and last Tuesday I caught her on two balls of soap."

In the afternoon the tall cow-puncher and I rode out to get an antelope.

After an hour, during which he was completely taciturn, he said: "I reckon maybe this hyeh lonesome country ain't been healthy for Em'ly to live in. It ain't for some humans. Them old trappers in the mountains gets skewed in the haid mighty often, an' talks out loud when nobody's nigher'n a hundred miles."

"Em'ly has not been solitary," I replied. "There are forty chickens here."

"That's so," said he. "It don't explain her."

He fell silent again, riding beside me, easy and indolent in the saddle. His long figure looked so loose and inert that the swift, light spring he made to the ground seemed an impossible feat. He had seen an antelope where I saw none.

"Take a shot yourself," I urged him, as he motioned me to be quick. "You never shoot when I'm with you."

"I ain't hyeh for that," he answered. "Now you've let him get away on yu'!"

The antelope had in truth departed.

"Why," he said to my protest, "I can hit them things any day. What's your notion as to Em'ly?"

"I can't account for her," I replied.

"Well," he said musingly, and then his mind took one of those particular turns that made me love him. "Taylor ought to see her. She'd be just the schoolmarm for Bear Creek!"

"She's not much like the eating-house lady at Medicine Bow," I said.

He gave a hilarious chuckle. "No, Em'ly knows nothing o' them joys. So yu' have no notion about her? Well, I've got one. I reckon maybe she was hatched after a big thunderstorm."

"A big thunderstorm!" I exclaimed.

"Yes. Don't yu' know about them, and what they'll do to aiggs? A big case o' lightnin' and thunder will addle aiggs and keep 'em from hatchin'. And I expect one came along, and all the other aiggs of Em'ly's set didn't hatch out, but got plumb addled, and she happened not to get addled that far, and so she just managed to make it through. But she cert'nly ain't got a strong haid."

"I fear she has not," said I.

"Mighty hon'ble intentions," he observed. "If she can't make out to lay anything, she wants to hatch somethin', and be a mother, anyways."

"I wonder what relation the law considers that a hen is to the chicken she hatched but did not lay?" I inquired.

The Virginian made no reply to this frivolous suggestion. He was gazing over the wide landscape gravely and with apparent inattention. He invariably saw game before I did, and was off his horse and crouched among the sage while I was still getting my left foot clear of the stirrup. I succeeded in killing an antelope, and we rode home with the head and hind quarters.

"No," said he. "It's sure the thunder, and not the lonesomeness. How do yu' like the lonesomeness yourself?"

I told him that I liked it.

"I could not live without it now," he said. "This has got into my system." He swept his hand out at the vast space of world. "I went back home to see my folks onced. Mother was dyin' slow, and she wanted me. I stayed a year. But them Virginia mountains could please me no more. Afteh she was gone, I told my brothers and sisters good-by. We like each other well enough, but I reckon I'll not go back."

We found Em'ly seated upon a collection of green California peaches, which the Judge had brought from the railroad.

"I don't mind her any more," I said. "I'm sorry for her."

"I've been sorry for her right along," said the Virginian. "She does hate the roosters so." And he said that he was making a collection of every class of object which he found her treating as eggs.

But Em'ly's egg-industry was terminated abruptly one morning, and her unquestioned energies diverted to a new channel. A turkey which had been sitting in the root-house appeared with twelve children, and a family of bantams occurred almost simultaneously. Em'ly was importantly scratching the soil inside Paladin's corral when the bantam tribe of newly born came by down the lane, and she caught sight of them through the bars. She crossed the corral at a run, and intercepted two of the chicks that were trailing somewhat behind their real mamma. These she undertook to appropriate, and assumed a high tone with the bantam, who was the smaller, and hence obliged to retreat with her still numerous family. I interfered, and put matters straight, but the adjustment was only temporary. In an hour I saw Em'ly immensely busy with two more bantams, leading them about and taking a care of them which I must admit seemed perfectly efficient.

And now came the first incident that made me suspect her to be demented.

She had proceeded with her changelings behind the kitchen, where one of the irrigation ditches ran under the fence from the hay-field to supply the house with water. Some distance along this ditch inside the field were the twelve turkeys in the short, recently cut stubble. Again Em'ly set off instantly like a deer. She left the dismayed bantams behind her. She crossed the ditch with one jump of her stout blue legs, flew over the grass, and was at once among the turkeys, where, with an instinct of maternity as undiscriminating as it was reckless, she attempted to huddle some of them away. But this other mamma was not a bantam, and in a few moments Em'ly was entirely routed in her attempt to acquire a new variety of family.

This spectacle was witnessed by the Virginian and myself, and it overcame him. He went speechless across to the bunk-house, by himself, and sat on his bed, while I took the abandoned bantams back to their own circle.

I have often wondered what the other fowls thought of all this. Some impression it certainly did make upon them. The notion may seem out of reason to those who have never closely attended to other animals than man; but I am convinced that any community which shares some of our instincts will share some of the resulting feelings, and that birds and beasts have conventions, the breach of which startles them. If there be anything in evolution, this would seem inevitable. At all events, the chicken-house was upset during the following several days. Em'ly disturbed now the bantams and now the turkeys, and several of these latter had died, though I will not go so far as to say that this was the result of her misplaced attentions. Nevertheless, I was seriously thinking of locking her up till the broods should be a little older, when another event happened, and all was suddenly at peace.

The Judge's setter came in one morning, wagging her tail. She had had her puppies, and she now took us to where they were housed, in between the floor of a building and the hollow ground. Em'ly was seated on the whole litter.

"No," I said to the Judge, "I am not surprised. She is capable of anything."

In her new choice of offspring, this hen had at length encountered an unworthy parent. The setter was bored by her own puppies. She found the hole under the house an obscure and monotonous residence compared with the dining room, and our company more stimulating and sympathetic than that of her children. A much-petted contact with our superior race had developed her dog intelligence above its natural level, and turned her into an unnatural, neglectful mother, who was constantly forgetting her nursery for worldly pleasures.

At certain periods of the day she repaired to the puppies and fed them, but came away when this perfunctory ceremony was accomplished; and she was glad enough to have a governess bring them up. She made no quarrel with Em'ly, and the two understood each other perfectly. I have never seen among animals any arrangement so civilized and so perverted. It made Em'ly perfectly happy. To see her sitting all day jealously spreading her wings over some blind puppies was sufficiently curious; but when they became large enough to come out from under the house and toddle about in the proud hen's wake, I longed for some distinguished naturalist. I felt that our ignorance made us inappropriate spectators of such a phenomenon. Em'ly scratched and clucked, and the puppies ran to her, pawed her with their fat limp little legs, and retreated beneath her feathers in their games of hide and seek. Conceive, if you can, what confusion must have reigned in their infant minds as to who the setter was!

"I reckon they think she's the wet-nurse," said the Virginian.

When the puppies grew to be boisterous, I perceived that Em'ly's mission was approaching its end. They were too heavy for her, and their increasing scope of playfulness was not in her line. Once or twice they knocked her over, upon which she arose and pecked them severely, and they retired to a safe distance, and sitting in a circle, yapped at her. I think they began to suspect that she was only a hen after all. So Em'ly resigned with an indifference which surprised me, until I remembered that if it had been chickens, she would have ceased to look after them by this time.

But here she was again "out of a job," as the Virginian said.

"She's raised them puppies for that triflin' setter, and now she'll be huntin' around for something else useful to do that ain't in her business."

Now there were other broods of chickens to arrive in the hen-house, and I did not desire any more bantam and turkey performances. So, to avoid confusion, I played a trick upon Em'ly. I went down to Sunk Creek and fetched some smooth, oval stones. She was quite satisfied with these, and passed a quiet day with them in a box. This was not fair, the Virginian asserted.

"You ain't going to jus' leave her fooled that a-way?"

I did not see why not.

"Why, she raised them puppies all right. Ain't she showed she knows how to be a mother anyways? Em'ly ain't going to get her time took up for nothing while I'm round hyeh," said the cow-puncher.

He laid a gentle hold of Em'ly and tossed her to the ground. She, of course, rushed out among the corrals in a great state of nerves.

"I don't see what good you do meddling," I protested.

To this he deigned no reply, but removed the unresponsive stones from the straw.

"Why, if they ain't right warm!" he exclaimed plaintively. "The poor, deluded son-of-a-gun!" And with this unusual description of a lady, he sent the stones sailing like a line of birds. "I'm regular getting stuck on Em'ly," continued the Virginian. "Yu' needn't to laugh. Don't yu' see she's got sort o' human feelin's and desires? I always knowed hawsses was like people, and my collie, of course. It is kind of foolish, I expect, but that hen's goin' to have a real aigg di-rectly, right now, to set on." With this he removed one from beneath another hen. "We'll have Em'ly raise this hyeh," said he, "so she can put in her time profitable."

It was not accomplished at once; for Em'ly, singularly enough, would not consent to stay in the box whence she had been routed. At length we found another retreat for her, and in these new surroundings, with a new piece of work for her to do, Em'ly sat on the one egg which the Virginian had so carefully provided for her.

Thus, as in all genuine tragedies, was the stroke of Fate wrought by chance and the best intentions.

Em'ly began sitting on Friday afternoon near sundown. Early next morning my sleep was gradually dispersed by a sound unearthly and continuous. Now it dwindled, receding to a distance; again it came near, took a turn, drifted to the other side of the house, then, evidently, whatever it was, passed my door close, and I jumped upright in my bed. The high, tense strain of vibration, nearly, but not quite, a musical note, was like the threatening scream of machinery, though weaker, and I bounded out of the house in my pajamas.

There was Em'ly, dishevelled, walking wildly about, her one egg miraculously hatched within ten hours. The little lonely yellow ball of down went cheeping along behind, following its mother as best it could. What, then, had happened to the established period of incubation? For an instant the thing was like a portent, and I was near joining Em'ly in her horrid surprise, when I saw how it all was. The Virginian had taken an egg from a hen which had already been sitting for three weeks.

I dressed in haste, hearing Em'ly's distracted outcry. It steadily sounded, without perceptible pause for breath, and marked her erratic journey back and forth through stables, lanes, and corrals. The shrill disturbance brought all of us out to see her, and in the hen-house I discovered the new brood making its appearance punctually.

But this natural explanation could not be made to the crazed hen. She continued to scour the premises, her slant tail and its one preposterous feather waving as she aimlessly went, her stout legs stepping high with an unnatural motion, her head lifted nearly off her neck, and in her brilliant yellow eye an expression of more than outrage at this overturning of a natural law. Behind her, entirely ignored and neglected, trailed the little progeny. She never looked at it. We went about our various affairs, and all through the clear, sunny day that unending metallic scream pervaded the premises. The Virginian put out food and water for her, but she tasted nothing. I am glad to say that the little chicken did. I do not think that the hen's eyes could see, except in the way that sleep-walkers do.

The heat went out of the air, and in the cañon the violet light began to show. Many hours had gone, but Em'ly never ceased. Now she suddenly flew up in a tree and sat there with her noise still going; but it had risen lately several notes into a slim, acute level of terror, and was not like machinery any more, nor like any sound I ever heard before or since. Below the tree stood the bewildered little chicken, cheeping, and making tiny jumps to reach its mother.

"Yes," said the Virginian, "it's comical. Even her aigg acted different from anybody else's." He paused, and looked across the wide, mellowing plain with the expression of easy-going gravity so common with him. Then he looked at Em'ly in the tree and the yellow chicken. "It ain't so damned funny," said he.

We went in to supper, and I came out to find the hen lying on the ground, dead. I took the chicken to the family in the hen-house.

No, it was not altogether funny any more. And I did not think less of the Virginian when I came upon him surreptitiously digging a little hole in the field for her.

"I have buried some citizens here and there," said he, "that I have respected less."

And when the time came for me to leave Sunk Creek, my last word to the Virginian was, "Don't forget Em'ly."

"I ain't likely to," responded the cow-puncher. "She is just one o' them parables."

Save when he fell into his native idioms (which, they told me, his wanderings had well-nigh obliterated until that year's visit to his home again revived them in his speech), he had now for a long while dropped the "seh," and all other barriers between us. We were thorough friends, and had exchanged many confidences both of the flesh and of the spirit. He even went the length of saying that he would write me the Sunk Creek news if I would send him a line now and then. I have many letters from him now. Their spelling came to be faultless, and in the beginning was little worse than George Washington's.

The Judge himself drove me to the railroad by another way— across the Bow Leg Mountains, and south through Balaam's Ranch and Drybone to Rock Creek.

"I'll be very homesick," I told him.

"Come and pull the latch-string whenever you please," he bade me.

I wished that I might! No lotus land ever cast its spell upon man's heart more than Wyoming had enchanted mine.

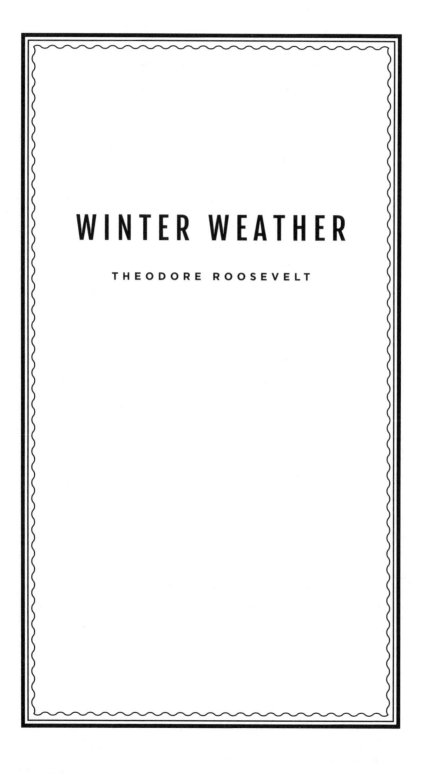

# WINTER WEATHER

## THEODORE ROOSEVELT

When the days have dwindled to their shortest, and the nights seem never ending, then all the great northern plains are changed into an abode of iron desolation. Sometimes furious gales blow out of the north, driving before them the clouds of blinding snow-dust, wrapping the mantle of death round every unsheltered being that faces their unshackled anger. They roar in a thunderous bass as they sweep across the prairie or whirl through the naked cañons; they shiver the great brittle cottonwoods, and beneath their rough touch the icy limbs of the pines that cluster in the gorges sing like the chords of an Æolian harp. Again, in the coldest midwinter weather, not a breath of wind may stir; and then the still, merciless, terrible cold that broods over the earth like the shadow of silent death seems even more dreadful in its gloomy rigor than is the lawless madness of the storms. All the land is like granite; the great rivers stand still in their beds, as if turned to frosted steel. In the long nights there is no sound to break the lifeless silence. Under the ceaseless, shifting play of the Northern Lights, or lighted only by the wintry brilliance of the stars, the snow-clad plains stretch out into dead and endless wastes of glimmering white.

Then the great fire-place of the ranch house is choked with blazing logs, and at night we have to sleep under so many blankets that the weight is fairly oppressive. Outside, the shaggy ponies huddle together in the corral, while long icicles hang from their lips, and the hoar-frost whitens the hollow backs of the cattle. For the ranchman the winter is occasionally a pleasant holiday, but more often an irksome period of enforced rest and gloomy foreboding.

In the winter there is much less work than at any other season, but what there is involves great hardship and exposure. Many of the men are discharged after the summer is over, and during much of the cold weather there is little to do except hunt now and then, and in very bitter days lounge listlessly about the house. But some of the men are out in the line camps, and the ranchman has occasionally to make the round of these; and besides that, one or more of the cowboys who are at home ought to be out every day when the cattle have become weak, so as to pick up and drive in any beast that will otherwise evidently fail to get through the season—a cow that has had an unusually early calf being particularly apt to need attention. The horses shift for themselves and need no help. Often, in winter, the Indians cut down the cottonwood trees and feed the tops to their ponies; but this is not done to keep them from starving, but only to keep them from wandering off in search of grass. Besides, the ponies are very fond of the bark of the young cottonwood shoots, and it is healthy for them.

The men in the line camps lead a hard life, for they have to be out in every kind of weather, and should be especially active and watchful during the storms. The camps are established along some line which it is proposed to make the boundary of the cattle's drift in a given direction. For example, we care very little whether our cattle wander to the Yellowstone; but we strongly object to their drifting east and south-east towards the granger country and the Sioux reservation, especially as when they drift that way they come out on flat, bare plains where there is danger of perishing. Accordingly, the cowmen along the Little Missouri have united in establishing a row of camps to the east of the river, along the line where the broken ground meets the prairie. The camps are usually for two men each, and some fifteen or twenty miles apart; then, in the morning, its two men start out in opposite ways, each riding till he meets his neighbor of the next camp nearest on that side, when he returns. The camp itself is sometimes merely a tent pitched in a sheltered coulée, but ought to be either made of logs or else a dug-out in the ground. A small corral and horse-shed is near by, with enough hay for the ponies, of which each rider has two or three. In riding over the beat each man drives any cattle that have come near it back into the Bad Lands, and if he sees by the hoof-marks that a few have strayed out over the line very recently, he will follow and fetch them home. They must be shoved well back into the Bad Lands before a great storm strikes them; for if they once begin to drift in masses before an icy gale it is impossible for a small number of men to hold them, and the only thing is to let them go, and then to organize an expedition to follow them as soon as possible. Line riding is very cold work, and dangerous too, when the men have to be out in a blinding snow-storm, or in a savage blizzard that takes the spirit in the thermometer far down below zero. In the worst storms it is impossible for any man to be out.

But other kinds of work besides line riding necessitate exposure to bitter weather. Once, while spending a few days over on Beaver Creek hunting up a lost horse, I happened to meet a cowboy who was out on the same errand, and made friends with him. We started home together across the open prairies, but were caught in a very heavy snow-storm almost immediately after leaving the ranch where we had spent the night. We were soon completely turned round, the great soft flakes—for, luckily, it was not cold—almost blinding us, and we had to travel entirely by compass. After feeling our way along for eight or nine hours, we finally got down into the broken country near Sentinel Butte and came across an empty hut, a welcome sight to men as cold, hungry, and tired as we were. In this hut we passed the night very comfortably, picketing our horses in a sheltered nook near by, with plenty of hay from an old stack. To while away the long evening, I read *Hamlet* aloud, from a little pocket Shakspere. The cowboy, a Texan,—one of the best riders I have seen, and also a very intelligent as well as a thoroughly good fellow in every way,—was greatly interested in it and commented most shrewdly on the parts he liked, especially Polonius's advice to Laertes, which he translated into more homely language with great relish, and ended with the just criticism that "old Shakspere saveyed human natur' some"—savey being a verb presumably adapted into the limited plains' vocabulary from the Spanish.

Even for those who do not have to look up stray horses, and who are not forced to ride the line day in and day out, there is apt to be some hardship and danger in being abroad during the bitter weather; yet a ride in midwinter is certainly fascinating. The great white country wrapped in the powdery snow-drift seems like another land; and the familiar landmarks are so changed that a man must be careful lest he lose his way, for the discomfort of a night in the open during such weather is very great indeed. When the sun is out the glare from the endless white stretches dazzles the eyes; and if the gray snow-clouds hang low and only let a pale, wan light struggle through, the lonely wastes become fairly appalling in their desolation. For hour after hour a man may go on and see no sign of life except, perhaps, a big white owl sweeping noiselessly by, so that in the dark it looks like a snow-wreath; the cold gradually chilling the rider to the bones, as he draws his fur cap tight over his ears and muffles his face in the huge collar of his wolf-skin coat, and making the shaggy little steed drop head and tail as it picks its way over the frozen soil. There are few moments more pleasant than the home-coming, when, in the gathering darkness, after crossing the last chain of ice-covered buttes, or after coming round the last turn in the wind-swept valley, we see, through the leafless trees, or across the frozen river, the red gleam of the firelight as it shines through the ranch windows and flickers over the trunks of the cottonwoods outside, warming a man's blood by the mere hint of the warmth awaiting him within.

The winter scenery is especially striking in the Bad Lands, with their queer fantastic formations. Among the most interesting features are the burning mines. These are formed by the coal seams that get on fire. They vary greatly in size. Some send up smoke-columns that are visible miles away, while others are not noticeable a few rods off. The old ones gradually burn away, while new ones unexpectedly break out. Thus, last fall, one suddenly appeared but half a mile from the ranch house. We never knew it was there until one cold moonlight night, when we were riding home, we rounded the corner of a ravine and saw in our path a tall white column of smoke rising from a rift in the snowy crags ahead of us. As the trail was over perfectly familiar ground, we were for a moment almost as startled as if we had seen a ghost.

The burning mines are uncanny places, anyhow. A strong smell of sulphur hangs round them, the heated earth crumbles and cracks, and through the long clefts that form in it we can see the lurid glow of the subterranean fires, with here and there tongues of blue or cherry colored flame dancing up to the surface.

The winters vary greatly in severity with us. During some seasons men can go lightly clad even in January and February, and the cattle hardly suffer at all; during other there will be spells of bitter weather, accompanied by furious blizzards, which render it impossible for days and weeks at a time for men to stir out-of-doors at all, save at the risk of their lives. Then line rider, ranchman, hunter, and teamster alike all have to keep within doors. I have known of several cases of men freezing to death when caught in shelterless places by such a blizzard, a strange fact being that in about half of them the doomed man had evidently gone mad before dying, and had stripped himself of most of his clothes, the body when found being nearly naked. On our ranch we have never had any bad accidents, although every winter some of us get more or less frost-bitten. My last experience in this line was while returning by moonlight from a successful hunt after mountain sheep. The thermometer was 26° below zero, and we had no food for twelve hours. I became numbed, and before I was aware of it had frozen my face, one foot, both knees, and one hand. Luckily, I reached the ranch before serious damage was done.

About once every six or seven years we have a season when these storms follow one another almost without interval throughout the winter months, and then the loss among the stock is frightful. One such winter occurred in 1880–81. This was when there were very few ranchmen in the country. The grass was so good that the old range stock escaped pretty well; but the trail herds were almost destroyed. The next severe winter was that of 1886–87, when the rush of incoming herds had overstocked the ranges, and the loss was in consequence fairly appalling, especially to the outfits that had just put on cattle.

The snow-fall was unprecedented, both for its depth and for the way it lasted; and it was this, and not the cold, that caused the loss. About the middle of November the storms began. Day after day the snow came down, thawing and then freezing and piling itself higher and higher. By January the drifts had filled the ravines and coulées almost level. The snow lay in great masses on the plateaus and river bottoms; and this lasted until the end of February. The preceding summer we had been visited by a prolonged drought, so that the short, scanty grass was already well cropped down; the snow covered what pasturage there was to the depth of several feet, and the cattle could not get at it at all, and could hardly move round. It was all but impossible to travel on horseback—except on a few well-beaten trails. It was dangerous to attempt to penetrate the Bad Lands, whose shape had been completely altered by the great white mounds and drifts. The starving cattle died by scores of thousands before the helpless owners' eyes. The bulls, the cows who were suckling calves, or who were heavy with calf, the weak cattle that had just been driven up on the trail, and the late calves suffered most; the old range animals did better, and the steers best of all; but the best was bad enough. Even many of the horses died. An outfit near me lost half its saddle-band, the animals having been worked so hard that they were very thin when fall came.

In the thick brush the stock got some shelter and sustenance. They gnawed every twig and bough they could get at. They browsed the bitter sage brush down to where the branches were the thickness of a man's finger. When near a ranch they crowded into the outhouses and sheds to die, and fences had to be built around the windows to keep the wild-eyed, desperate beasts from thrusting their heads through the glass panes. In most cases it was impossible either to drive them to the haystacks or to haul the hay out to them. The deer even were so weak as to be easily run down; and on one or two of the plateaus where there were bands of antelope, these wary creatures grew so numbed and feeble that they could have been slaughtered like rabbits. But the hunters could hardly get out, and could bring home neither hide nor meat, so the game went unharmed.

The way in which the cattle got through the winter depended largely on the different localities in which the bands were caught when the first heavy snows came. A group of animals in a bare valley, without underbrush and with steep sides, would all die, weak and strong alike; they could get no food and no shelter, and so there would not be a hoof left. On the other hand, hundreds wintered on the great thickly wooded bottoms near my ranch house with little more than ordinary loss, though a skinny sorry-looking crew by the time the snow melted. In intermediate places the strong survived and the weak perished.

It would be impossible to imagine any sight more dreary and melancholy than that offered by the ranges when the snow went off in March. The land was a mere barren waste; not a green thing could be seen; the dead grass eaten off till the country looked as if it had been shaved with a razor. Occasionally among the desolate hills a rider would come across a band of gaunt, hollow-flanked cattle feebly cropping the sparse, dry pasturage, too listless to move out of the way; and the blackened carcasses lay in the sheltered spots, some stretched out, others in as natural a position as if the animals had merely lain down to rest. It was small wonder that cheerful stockmen were rare objects that spring.

Our only comfort was that we did not, as usual, suffer a heavy loss from weak cattle getting mired down in the springs and mud-holes when the ice broke up—for all the weak animals were dead already. The truth is, ours is a primitive industry, and we suffer the reverses as well as enjoy the successes only known to primitive peoples. A hard winter is to us in the north what a dry summer is to Texas or Australia—what seasons of famine once were to all peoples. We still live in an iron age that the old civilized world has long passed by. The men of the border reckon upon stern and unending struggles with their iron-bound surroundings; against the grim harshness of their existence they set the strength and the abounding vitality that come with it. They run risks to life and limb that are unknown to the dwellers in cities; and what the men freely brave, the beasts that they own must also sometimes suffer.

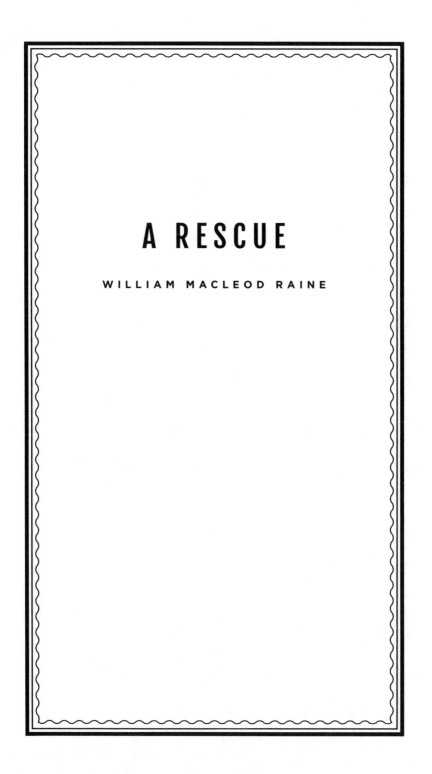

# A RESCUE

WILLIAM MACLEOD RAINE

He swung from the horse and offered a hand to help her dismount. A reckless, unholy light burned in his daring eyes.

"Home at last, Miss Messiter. Let me offer you a thousand welcomes."

An icy hand seemed to clutch at her heart. "Home! What do you mean? This isn't the Lazy D."

"Not at all. The Lazy D is sixty miles from here. This is where I hang out—and you, for the present."

"But—I don't understand. How dare you bring me here?"

"The desire for your company, Miss Messiter, made of me a Lochinvar."

She saw, with a shiver, that the ribald eyes were mocking her.

"Take me back this instant—this instant," she commanded, but her imperious voice was not very sure of itself. "Take me home at once, you liar."

"I expect you don't quite understand," he exclaimed, with gentle derision. "You're a prisoner of war, Miss Messiter."

"And who are you?" she faltered.

But before he spoke she found an answer to her question, found it by a flash of divination she could never afterward explain.

"You're the man I met at Fraser's dance—the man they call the King of the Bighorn country."

He accepted identification with an elaborate bow. "Correct, ma'am. I'm Ned Bannister the king."

An instant before she had been sitting rigid with a face of startled fear, but as he spoke a great wave of joy beat into her heart. For if this man were the terror of the country the one she had left wounded at her house could not be. She forgot that she was herself in peril, forgot everything in the swift conviction that the man she loved was an honest gentleman and worthy of her.

The man standing by the horse could not understand the light that had so immediately leaped to her eyes. Even *his* vanity hesitated at the obvious deduction that she had already succumbed to his attractions.

"But I don't understand—that isn't your real name, is it? I know another man who calls himself Ned Bannister."

He laughed scornfully. "My cousin, the sheepherder. Yes, that's his name, too. We both have a right to it."

"Your cousin?"

The familiarity in him that had been haunting her all day and that had deceived her at the dance was now explained. It was her lover of which this man reminded her. Now that she had been given the clue she could trace kinship in manner, gait and appearance.

"I'm not proud of my mealy-mouthed namesake," he replied.

"Nor he of you, I am sure," she quickly answered.

"I dare say not. But won't y'u 'light, Miss Messiter?"

She slipped immediately to the ground beside him. Her eyes looked him over with quiet scorn.

"From first to last you have done nothing but lie to me. When we were out last night you knew that ranch was close at hand. You lied to me again when you said it was deserted."

"Very well. We'll say I lied, though it's not a nice word in so pretty a mouth as yours, Miss Messiter. Y'u ought to read up again the fable about the toads dropping from the beautiful lady's lips."

"What's your object? What do you expect to gain by it?"

"Up to date I've gained a right interesting guest. Y'u will be diverting enough. With so charming a lady visiting me I'm not worrying about getting bored."

"So you war on women, you coward."

The change in him was instantaneous. It was as if a thousand years of civilization had been sponged out in an eyebeat. He stood before her a savage primeval, his tight-lipped smile cruel in its triumph.

"Did I begin this fight? Didn't y'u and your punchers try to balk me by taking that sheepherder from me after I had bagged him? That was your hour. By God, this is mine! I'll teach y'u it isn't safe to interfere with me. What I want I get one way or another, and don't y'u forget it, my girl."

She was afraid to the very marrow of her. But she would not show her fear, nor could he read it in the slim superb erectness with which she gave him defiance.

"You coward!"

"That's twice you've called me that," he cried, his face flushing darkly and his eyes glittering. "Y'u'll crawl on your knees to me and beg pardon before I'm through with y'u, my beauty. Y'u'll learn to lick the hand that strikes y'u. You're mine—mine to do with as I please. Don't forget that for a moment. I'll break your spirit or I'll break your heart."

His ferocity appalled her, but her brave eyes held their own. With an oath he turned on his heel and struck the palms of his hands together. An Indian squaw came running from one of the cabins. He flung at her a sentence or two in the native tongue and pointed at his captive. She asked a question impassively and he jabbed out a threat. The squaw nodded her head, and motioned to the girl to follow her.

When Helen Messiter was alone in the room that was to serve as her prison she sank into a chair and covered her face with her hands in a despair that was for the moment utter.

~~~~~~~~~~~~~~~~~~~~~~~~~~~~~~~~~~~~~~~~~~~~~~~~~~~~~~~~~~~~~~~~~~~~

Helen Messiter was left alone until darkness fell, when the Cheyenne squaw brought in a kerosene lamp and shortly afterward her supper. The woman either could not or would not speak English, and her only answer to her captive's advances was by sullen grunts. At the expiration of half an hour she returned for the dishes, locking the door after her when she left.

The room itself was comfortable enough. It was evidently Bannister's own, judging from its contents. Two or three rifles hung in racks. On top of the bookcase was a half-filled tobacco pouch and several pipes, all of them lying carelessly on a pile of music which ran from Verdi to ragtime. In his books she found the same shallow catholicity. Side by side with Montaigne's "Essays," a well-worn Villon in the original, Stevenson's "Letters" and "Anna Karenina," dozens of paper-covered novels, mostly the veriest trash, held their disreputable own. Some of them were French, others detective stories, still others melodramatic tales of love. The piano was an expensive one, but not in the best of tune. Everything in the room contributed to the effect of capacity untempered by discipline and discrimination. Plainly he was a man of taste who had outraged and deadened his power of differentiation by abuse.

For Helen the silent night was alive with alarms. The moaning of the wind, the slightest rustle outside, the creaking of a board, were enough to set her heart wildly beating. She did not undress, but by the light of her dim, ragged wick sought for composure from the pages of Montaigne and Stevenson. When the first gray day streaks came she was still reading, but with their coming she blew out her light and lay down. She fell asleep at once, and it was five hours later that the knock of her attendant awakened her from heavy slumber.

With the bright sunlit day she was again mistress of her nerves, prepared to meet resolutely whatever danger might confront her. But the morning passed quietly enough, and after lunch the Indian woman led her into the little valley promenade in front of the buildings and sat down on a rock while her captive enjoyed the sunshine.

The course of Helen's saunterings took her toward the rock slide that made the gateway of the valley. She was wondering if it could have been left unguarded, when a rough voice warned her back. Looking round, she caught sight of a man seated cross-legged on a great boulder. It took only a second glance to certify that the man was her former foreman, Judd Morgan.

She had never seen anything more malevolent than his triumph.

"Better stay in the valley, Miss Messiter. Y'u might right easily get lost outside," he jeered.

Without reply she turned her back on him and began to retrace her way to the house. Stung by her contempt, he sprang up and strode after her.

"So y'u won't speak to me, eh? Think yourself too good to speak to a common everyday God damned white man, do y'u?"

Apparently she did not know he was on the map. In a fury he caught at her shoulder and whirled her round.

"Now, by God, do y'u see me? I'm Judd Morgan, the man y'u kicked off the Lazy D. I told y'u then y'u were going to be sorry long as y'u lived."

"Don't you dare touch me, you hound!" Her blazing eyes menaced him so fiercely that he hesitated.

There was the sound of a quick, light step running toward them. Morgan half turned, was caught in a grip of steel and hurled headlong among a pile of broken rocks.

"Y'u would dare, would y'u?" panted his assailant, passionately, ready to obliterate the offender if he showed fight.

Morgan got up slowly, his head bleeding from contact with the sharp rocks. There was murder in his bloodshot eye, but he knew his master, and after trying vainly to face him down he swung away with an oath.

"I'll have to apologize for that coyote, Miss Messiter. These fellows need a hint occasionally as to how to behave," said Bannister.

"Your hints are rather forceful, are they not?"

"I ain't running a Sunday school," he admitted.

"So I have gathered. I wonder where he learned to bully women," she mused aloud.

"Putting it another way, you think there ought to be some one to apologize for his master."

He was smiling at her without the least rancor, and it came on her with a woman's swift instinct that safety lay in humoring his volatile moods and diverting him from those that were dangerous.

"Since I'm a prisoner of war I wouldn't dare think that—not aloud, at least. You might starve me," she told him, saucily.

"Still, down in your heart y'u think—"

"That there is a great deal of difference between master and man. One is a gentleman in his best moments; the other is always a ruffian."

She had touched his vanity. As he walked beside her she could almost see his complacency purr.

"I'm a miscreant, I reckon, but I was a gentleman first."

Fortunately he did not see the flash of veiled scorn she shot at him under her long lashes.

With her breakfast next morning the Cheyenne woman brought a note signed "Shepherd-of-the-Desert." In it Bannister asked permission to pay his respects. The girl divined that he was in his better mood, and penciled on his note the favor she could scarce refuse.

But she was scarcely prepared for the impudent air of jocund spring he brought into her prison, the gay assumption of *camaraderie* so inconsistent with the facts. Yet since safety lay in an avoidance of the tragic, she set herself to match his mood.

At sight of the open Tennyson on the table he laughed and quoted:

> "She only said, 'The day is dreary,
> He cometh not,' she said"

"But, you see, he comes," he added. "What say, Mariana of the Robbers' Roost, to making a picnic day of it? We'll climb the Crags and lunch on the summit."

"The Crags?"

"That Matterhorn-shaped peak that begins at our back door. Are you for it?"

While this mood was uppermost in him she felt reasonably safe. It was a phase of him she certainly did not mean to discourage. Besides, she had a youthful confidence in her powers that she was loath to give up without an effort to find the accessible side of his ruthless heart.

"I'll try it; but you must help me when we come to the bad places," she said.

"Sure thing! It's a deal. You're a right good mountaineer, I'll bet."

"Thank you; but you had better save your compliments till I make good," she told him, with the most piquant air of gayety in the world.

They started on horseback, following a mountain trail that zig-zagged across the foothills toward the Crags. He had unearthed some-where a boy's saddle that suited her very well, and the pony she rode was one of the easiest she had ever mounted. At the end of an hour's ride they left the horses and began the ascent on foot. It was a stiff climb, growing steeper as they ascended, but Helen Messiter had not tramped over golf links for nothing. She might grow leg weary, but she would not cry "Enough!" And he, on his part, showed the tactful con-sideration for the resources of her strength he had already taught her to expect from that other day's experience on the plains. It was a very rare hand of assistance that he offered her, but often he stopped to admire the beautiful view that stretched for many miles below them, in order that she might get a minute's breathing space.

Once he pointed out, far away on the horizon, a bright gleam that caught the sunlight like a heliograph.

"That's the big rock slide back of the Lazy D," he explained.

She drew a long breath, and flashed a stealthy look at him.

"It's a long way from here, isn't it?"

"I didn't find it so far last time I took the trip—not the last half of the journey, anyhow," he answered.

"You're very complimentary. I was only wondering whether I could find it if I should manage to escape."

He stroked his black mustache and smiled gallantly at her. "I reckon I won't let so pretty a prisoner escape."

"Do you expect me to burden your hospitality forever and a day? Wouldn't that be a little too much of Mariana of the Robbers' Roost?" she asked, lightly.

"I'm willing to risk it."

He looked with half-shut smoldering eyes at her slender exquisite-ness, so instinct with the vital charm of sex. There was veiled passion in his eyes, but there was in them, too, a desire to stand well with her. He meant to win her, but if possible he would win with her own reluctant consent. She must bring him with hesitant feet a heart surrendered in spite of her pride and flinty puritanism. The vanity of the man craved a victory that should be of the spirit as well as of the flesh.

Deftly she guided the conversation back to less dangerous channels. In this the increasing difficulty of the climb assisted her, for after they reached the last ascent sustained talk became impossible.

"See that trough above us near the summit? Y'u'll have to hang on by your eyelashes, pardner." He always burlesqued the word of comradeship a little to soften its familiarity.

"Dear me! Is it that bad?"

"It is so bad that at the top y'u have to jump for a grip and draw yourself up by your arms."

"I'll never be able to do it."

"I'm here to help."

"But if one should miss?"

He shrugged. "Ah! That's a theological question. If the sky pilots guess right, for y'u heaven and for me hell."

They negotiated the trough successfully to its uptilted end. She had a bad moment when he leaped for the rock rim above from the narrow ledge on which they stood. But he caught it, drew himself up without the least trouble and turned to assist her. He sat down on the rock edge facing the abyss beneath them, and told her to lock her hands together above his left foot. Then slowly, inch by inch, he drew her up till with one of his hands he could catch her wrist. A moment later she was standing on his rigid toes, from which position she warily edged to safety above.

"Well done, little pardner. You're the first woman ever climbed the Crags." He offered a hand to celebrate the achievement.

"If I am it is all due to you, big pardner. I could never have made that last bit alone."

They ate lunch merrily in the pleasant sunlight, and both of them seemed as free from care as a schoolboy on a holiday.

"It's good to be alive, isn't it?" he asked her after they had eaten, as he lay on the warm ground at her feet. "And what a life it is here! To be riding free, with your knees pressing a saddle, in the wind and sun. There's something in a man to which the wide spaces call. I'd rather lie here in the sunbeat with you beside me than be a king. You remember the 'Last Ride' that fellow Browning tells about? I reckon he's dead right. If a man could only capture his best moments and hold them forever it would be heaven to the $n$th degree."

She studied her sublimated villain with that fascination his vagaries always excited in her. Was ever a more impossible combination put together than this sentimental scamp with the long record of evil?

"Say it," he laughed. "Whang it out! Ask anything you like, pardner."

Pluckily daring, she took him at his word. "I was only wondering at the different men I find in you. Before I have known you a dozen hours I discover in you the poet and the man of action, the schoolboy and the philosopher, the sentimentalist and the cynic, and—may I say it?—the gentleman and the blackguard. One feels a sense of loss. You should have specialized. You would have made such a good soldier, for instance. Pity you didn't go to West Point."

"Think so?" He was immensely flattered at her interest in him.

"Yes. You surely missed your calling. You were born for a soldier; cavalry, I should say. What an ornament to society you would have been if your energies had found the right vent! But they didn't find it—and you craved excitement, I suppose. Perhaps you had to go the way you did."

"Therefore I am what I am? Please particularize."

"I can't, because I don't understand you. But I think this much is true, that you have set yourself against all laws of God and man. Yet you are not consistent, since you are better than your creed. You tell yourself there shall be no law for you but your own will, and you find there is something in you stronger than desire that makes you shrink at many things. You can kill in fair fight, but you can't knife a man in the back, can you?"

"I never have."

"You have a dreadfully perverted set of rules, but you play by them. That's why I know I'm safe with you, even when you are at your worst." She announced this boldly, just as if she had no doubts.

"Oh, you know you're safe, do you?"

"Of course I do. You were once a gentleman and you can't forget it entirely. That's the weakness in your philosophy of total depravity."

"You speak with an assurance you don't always feel, I reckon. And I expect I wouldn't bank too much on those divinations of yours, if I were you." He rolled over so that he could face her more directly. "You've been mighty frank, Miss Messiter, and I take off my hat to your sand. Now I'm going to be frank awhile. You interest me. I never met a woman that interested me so much. But you do a heap more than interest me. No, you sit right there and listen. Your cheeky pluck and that insolent, indifferent beauty of yours made a hit with me the first minute I saw you that night. I swore I'd tame you, and that's why I brought you to the ranch. Your eye flashed a heap too haughty for me to give you the go-by. Mind you, I meant to be master. I meant to make you mine as much as that dog that licked my hand before we started. What I meant then I still mean, but in a different way.

"That's as far as it went with me then, but before we reached here next day I knew the thing cut deeper with me. I ain't saying that I love you, because I'm a sweep and it's just likely I don't know passion from love. But I'll tell you this—there hasn't been a waking moment since then I haven't been on fire to be with you. That's why I stayed away until I knew I wasn't so likely to slop over. But here, I'm doing it right this minute. I care more for you than I do for anything else on this earth. But that makes it worse for you. I never cared for anybody without bringing ruin on them. I broke my mother's heart and spoiled the life of a girl I was going to marry. That's the kind of scoundrel I am. Even if I can make you care for me—and I reckon I can if y'u are like other women—I'll likely drag you through hell after me."

The simulation of despair in his beautiful eyes spoke more impressively than his self-scorning words. She was touched in spite of herself, despite, too, his colossal egotism. For there is an appeal about the engaging sinner that drums in a woman's head and calls to her heart. All good women are missionaries in the last analysis, and Miss Messiter was not an exception to her sex. Even though she knew he was half a fraud and that his emotion was theatric, she could not let the moment pass.

She leaned forward, a sweet, shy dignity in her manner. "Is it too late to change? Why not begin now? There is still a to-morrow, and it need not be the slave of yesterday. Life for all of us is full of milestones."

"And how shall I begin my new career of saintliness?" he asked, with a swift return to blithe irony.

"The nearest duty. Take me back to my ranch. Begin a life of rigid honesty."

"Give you up now that I have found you? That is just the last thing I would do," he cried, with glancing eyes. "No—no. The clock can't be turned back. I have sowed and I must reap."

He leaped to his feet. "Come! We must be going."

She rose sadly, for she knew the mood of sentimental regret for his wasted life had passed, and she had failed.

They descended the trough and reached the boulder field that had marked the terminal of the glacier. At the farther edge of it the outlaw turned to point out to the girl a great bank of snow on a mountainside fifteen miles away.

He changed his weight as he turned, when a rock slipped under his foot and he came down hard. He was up again in an instant, but Helen Messiter caught the sharp intake of his breath when he set foot on the ground.

"You've sprained your ankle!" she cried.

"Afraid so. It's my own rotten carelessness." He broke into a storm of curses and limped forward a dozen steps, but he had to set his teeth to stand the pain.

"Lean on me," she said, gently.

"I reckon I'll have to," he grimly answered.

They covered a quarter of a mile, with many stops to rest the swollen ankle. Only by the irregularity of his breathing and the damp moisture on his forehead could she tell the agony he was enduring.

"It must be dreadful," she told him once.

"I've got to stand for it, I reckon."

Again she said, when they had reached a wooden grove where pines grew splendid on a carpet of grass: "Only two hundred yards more. I think I can bring your pony as far as the big cottonwood."

She noticed that he leaned heavier and heavier on her. However, when they reached the cottonwood he leaned no more, but pitched forward in a faint. The water bottle was empty, but she ran down to where the ponies had been left, and presently came back with his canteen. She had been away perhaps twenty minutes, and when she came back he waved a hand airily at her.

"First time in my life that ever happened," he apologized, gayly. "But why didn't y'u get on Jim and cut loose for the Lazy D while you had the chance?"

"I didn't think of it. Perhaps I shall next time."

"I shouldn't. Y'u see, I'd follow you and bring you back. And if I didn't find you there would be a lamb lost again in these hills."

"The sporting thing would be to take a chance."

"And leave me here alone? Well, I'm going to give you a show to take it." He handed her his revolver. "Y'u may need this if you're going traveling."

"Are you telling me to go?" she asked, amazed.

"I'm telling you to do as you think best. Y'u may take a hike or y'u may bring back Two-step to me. Suit yourself."

"I tell you plainly, I sha'n't come back."

"And I'm sure y'u will."

"But I won't. The thing's absurd. Would you?"

"No, I shouldn't. But y'u will."

"I won't. Good-bye." She held out her hand.

He shook his head, looking steadily at her. "What's the use? You'll be back in half an hour."

"Not I. Did you say I must keep the Antelope Peaks in a line to reach the Lazy D?"

"Yes, a little to the left. Don't be long, little pardner."

"I hate to leave you here. Perhaps I'll send a sheriff to take care of you."

"Better bring Two-step up to the south of that bunch of cottonwoods. It's not so steep that way."

"I'll mention it to the sheriff. I'm not coming myself."

She left him apparently obstinate in the conviction that she would return. In reality he was taking a gambler's chance, but it was of a part with the reckless spirit of the man that the risk appealed to him. It was plain he could not drag himself farther. Since he must let her go for the horse alone, he chose that she should go with her eyes open to his knowledge of the opportunity of escape.

But Helen Messiter had not the slightest intention of returning. She had found her chance, and she meant to make the most of it. As rapidly as her unaccustomed fingers would permit she saddled and cinched her pony. She had not ridden a hundred yards before Two-step came crashing through the young cottonwood grove after her. Objecting to being left alone, he had broken the rein that tied him. The girl tried to recapture the horse in order that the outlaw might not be left entirely without means of reaching camp, but her efforts were unsuccessful. She had to give it up and resume her journey.

Of course the men at his ranch would miss their chief and search for him. There could be no doubt but that they would find him. She bolstered up her assurance of this as she rode toward the Antelope Peaks, but her hope lacked buoyancy, because she doubted if they had any idea of where he had been going to spend the day.

She rode slower and slower, and finally came to a long halt for consideration. Vividly there rose before her a picture of the miscreant waiting grimly for death or rescue. Well, she was not to blame. If she deserted him it was to save herself. But to leave him helpless——

No, she could not leave a crippled man to die alone, even though he were her enemy. That was the goal to which her circling thoughts came always home, and with a sob she turned her horse's head. It was a piece of soft-headed folly, she confessed, but she could not help it.

So back she went and found him lying just where she had left him. His derisive smile offered her no thanks. She doubted, indeed, whether he felt any sense of gratitude.

"Y'u didn't break your neck hurrying," he said.

She made her confession with a palpable chagrin, "I meant to ride away. I rode a mile or two. But I had to come back. I couldn't leave you here alone."

His eyes sparkled triumphantly. She saw that he had misunderstood the reason of her return, that he was pluming himself on a conquest of his fascinated victim.

"One couldn't leave even a broken-legged dog without help," she added, quietly.

"So how could we expect a woman to leave the man she's getting ready to love?"

She let her contemptuous eyes rest on him in silence.

"That's right. Look at me as if I were dirt under your feet. Hate me, if it makes y'u feel better. But y'u'll have to come to loving me just the same."

"Can you get on without help?" she asked, ranging the pony alongside him.

"Yes." He dragged himself to the saddle and smiled down at her. "So y'u better make up your mind to that soon as convenient."

Disdaining answer, she walked in front of the pony down the trail. She was tired, but her elastic tread would not admit it to him. For she was dramatizing unconsciously, with firmly clenched fingers that bit into her palms, the march of the unconquerable.

Evening had fallen before they reached the ranch. It was beautifully still, except for the call of the quails. The hazy violet outline of the mountains came to silhouette against the skyline with a fine edge.

As they passed the pony corral he spoke again. "I'll never forget to-day. I've got it fenced from all the yesterdays and to-morrows. I have surely enjoyed our little picnic."

"Nor will I forget it," she flung back quickly, as she followed him into the house. "For I never before met a man wholly incapable of gratitude and entirely lacking in all the elements that go to distinguish a human being from a wolf."

He turned to speak to her, and as he did so a quiet voice cautioned him:

"Don't move, seh, except to throw up your hands."

At the sound of that pleasant drawl Helen's heart jumped to her throat. Jim McWilliams, half seated on the edge of the table, was looking intently at Bannister, and there was a revolver in his hand. On the other side of the room sat Morgan and the Cheyenne woman, apparently in charge of the young giant Denver.

Bannister's hands went up, even as he whirled with a snarl toward the man Morgan.

"I told y'u to watch out, y'u muttonhead!"

"But y'u clean forgot to remember to watch out your own self," spoke up McWilliams, unbuckling the belt from the waist of his new captive.

"Oh, Mac, you blessed boy!" cried Helen, with an hysterical laugh that was half a sob. "How did you ever find me?"

"Followed the track of the gas wagon to where it ran out of juice. We lost your trail after that, but Denver and me had the good luck to pick it up again where y'u'd camped that night. We mislaid it again up in the hills, and Denver he knew about this place. We dropped in just casual for information, but when we set our peepers on Judd we allowed we would stay awhile, him being so anxious to have us."

"You dear boys! I'm so glad! You don't know," she sobbed, dropping weakly into the nearest chair.

"We can guess, ma'am," her foreman answered grimly, his eyes on Bannister. "And if either of these scoundrels have treated y'u so they need their light put out all y'u have got to do is to say so."

"No, no, Mac. Let us go away from here and leave them. Can't we go now—this very minute?"

The foreman's eyes found those of Denver and the latter nodded. Neither of them had had a bite to eat since the previous evening, and they were naturally ravenous.

"All right. We'll go right now, ma'am. Denver, I'll take care of these beauties while y'u step into the pantry with Mrs. Lo-the-poor-Indian and put up a lunch. Y'u don't want to forget we're hungry enough to eat the wool off a pair of chaps."

"I ain't likely to forget it, am I?" grinned Denver, as he rose.

"You poor boys! I know you are starved. I'll see about the lunch if one of you will get the horses round," Helen broke in. "Only let us hurry and get away from here."

Ten minutes later they were in the saddle. For the sake of precaution Mac walked two of his captives with them for about a mile before releasing them. Bannister, unable to travel, they left behind.

"We'll get down out of the hills and then cut acrost to the Meeker ranch," said McWilliams, after they had ridden forward a few miles. "I'll telephone from there to Slauson's and have the old man send a boy over to the Lazy D with the good word. We'll get an early start from Meeker's and make it home in the afternoon."

"How did you leave Mr. Bannister?" asked Helen, in a carefully careless voice.

She had held back this question for nearly an hour till Denver, who was guiding the party, had passed out of earshot.

"Left him with two of the boys holding him down. He was plumb anxious to commit suicide by joining the hunt for y'u, but I had other thoughts," grinned Mac.

She felt herself flushing in the darkness. "We've made a great mistake about him, Mac. It's his cousin of the same name that is the desperado—the man we just left."

"Yes, that's what Judd let out before y'u and the King arrived. It made me plumb glad to my gizzard to hear it."

"I was pleased, too."

"Somehow I suspicioned that," he made answer, with banter in his dry tones.

"Of course I would be glad to know that he is not a villain," she defended.

"Sure!"

"Well, one doesn't like to think that a friend———"

"He's your friend, is he?" chuckled Mac.

"Why shouldn't he be?"

"I'm offering no objection, ma'am."

"You act as if———"

"Sho! Don't pay any attention to me. Sometimes I get these spells of laughing in to myself. They just come. Doctors never could find a reason."

"Oh, well!"

"He was your enemy and now he's your friend. Course since I'm your foreman I got to keep posted on how we stand with our neighbors. If your feelings change to him again y'u'll let me know, I expect."

"Why should they change?" she asked in a cold voice that her rising color belied.

"Search *me!* I just thought mebbe———"

"You think too much," she cut in, shortly.

"Yes, ma'am," admitted the youth, meekly, but from time to time as they rode she could hear faint sounds of mirth from his direction.

McWilliams telephoned from the Meeker ranch to Slauson's, and inside of two hours the Lazy D knew that its owner had been found. As one puncher after another reported there on jaded ponies to get the latest word they heard that all was well. Each one at once unsaddled, ate and turned in for the first night's sleep he had had since his mistress had been missing. Next morning they rode in a body to meet her.

She saw them galloping toward her in a cloud of dust, and presently she was the center of a circle of her happy family. They were like boys—exuberant in their joy at her deliverance and eager to set out at once to avenge her wrongs.

Ned Bannister, from his window, saw them coming. When the group separated at the corral and she rode from among them with McWilliams toward the house the sheepman could sit still no longer. He limped to the front door and waved the American flag which he had unearthed for the occasion.

# A RODEO AT LOS OJOS

### FREDERIC REMINGTON

The sun beat down on the dry grass, and the punchers were squatting about in groups in front of the straggling log and *adobe* buildings which constituted the outlying ranch of Los Ojos.

Mr. Johnnie Bell, the *capitan* in charge, was walking about in his heavy *chaparras*, a slouch hat, and a white "biled" shirt. He was chewing his long yellow mustache, and gazing across the great plain of Bavicora with set and squinting eyes. He passed us and repassed us, still gazing out, and in his long Texas drawl said, "Thar's them San Miguel fellers."

I looked, but I could not see any San Miguel fellows in the wide expanse of land.

"Hyar, crawl some horses, and we'll go out and meet 'em," continue Mr. Bell; and, suiting the action, we mounted our horses and followed him. After a time I made out tiny specks in the atmospheric wave which rises from the heated land, and in half an hour could plainly make out a cavalcade of horsemen. Presently breaking into a gallop, which movement was imitated by the other party, we bore down on each other, and only stopped when near enough to shake hands, the half-wild ponies darting about and rearing under the excitement. Greetings were exchanged in Spanish, and the peculiar shoulder tap, or abbreviated embrace, was indulged in. Doubtless a part of our outfit was as strange to Governor Terraza's men—for he is the *patron* of San Miguel—as they were to us.

My imagination had never before pictured anything so wild as these leather-clad *vaqueros*. As they removed their hats to greet Jack, their unkempt locks blew over their faces, back off their foreheads, in the greatest disorder. They were clad in terra-cotta buckskin, elaborately trimmed with white leather, and around their lower legs wore heavy cowhide as a sort of legging. They were fully armed, and with their jingling spurs, their flapping ropes and buckskin strings, and with their gay *serapes* tied behind their saddles, they were as impressive a cavalcade of desert-scamperers as it has been my fortune to see. Slowly we rode back to the corrals, where they dismounted.

Shortly, and unobserved by us until at hand, we heard the clatter of hoofs, and, leaving in their wake a cloud of dust, a dozen punchers from another outfit bore down upon us as we stood under the *ramada* of the ranchhouse, and pulling up with a jerk, which threw the ponies on their haunches, the men dismounted and approached, to be welcomed by the master of the *rodeo*.

A few short orders were given, and the three mounted men started down to the springs, and, after charging about, we could see that they had roped a steer, which they led, bawling and resisting, to the ranch, where it was quickly thrown and slaughtered. Turning it on its back, after the manner of the old buffalo-hunters, it was quickly disrobed and cut up into hundreds of small pieces, which is the method practised by the Mexican butchers, and distributed to the men.

In Mexico it is the custom for the man who gives the "round-up" to supply fresh beef to the visiting cow-men; and on this occasion it seemed that the pigs, chickens, and dogs were also embraced in the bounty of the *patron*, for I noticed one piece which hung immediately in front of my quarters had two chickens roosting on the top of it, and a pig and a dog tugging vigorously at the bottom.

The horse herds were moved in from the *llano* and rounded up in the corral, from which the punchers selected their mounts by roping, and as the sun was westering they disappeared, in obedience to orders, to all points of the compass. The men took positions back in the hills and far out on the plain; there, building a little fire, they cook their beef, and, enveloped in their *serapes*, spend the night. At early dawn they converge on the ranch, driving before them such stock as they may.

In the morning we could see from the ranch-house a great semicircle of gray on the yellow plains. It was the thousands of cattle coming to the *rodeo*. In an hour more we could plainly see the cattle, and behind them the *vaqueros* dashing about, waving their *serapes*. Gradually they converged on the *rodeo* ground, and, enveloped in a great cloud of dust and with hollow bellowings, like the low pedals of a great organ, they began to mill, or turn about a common centre, until gradually quieted by the enveloping cloud of horsemen. The *patron* and the captains of the neighboring ranches, after an exchange of long-winded Spanish formalities, and accompanied by ourselves, rode slowly from the ranch to the herd, and, entering it, passed through and through and around in solemn procession. The cattle part before the horsemen, and the dust rises so as to obscure to unaccustomed eyes all but the silhouettes of the moving thousands. This is an important function in a cow country, since it enables the owners or their men to estimate what numbers of the stock belong to them, to observe the brands, and to inquire as to the condition of the animals and the numbers of calves and "mavericks," and to settle any disputes which may arise therefrom.

All controversy, if there be any, having been adjusted, a part of the punchers move slowly into the herd, while the rest patrol outside, and hold it. Then a movement soon begins. You see a figure dash about at full speed through an apparently impenetrable mass of cattle; the stock becomes uneasy and moves about, gradually beginning the milling process, but the men select the cattle bearing their brand, and course them through the herd; all becomes confusion, and the cattle simply seek to escape from the ever-recurring horsemen. Here one sees the matchless horsemanship of the punchers. Their little ponies, trained to the business, respond to the slightest pressure. The cattle make every attempt to escape, dodging in and out and crowding among their kind; but right on their quarter, gradually forcing them to the edge of the herd, keeps the puncher, until finally, as a last effort, the cow and the calf rush through the supporting line, when, after a terrific race, she is turned into another herd, and is called "the cut."

One who finds pleasure in action can here see the most surprising manifestations of it. A huge bull, wild with fright, breaks from the herd, with lowered head and whitened eye, and goes charging off indifferent to what or whom he may encounter, with the little pony pattering in his wake. The cattle run at times with nearly the intensity of action of a deer, and whip and spur are applied mercilessly to the little horse. The process of "tailing" is indulged in, although it is a dangerous practice for the man, and reprehensible from its brutality to the cattle. A man will pursue a bull at top speed, will reach over and grasp the tail of the animal, bring it to his saddle, throw his right leg over the tail, and swing his horse suddenly to the left, which throws the bull rolling over and over. That this method has its value I have seen in the case of pursuing "mavericks," where an unsuccessful throw was made with the rope, and the animal was about to enter the thick timber; it would be impossible to coil the rope again, and an escape would follow but for the wonderful dexterity of these men in this accomplishment. The little calves become separated from their mothers, and go bleating about; their mothers respond by bellows, until pandemonium seems to reign. The dust is blinding, and the puncher becomes grimy and soiled; the horses lather; and in the excitement the desperate men do deeds which convince you of their faith that "a man can't die till his time comes." At times a bull is found so skilled in these contests that he cannot be displaced from the herd; it is then necessary to rope and drag him to the point desired; and I noticed punchers ride behind recalcitrant bulls and, reaching over, spur them. I also saw two men throw simultaneously for an immense creature, when, to my great astonishment, he turned tail over head and rolled on the ground. They had both sat back on their ropes together.

The whole scene was inspiring to a degree, and well merited Mr. Yorick's observation that "it is the sport of kings; the image of war, with twenty-five per cent of its danger."

Fresh horses are saddled from time to time, but before high noon the work is done, and the various "cut-offs" are herded in different directions. By this time the dust had risen until lost in the sky above, and as the various bands of cowboys rode slowly back to the ranch, I observed their demoralized condition. The economy *per force* of the Mexican people prompts them to put no more cotton into a shirt than is absolutely necessary, with the consequences that, in these cases, their shirts had pulled out from their belts and their *serapes*, and were flapping in the wind; their mustaches and their hair were perfectly solid with dust, and one could not tell a bay horse from a black.

Now come the cigarettes and the broiling of beef. The bosses were invited to sit at our table, and as the work of cutting and branding had yet to be done, no time was taken for ablutions. Opposite me sat a certain individual who, as he engulfed his food, presented a grimy waste of visage only broken by the rolling of his eyes and the snapping of his teeth.

We then proceeded to the corrals, which were made in stockaded form from gnarled and many-shaped posts set on an end. The cows and calves were bunched on one side in fearful expectancy. A fire was built just outside of the bars, and the branding-irons set on. Into the corrals went the punchers, with their ropes coiled in their hands. Selecting their victims, they threw their ropes, and, after pulling and tugging, a bull calf would come out of the bunch, whereat two men would set upon him and "rastle" him to the ground. It is a strange mixture of humor and pathos, this mutilation of calves—humorous when the calf throws the man, and pathetic when the man throws the calf. Occasionally an old cow takes an unusual interest in her offspring, and charges boldly into their midst. Those men who cannot escape soon enough throw dust in her eyes, or put their hats over her horns. And in this case there were some big steers which had been "cut out" for purposes of work at the plough and turned in with the young stock; one old grizzled veteran manifested an interest in the proceedings, and walked boldly from the bunch, with his head in the air and bellowing; a wild scurry ensued, and hats and *serapes* were thrown to confuse him. But over all this the punchers only laugh, and go at it again. In corral roping they try to catch the calf by the front feet, and in this they become so expert that they rarely miss. As I sat on the fence, one of the foremen, in play, threw and caught my legs as they dangled.

When the work is done and the cattle are again turned into the herd, the men repair to the *casa* and indulge in games and pranks. We had shooting-matches and hundred-yard dashes; but I think no records were broken, since punchers on foot are odd fish. They walk as though they expected every movement to sit down. Their knees work outward, and they have a decided "hitch" in their gait; but once let them get a foot in a stirrup and a grasp on the horn of the saddle, and a dynamite cartridge alone could expel them from their seat. When loping over the plain the puncher is the epitome of equine grace, and if he desires to look behind him he simply shifts his whole body to one side and lets the horse go as he pleases. In the pursuit of cattle at a *rodeo* he leans forward in his saddle, and with his arms elevated to his shoulders he "plugs" in his spurs and makes his pony fairly sail. While going at this tremendous speed he turns his pony almost in his stride, and no matter how a bull may twist and swerve about, he is at his tail as true as a magnet to the pole. The Mexican punchers all use the "ring bit," and it is a fearful contrivance. Their saddle-trees are very short, and straight and quite as shapeless as a "sawbuck pack-saddle." The horn is as big as a dinner plate, and taken altogether it is inferior to the California tree. It is very hard on horses' backs, and not at all comfortable for a rider who is not accustomed to it.

They all use hemp ropes which are imported from some of the southern states of the republic, and carry a lariat of hair which they make themselves. They work for from eight to twelve dollars a month in Mexican coin, and live on the most simple diet imaginable. They are mostly *peoned*, or in hopeless debt to their *patrons*, who go after any man who deserts the range and bring him back by force. A puncher buys nothing but his gorgeous buckskin clothes, and his big rings. He makes his *teguas* or buckskin boots, his heavy leggings, his saddle, and the *patron* furnishes his arms. On the round-up, which lasts about half of the year, he is furnished beef, and also kills game. The balance of the year he is kept in an outlying camp to turn stock back on the range. These camps are often the most simple things, consisting of a pack containing his "grub," his saddle, and *serape*, all lying under a tree, which does duty as a house. He carries a flint and steel, and has a piece of sheet-iron for a stove, and a piece of pottery for boiling things in. This part of their lives is passed in a long siesta, and a man of the North who has a local reputation as a lazy man should see a Mexican puncher loaf, in order to comprehend that he could never achieve distinction in the land where *poco tiempo* means forever. Such is the life of the *vaquero*, a brave fellow, a fatalist, with less wants than the pony he rides, a rather thoughtless man, who lacks many virtues, but when he mounts his horse or casts his riata all men must bow and call him master.

The *baile*, the song, the man with the guitar—and under all this *dolce far niente* are their little hates and bickerings, as thin as cigarette smoke and as enduring as time. They reverence their parents, they honor their *patron*, and love their *compadre*. They are grave, and grave even when gay; they eat little, they think less, they meet death calmly, and it's a terrible scoundrel who goes to hell from Mexico.

The Anglo-American foremen are another type entirely. They have all the rude virtues. The intelligence which is never lacking and the perfect courage which never fails are found in such men as Tom Bailey and Johnnie Bell—two Texans who are the superiors of any cow-men I have ever seen. I have seen them chase the "mavericks" at top speed over a country so difficult that a man could hardly pass on foot out of a walk. On one occasion Mr. Bailey, in hot pursuit of a bull, leaped a tremendous fallen log at top speed, and in the next instant "tailed" and threw the bull as it was about to enter the timber. Bell can ride a pony at a gallop while standing up on his saddle, and while Cossacks do this trick they are enabled to accomplish it easily from the superior adaptability of their saddles for the purpose. In any association with these men of the frontier I have come to greatly respect their moral fibre and their character. Modern civilization, in the process of educating men beyond their capacity, often succeeds in vulgarizing them; but these natural men possess minds which, though lacking all embellishments, are chaste and simple, utterly devoid of a certain flippancy which passes for smartness in situations where life is not so real. The fact that a man bolts his food or uses his table-knife as though it were a deadly weapon counts for very little in the game these men play in their lonely range life. They are not complicated, these children of nature, and they never think one thing and say another. Mr. Bell was wont to squat against a fireplace—*a' la* Indian—and dissect the peculiarities of the audience in a most ingenuous way. It never gave offence either, because so guileless. Mr. Bailey, after listening carefully to a theological tilt, observed that "he believed he would be religious if he knowed how."

The jokes and pleasantries of the American puncher are so close to nature often, and so generously veneered with heart-rending profanity, as to exclude their becoming classic. The cow-men are good friends and virulent haters, and, if justified in their own minds, would shoot a man instantly, and regret the necessity, but not the shooting, afterwards.

Among the dry, saturnine faces of the cow punchers of the Sierra Madre was one which beamed with human instincts, which seemed to say, "Welcome, stranger!" He was the first impression my companion and myself had of Mexico, and as broad as are its plains and as high as its mountains, yet looms up William on a higher pinnacle of remembrance.

We crawled out of a Pullman in the early morning at Chihuahua, and fell into the hands of a little black man, with telescopic pantaloons, a big sombrero with the edges rolled up, and a grin on his good-humored face like a yawning *barranca*.

"Is you frens of Mista Jack's?"

"We are."

"Gimme your checks. Come dis way," he said; and without knowing why we should hand ourselves and our property over to this uncouth personage, we did it, and from thence on over the deserts and in the mountains, while shivering in the snow by night and by day, there was Jack's man to bandage our wounds, lend us tobacco when no one else had any, to tuck in our blankets, to amuse us, to comfort us in distress, to advise and admonish, until the last *adios* were waved from the train as it again bore us to the borderland.

On our departure from Chihuahua to meet Jack out in the mountains the stage was overloaded, but a proposition to leave William behind was beaten on the first ballot; it was well vindicated, for without William the expedition would have been a "march from Moscow." There was only one man in the party with a sort of bass-relief notion that he could handle the Spanish language, and the relief was a very slight one—almost imperceptible—the politeness of the people only keeping him from being mobbed. But William could speak German, English, and Spanish, separately, or all at once.

William was so black that he would make a dark hole in the night, and the top of his head was not over four and a half feet above the soles of his shoes. His legs were all out of drawing, but forty-five winters had not passed over him without leaving a mind which, in its sphere of life, was agile, resourceful, and eminently capable of grappling with any complication which might arise. He had personal relations of various kinds with every man, woman, and child whom we met in Mexico. He had been thirty years a cook in a cow camp, and could evolve banquets from the meat on a bull's tail, and was wont to say, "I don't know so much 'bout dese yar stoves, but gie me a camp-fire an' I can make de bes' thing yo' ever threw your lip ober."

When in camp, with his little cast-off English tourist cap on one side of his head, a short black pipe tipped at the other angle to balance the effect, and two or three stripes of white corn-meal across his visage, he would move round the camp-fire like a cub bear around a huckleberry bush, and in a low, authoritative voice have the Mexicans all in action, one hurrying after water, another after wood, some making *tortillas* or cutting up venison, grinding coffee between two stones, dusting bedding, or anything else. The British Field-Marshal air was lost in a second when he addressed "Mister Willie" or "Mister Jack," and no fawning courier of the Grand Monarch could purr so low.

On our coach ride to Bavicora, William would seem to go up to any ranch-house on the road, when the sun was getting low, and after ten minutes' conversation with the grave Don who owned it, he would turn to us with a wink, and say: "Come right in, gemmen. Dis ranch is yours." Sure enough, it was. Whether he played us for major-generals or governors of states I shall never know, but certainly we were treated as such.

On one occasion William had gotten out to get a hat blown off by the wind, and when he came up to view the wreck of the turn-over of the great Concord coach, and saw the mules going off down the hill with the front wheels, the ground littered with boxes and débris, and the men all lying about, groaning or fainting in agony, William scratched his wool, and with just a suspicion of humor on his face he ventured, "If I'd been hyar, I would be in two places 'fore now, shuah," which was some consolation to William, if not to us.

In Chihuahua we found William was in need of a clean shirt, and we had got one for him in a shop. He had selected one with a power of color enough to make the sun stand still, and with great glass diamonds in it. We admonished him that when he got to the ranch the punchers would take it away from him.

"No, sah; I'll take it off 'fore I get thar."

William had his commercial instincts developed in a reasonable degree, for he was always trying to trade a silver watch, of the Captain Cuttle kind, with the Mexicans. When asked what time it was,

William would look at the sun and then deftly cant the watch around, the hands of which swung like compasses, and he would show you the time within fifteen minutes of right, which little discrepancy could never affect the value of a watch in the land of *mañana*.

That he possessed tact I have shown, for he was the only man at Bavicora whose relations with the *patron* and the smallest, dirtiest Indian "kid," were easy and natural. Jack said of his popularity, "He stands 'way in with the Chinese cook; gets the warm corner behind the stove." He also had courage, for didn't he serve out the ammunition in Texas when his "outfit" was in a life-and-death tussle with the Comanches? Did he not hold a starving crowd of Mexican teamsters off the grub-wagon until the boys came back?

There was only one feature of Western life with which William could not assimilate, and that was the horse. He had trusted a bronco too far on some remote occasion, which accounted partially for the kinks in his legs; but after he had recovered fully his health he had pinned his faith to *burros*, and forgotten the glories of the true cavalier.

"No, sah, Mister Jack, I don' care for to ride dat horse. He's a good horse, but I jes hit de flat for a few miles 'fore I rides him," he was wont to say when the cowboys gave themselves over to an irresponsible desire to see a horse kill a man. He would then go about his duties, uttering gulps of suppressed laugher, after the negro manner, safe in the knowledge that the *burro* he affected could "pack his freight."

One morning I was taking a bath out of our washbasin, and William, who was watching me and the coffeepot at the same time, observed that "if one of dese people down hyar was to do dat dere, dere'd be a funeral 'fo' twelve o'clock."

William never admitted any social affinity with Mexicans, and as to his own people he was wont to say: "Never have went with people of my own color. Why, you go to Brazos to-day, and dey tell you dere was Bill, he go home come night, an' de balance of 'em be looking troo de grates in de morning." So William lives happily in the "small social puddle," and always reckons to "treat any friends of Mister Jack's right." So if you would know William, you must do it through Jack.

It was on rare occasions that William, as master of ceremonies, committed any indiscretion, but one occurred in the town of Guerrero. We had gotten in rather late, and William was sent about the town to have some one serve supper for us. We were all very busy when William "blew in" with a great sputtering, and said, "Is yous ready for dinner, gemmen?" "Yes, William," we answered, whereat William ran off. After waiting a long time, and being very hungry, we concluded to go and "rustle" for ourselves, since William did not come back and had not told us where he had gone. After we had found and eaten a dinner, William turned up, gloomy and dispirited. We inquired as to his mood. "I do declar', gemmen, I done forget dat you didn't know where I had ordered dat dinner; but dere's de dinner an' nobody to eat it, an' I's got to leave dis town 'fore sunup, pay for it, or die." Unless some one had advanced the money, William's two other alternatives would have been painful.

The romance in William's life even could not be made mournful, but it was the "mos' trouble" he ever had, and it runs like this: Some years since William had saved up four hundred dollars, and he had a girl back in Brazos to whom he had pinned his faith. He had concluded to assume responsibilities, and to create a business in a little mud town down the big road. He had it arranged to start a travellers' eating-house; he had contracted for a stove and some furniture; and at about that time his dishonest employer had left Mexico for parts unknown, with all his money. The stove and furniture were yet to be paid for, so William entered into hopeless bankruptcy, lost his girl, and then, attaching himself to Jack, he bravely set to again in life's battle.

But I was glad to know that he had again conquered, for before I left I overheard a serious conversation between William and the *patron*. William was cleaning a frying-pan by the camp-fire light, and the *patron* was sitting enveloped in his *serape* on the other side.

"Mist' Jack, I's got a girl. She's a Mexican."

"Why, William, how about that girl up in the Brazos?" inquired the *patron*, in surprise.

"Don't care about her now. Got a new girl."

"Well, I suppose you can have her, if you can win her," replied the *patron*.

"Can I, sah? Well, den, I's win her already, sah—dar!" chuckled William.

"Oh! Very well, then, William, I will give you a wagon, with two yellow ponies, to go down and get her; but I don't want you to come back to Bavicora with an empty wagon."

"No, sah; I won't sah," pleasedly responded the lover.

"Does that suit you, then?" asked the *patron*.

"Yes, sah; but, sah, wonder, sah, might I have the two old whites?"

"All right! You can have the two old white ponies;" and, after a pause, "I will give you that old *adobe* up in La Pinta, and two speckled steers; and I don't want you to come down to the ranch except on *Baile* night, and I want you to slide in then just as quiet as any other outsider," said the *patron*, who was testing William's loyalty to the girl.

"All right! I'll do that."

"William, do you know that no true Mexican girl will marry a man who don't know how to ride a charger?" continued the *patron*, after a while.

"Yes; I's been thinking of dat; but dar's dat Timbrorello, he's a good horse what a man can 'pend on," replied William, as he scoured at the pan in a very wearing way.

"He's yours, William; and now all you have got to do is to win the girl."

After that William was as gay as a robin in the spring; and as I write this I suppose William is riding over the pass in the mountains, sitting on a board across his wagon, with his Mexican bride by his side, singing out between the puffs of his black pipe, "Go on, dar, you muchacos; specks we ever get to Bavicora dis yar gait?"

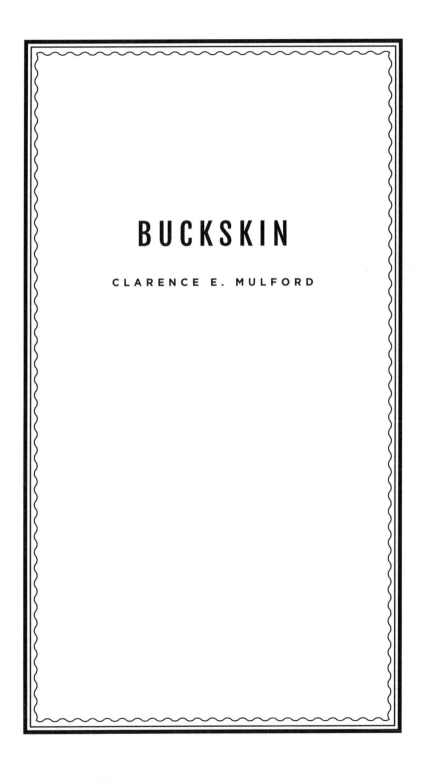

# BUCKSKIN

CLARENCE E. MULFORD

The town lay sprawled over half a square mile of alkali plain, its main street depressing in its width, for those who were responsible for its inception had worked with a generosity born of the knowledge that they had at their immediate and unchallenged disposal the broad lands of Texas and New Mexico on which to assemble a grand total of twenty buildings, four of which were of wood. As this material was scarce, and had to be brought from where the waters of the Gulf lapped against the flat coast, the last-mentioned buildings were a matter of local pride, as indicating the progressiveness of their owners. These creations of hammer and saw were of one story, crude and unpainted; their cheap weather sheathing, warped and shrunken by the pitiless sun, curled back on itself and allowed unrestricted entrance to alkali dust and air. The other shacks were of adobe and reposed in that magnificent squalor dear to their owners, Indians and Mexicans.

It was an incident of the Cattle Trail, that most unique and stupendous of all modern migrations, and its founders must have been inspired with a malicious desire to perpetrate a crime against geography, or else they reveled in a perverse cussedness, for within a mile on every side lay broad prairies, and two miles to the east flowed the indolent waters of the Rio Pecos itself. The distance separating the town from the river was excusable, for at certain seasons of the year the placid stream swelled mightily and swept down in a broad expanse of turbulent, yellow flood.

Buckskin was a town of one hundred inhabitants, located in the valley of the Rio Pecos fifty miles south of the Texas–New Mexico line. The census claimed two hundred, but it was a well-known fact that it was exaggerated. One instance of this is shown by the name of Tom Flynn. Those who once knew Tom Flynn, alias Johnny Redmond, alias Bill Sweeney, alias Chuck Mullen, by all four names, could find them in the census list. Furthermore, he had been shot and killed in the March of the year preceding the census, and now occupied a grave in the young but flourishing cemetery. Perry's Bend, twenty miles up the river, was cognizant of this and other facts, and, laughing in open derision at the padded list, claimed to be the better town in all ways, including marksmanship.

One year before this tale opens, Buck Peters, an example for the more recent Billy the Kid, had paid Perry's Bend a short but busy visit. He had ridden in at the north end of Main Street and out at the south. As he came in he was fired at by a group of ugly cowboys from a ranch known as the C-80. He was hit twice, but he unlimbered his artillery, and before his horse had carried him, half dead, out on the prairie, he had killed one of the group. Several citizens had joined the cowboys and added their bullets against Buck. The deceased had been the best bartender in the country, and the rage of the suffering citizens can well be imagined. They swore vengeance on Buck, his ranch, and his stamping ground.

The difference between Buck and Billy the Kid is that the former never shot a man who was not trying to shoot him, or who had not been warned by some action against Buck that would call for it. He minded his own business, never picked a quarrel, and was quiet and pacific up to a certain point. After that had been passed he became like a raging cyclone in a tenement house, and storm-cellars were much in demand.

"Fanning" is the name of a certain style of gun play not unknown among the bad men of the West. While Buck was not a bad man, he had to rub elbows with them frequently, and he believed that the sauce for the goose was the sauce for the gander. So he had removed the trigger of his revolver and worked the hammer with the thumb of the "gun hand" or the heel of the unencumbered hand. The speed thus acquired was greater than that of the more modern double-action weapon. Six shots in three seconds was his average speed when that number was required, and when it is thoroughly understood that at least some of them found their intended billets it is not difficult to realize that fanning was an operation of danger when Buck was doing it.

He was a good rider, as all cowboys are, and was not afraid of anything that lived. At one time he and his chums, Red Connors and Hopalong Cassidy, had successfully routed a band of fifteen Apaches who wanted their scalps. Of these, twelve never hunted scalps again, nor anything else on this earth, and the other three returned to their tribe with the report that three evil spirits had chased them with "wheel guns" (cannons).

So now, since his visit to Perry's Bend, the rivalry of the two towns had turned to hatred and an alert and eager readiness to increase the inhabitants of each other's graveyard. A state of war existed, which for a time resulted in nothing worse than acrimonious suggestions. But the time came when the score was settled to the satisfaction of one side, at least.

Four ranches were also concerned in the trouble. Buckskin was surrounded by two, the Bar-20 and the Three Triangle. Perry's Bend was the common point for the C-80 and the Double Arrow. Each of the two ranch contingents accepted the feud as a matter of course, and as a matter of course took sides with their respective towns. As no better class of fighters ever lived, the trouble assumed Homeric proportions and insured a danger zone well worth watching.

Bar-20's northern line was C-80's southern one, and Skinny Thompson took his turn at outriding one morning after the season's round-up. He was to follow the boundary and turn back stray cattle. When he had covered the greater part of his journey he saw Shorty Jones riding toward him on a course parallel to his own and about long revolver range away. Shorty and he had "crossed trails" the year before and the best of feelings did not exist between them.

Shorty stopped and stared at Skinny, who did likewise at Shorty. Shorty turned his mount around and applied the spurs, thereby causing his indignant horse to raise both heels at Skinny. The latter took it all in gravely and, as Shorty faced him again, placed his left thumb to his nose, wiggling his fingers suggestively. Shorty took no apparent notice of this but began to shout:

"Yu wants to keep yore busted-down cows on yore own side. They was all over us day afore yesterday. I'm goin' to salt any more what comes over, and don't yu fergit it, neither."

Thompson wigwagged with his fingers again and shouted in reply: "Yu c'n salt all yu wants to, but if I ketch yu adoin' it yu won't have to work no more. An' I kin say right here thet they's more C-80 cows over here than they's Bar-20's over there."

Shorty reached for his revolver and yelled, "Yore a liar!"

Among the cowboys in particular and the Westerners in general at that time, the three suicidal terms, unless one was an expert in drawing quick and shooting straight with one movement, were the words "liar," "coward," and "thief." Any man who was called one of these in earnest, and he was the judge, was expected to shoot if he could and save his life, for the words were seldom used without a gun coming with them. The movement of Shorty's hand toward his belt before the appellation reached him was enough for Skinny, who let go at long range—and missed.

The two reports were as one. Both urged their horses nearer and fired again. This time Skinny's sombrero gave a sharp jerk and a hole appeared in the crown. The third shot of Skinny's sent the horse of the other to its knees and then over on its side. Shorty very promptly crawled behind it and, as he did so, Skinny began a wide circle, firing at intervals as Shorty's smoke cleared away.

Shorty had the best position for defense, as he was in a shallow coulée, but he knew that he could not leave it until his opponent had either grown tired of the affair or had used up his ammunition. Skinny knew it, too. Skinny also knew that he could get back to the ranch house and lay in a supply of food and ammunition and return before Shorty could cover the twelve miles he had to go on foot.

Finally Thompson began to head for home. He had carried the matter as far as he could without it being murder. Too much time had elapsed now, and, besides, it was before breakfast and he was hungry. He would go away and settle the score at some time when they would be on equal terms.

He rode along the line for a mile and chanced to look back. Two C-80 punchers were riding after him, and as they saw him turn and discover them they fired at him and yelled. He rode on for some distance and cautiously drew his rifle out of its long holster at his right leg. Suddenly he turned around in the saddle and fired twice. One of his pursuers fell forward on the neck of his horse, and his comrade turned to help him. Thompson wigwagged again and rode on, reaching the ranch as the others were finishing their breakfast.

At the table Red Connors remarked that the tardy one had a hole in his sombrero, and asked its owner how and where he had received it.

"Had a argument with C-80 out'n th' line."

"Go 'way! Ventilate enny?"

"One."

"Good boy, sonny! Hey, Hopalong, Skinny perforated C-80 this mawnin'!"

Hopalong Cassidy was struggling with a mouthful of beef. He turned his eyes toward Red without ceasing, and grinning as well as he could under the circumstances managed to grunt out "Gu—," which was as near to "Good" as the beef would allow.

Lanky Smith now chimed in as he repeatedly stuck his knife into a reluctant boiled potato, "How'd yu do it, Skinny?"

"Bet he sneaked up on him," joshed Buck Peters; "did yu ask his pardin, Skinny?"

"Ask nothin'," remarked Red, "he jest nachurly walks up to C-80 an' sez, 'Kin I have the pleasure of ventilatin' yu?' an' C-80 he sez, 'If yu do it easy like,' sez he. Didn't he, Thompson?"

"They'll be some ventilatin' under th' table if yu fellows don't lemme alone; I'm hungry," complained Skinny.

"Say, Hopalong, I bets yu I kin clean up C-80 all by my lonesome," announced Buck, winking at Red.

"Yah! Yu onct tried to clean up the Bend, Buckie, an' if Pete an' Billy hadn't afound yu when they come by Eagle Pass that night yu wouldn't be here eatin' beef by th' pound," glancing at the hard-working Hopalong. "It was plum lucky fer yu that they was acourtin' that time, wasn't it, Hopalong?" suddenly asked Red. Hopalong nearly strangled in his efforts to speak. He gave it up and nodded his head.

"Why can't yu git it straight, Connors? I wasn't doin' no courtin', it was Pete. I runned into him on th' other side o' th' pass. I'd look fine acourtin', wouldn't I?" asked the downtrodden Williams.

Pete Wilson skillfully flipped a potato into that worthy's coffee, spilling the beverage of the questionable name over a large expanse of blue flannel shirt. "Yu's all right, yu are. Why, when I meets yu, yu was lost in th' arms of yore ladylove. All I could see was yore feet. Go an' git tangled up with a two hundred and forty pound half-breed squaw an' then try to lay it onter me! When I proposed drownin' yore troubles over at Cowan's, yu went an' got mad over what yu called th' insinooation. An' yu shore didn't look any too blamed fine, neither."

"All th' same," volunteered Thompson, who had taken the edge from his appetite, "we better go over an' pay C-80 a call. I don't like what Shorty said about saltin' our cattle. He'll shore do it, unless I camps on th' line, which same I hain't hankerin' after."

"Oh, he wouldn't stop th' cows that way, Skinny; he was only afoolin'," exclaimed Connors meekly.

"Foolin' yore gran'mother! That there bunch'll do anything if we wasn't lookin'," hotly replied Skinny.

"That's shore nuff gospel, Thomp. They's sore fer mor'n one thing. They got aplenty when Buck went on th' warpath, an they's hankerin' to git square," remarked Johnny Nelson, stealing the pie, a rare treat, of his neighbor when that unfortunate individual was not looking. He had it halfway to his mouth when its former owner, Jimmy Price, a boy of eighteen, turned his head and saw it going.

"Hi-yi! Yu clay-bank coyote, drap thet pie! Did yu ever see such a son-of-a-gun fer pie?" he plaintively asked Red Connors, as he grabbed a mighty handful of apples and crust. "Pie'll kill yu some day, yu bob-tailed jack! I had an uncle that died onct. He et too much pie an' he went an' turned green, an so'll yu if yu don't let it alone."

"Yu ought'r seed th' pie Johnny had down in Eagle Flat," murmured Lanky Smith reminiscently. "She had feet that'd stop a stampede. Johnny was shore loco about her. Swore she was the finest blossom that ever growed." Here he choked and tears of laughter coursed down his weather-beaten face as he pictured her. "She was a dainty Mexican, about fifteen han's high an' about sixteen han's around. Johnny used to chalk off when he hugged her, usen't yu, Johnny? One night when he had got purty well around on th' second lap he run inter a feller jest startin' out on his fust. They hain't caught that Mexican yet."

Nelson was pelted with everything in sight. He slowly wiped off the pie crust and bread and potatoes. "Anybody'd think I was a busted grub wagon," he grumbled. When he had fished the last piece of beef out of his ear he went out and offered to stand treat. As the round-up was over, they slid into their saddles and raced for Cowan's saloon at Buckskin.

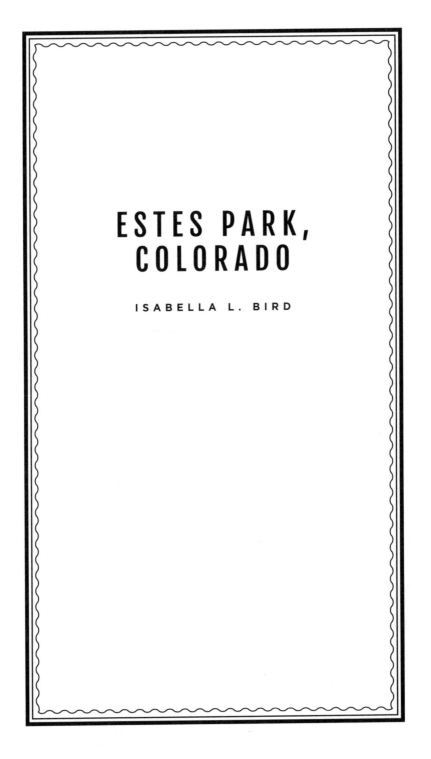

# ESTES PARK, COLORADO

ISABELLA L. BIRD

This afternoon, as I was reading in my cabin, little Sam Edwards ran in, saying, "Mountain Jim wants to speak to you." This brought to my mind images of infinite worry, *gauche* servants, "please Ma'am," *contretemps*, and the habit growing out of our elaborate and uselessly conventional life of magnifying the importance of similar trifles. Then "things" came up, with the tyranny they exercise. I *really* need nothing more than this log cabin offers. But elsewhere one must have a house and servants, and burdens and worries—not that one may be hospitable and comfortable, but for the "thick clay" in the shape of "things" which one has accumulated. My log house takes me about five minutes to "do," and you could eat off the floor, and it needs no lock, as it contains nothing worth stealing.

But "Mountain Jim" was waiting while I made these reflections to ask us to take a ride; and he, Mr. and Mrs. Dewy, and I, had a delightful stroll through colored foliage, and then, when they were fatigued, I changed my horse for his beautiful mare, and we galloped and raced in the beautiful twilight, in the intoxicating frosty air. Mrs. Dewy wishes you could have seen us as we galloped down the pass, the fearful-looking ruffian on my heavy wagon horse, and I on his bare wooden saddle, from which beaver, mink, and marten tails, and pieces of skin, were hanging raggedly, with one spur, and feet not in the stirrups, the mare looking so aristocratic and I so beggarly! Mr. Nugent is what is called "splendid company." With a sort of breezy mountain reckless-ness in everything, he passes remarkably acute judgments on men and events; on women also. He has pathos, poetry, and humor, an intense love of nature, strong vanity in certain directions, an obvious desire to act and speak in character, and sustain his reputation as a desperado, a considerable acquaintance with literature, a wonderful verbal memory, opinions on every person and subject, a chivalrous respect for women in his manner, which makes it all the more amusing when he suddenly turns round upon one with some graceful raillery, a great power of fascination, and a singular love of children. The children of this house run to him, and when he sits down they climb on his broad shoulders and play with his curls. They say in the house that "no one who has been here thinks any one worth speaking to after Jim," but I think that this is probably an opinion which time would alter. Somehow, he is kept always before the public of Colorado, for one can hardly take up a newspaper without finding a paragraph about him, a contribution by him, or a fragment of his biography. Ruffian as he looks, the first word he speaks—to a lady, at least—places him on a level with educated gentlemen, and his conversation is brilliant, and full of the light and fit-fulness of genius. Yet, on the whole, he is a most painful spectacle. His magnificent head shows so plainly the better possibilities which might have been his. His life, in spite of a certain dazzle which belongs to it, is a ruined and wasted one, and one asks what of good can the future have in store for one who has for so long chosen evil?*

---

*September of the next year answered the question by laying him down in a dishonored grave, with a rifle bullet in his brain.

Shall I ever get away? We were to have had a grand cattle hunt yesterday, beginning at 6:30, but the horses were all lost. Often out of fifty horses all that are worth anything are marauding, and a day is lost in hunting for them in the canyons. However, before daylight this morning Evans called through my door, "Miss Bird, I say we've got to drive cattle fifteen miles, I wish you'd lend a hand; there's not enough of us; I'll give you a good horse."

The scene of the drive is at a height of 7,500 feet, watered by two rapid rivers. On all sides mountains rise to an altitude of from 11,000 to 15,000 feet, their skirts shaggy with pitch-pine forests, and scarred by deep canyons, wooded and boulder strewn, opening upon the mountain pasture previously mentioned. Two thousand head of half-wild Texan cattle are scattered in herds throughout the canyons, living on more or less suspicious terms with grizzly and brown bears, mountain lions, elk, mountain sheep, spotted deer, wolves, lynxes, wild cats, beavers, minks, skunks, chipmunks, eagles, rattlesnakes, and all the other two-legged, four-legged, vertebrate, and invertebrate inhabitants of this lonely and romantic region. On the whole, they show a tendency rather to the habits of wild than of domestic cattle. They march to water in Indian file, with the bulls leading, and when threatened, take strategic advantage of ridgy ground, slinking warily along in the hollows, the bulls acting as sentinels, and bringing up the rear in case of an attack from dogs. Cows have to be regularly broken in for milking, being as wild as buffaloes in their unbroken state; but, owing to the comparative dryness of the grasses, and the system of allowing the calf to have the milk during the daytime, a dairy of 200 cows does not produce as much butter as a Devonshire dairy of fifty. Some "necessary" cruelty is involved in the stockman's business, however humane he may be. The system is one of terrorism, and from the time that the calf is bullied into the branding pen, and the hot iron burns into his shrinking flesh, to the day when the fatted ox is driven down from his boundless pastures to be slaughtered in Chicago, "the fear and dread of man" are upon him.

The herds are apt to penetrate the savage canyons which come down from the Snowy Range, when they incur a risk of being snowed up and starved, and it is necessary now and then to hunt them out and drive them down to the "park." On this occasion, the whole were driven down for a muster, and for the purpose of branding the calves.

After a 6:30 breakfast this morning, we started, the party being composed of my host, a hunter from the Snowy Range, two stockmen from the Plains, one of whom rode a violent buck-jumper, and was said by his comrade to be the "best rider in North Americay," and myself. We were all mounted on Mexican saddles, rode, as the custom is, with light snaffle bridles, leather guards over our feet, and broad wooden stirrups, and each carried his lunch in a pouch slung on the lassoing horn of his saddle. Four big, badly-trained dogs accompanied us. It was a ride of nearly thirty miles, and of many hours, one of the most splendid I ever took. We never got off our horses except to tighten the girths, we ate our lunch with our bridles knotted over our saddle horns, started over the level at full gallops, leapt over trunks of trees, dashed madly down hillsides rugged with rocks or strewn with great stones, forded deep, rapid streams, saw lovely lakes and views of surpassing magnificence, startled a herd of elk with uncouth heads and in the chase, which for some time was unsuccessful, rode to the very base of Long's Peak, over 14,000 feet high, where the bright waters of one of the affluents of the Platte burst from the eternal snows through a canyon of indescribable majesty. The sun was hot, but at a height of over 8,000 feet the air was crisp and frosty, and the enjoyment of riding a good horse under such exhilarating circumstances was extreme. In one wild part of the ride we had to come down a steep hill, thickly wooded with pitch pines, to leap over the fallen timber, and steer between the dead and living trees to avoid being "snagged," or bringing down a heavy dead branch by an unwary touch.

Emerging from this, we caught sight of a thousand Texan cattle feeding in a valley below. The leaders scented us, and, taking fright, began to move off in the direction of the open "park," while we were about a mile from and above them. "Head them off, boys!" our leader shouted; "all aboard; hark away!" and with something of the "High, tally-ho in the morning!" away we all went at a hard gallop downhill. I could not hold my excited animal; down-hill, up-hill, leaping over rocks and timber, faster every moment the pace grew, and still the leader shouted, "Go it, boys!" and the horses dashed on at racing speed, passing and repassing each other, till my small but beautiful bay was keeping pace with the immense strides of the great buck-jumper ridden by "the finest rider in North Americay," and I was dizzied and breathless by the pace at which we were going. A shorter time than it takes to tell it brought us close to and abreast of the surge of cattle. The bovine waves were a grand sight: huge bulls, shaped like buffaloes, bellowed and roared, and with great oxen and cows with yearling calves, galloped like racers, and we galloped alongside of them, and shortly headed them and in no time were placed as sentinels across the mouth of the valley. It seemed like infantry awaiting the shock of cavalry as we stood as still as our excited horses would allow. I almost quailed as the surge came on, but when it got close to us my comrades hooted fearfully, and we dashed forward with the dogs, and, with bellowing, roaring, and thunder of hoofs, the wave receded as it came. I rode up to our leader, who received me with much laughter. He said I was "a good cattleman," and that he had forgotten that a lady was of the party till he saw me "come leaping over the timber, and driving with the others."

It was not for two hours after this that the real business of driving began, and I was obliged to change my thoroughbred for a well-trained cattle horse—a *bronco*, which could double like a hare, and go over any ground. I had not expected to work like a *vachero*, but so it was, and my Hawaiian experience was very useful. We hunted the various canyons and known "camps," driving the herds out of them; and, until we had secured 850 head in the *corral* some hours afterwards, we scarcely saw each other to speak to. Our first difficulty was with a herd which got into some swampy ground, when a cow, which afterwards gave me an infinity of trouble, remained at bay for nearly an hour, tossing the dog three times, and resisting all efforts to dislodge her. She had a large yearling calf with her, and Evans told me that the attachment of a cow to her first calf is sometimes so great that she will kill her second that the first may have the milk. I got a herd of over a hundred out of a canyon by myself, and drove them down to the river with the aid of one badly-broken dog, which gave me more trouble than the cattle. The getting over was most troublesome; a few took to the water readily and went across, but others smelt it, and then, doubling back, ran in various directions; while some attacked the dog as he was swimming, and others, after crossing, headed back in search of some favorite companions which had been left behind, and one specially vicious cow attacked my horse over and over again. It took an hour and a half of time and much patience to gather them all on the other side.

It was getting late in the day, and a snowstorm was impending, before I was joined by the other drivers and herds, and as the former had diminished to three, with only three dogs, it was very difficult to keep the cattle together. You drive them as gently as possible, so as not to frighten or excite them,* riding first on one side, then on the other, to guide them; and if they deliberately go in a wrong direction, you gallop in front and head them off. The great excitement is when one breaks away from the herd and gallops madly up and down-hill, and you gallop after him anywhere, over and among the rocks and trees, doubling when he doubles, and heading him till you get him back again. The bulls were quite easily managed, but the cows with calves, old or young, were most troublesome. By accident I rode between one cow and her calf in a narrow place, and the cow rushed at me and was just getting her big horns under the horse, when he reared, and spun dexterously aside. This kind of thing happened continually. There was one very handsome red cow which became quite mad. She had a calf with her nearly her own size, and thought every one its enemy, and though its horns were well developed, and it was quite able to take care of itself, she insisted on protecting it from all fancied dangers. One of the dogs, a young, foolish thing, seeing that the cow was excited, took a foolish pleasure in barking at her, and she was eventually quite infuriated. She turned to bay forty times at least; tore up the ground with her horns, tossed and killed the calves of two other cows, and finally became so dangerous to the rest of the herd that, just as the drive was

---

*In several visits to America I have observed that the Americans are far in advance of us and our colonial kinsmen in their treatment of horses and other animals. This was very apparent with regard to this Texan herd. There were no stock whips, no needless worrying of the animals in the excitement of the sport. Any dog seizing a bullock by his tail or heels would have been called off and punished, and quietness and gentleness were the rule. The horses were ridden without whips, and with spurs so blunt that they could not hurt even a human skin, and were ruled by the voice and a slight pressure on the light snaffle bridle. This is the usual plan, even where, as in Colorado, the horses are *bronchos*, and inherit ineradicable vice. I never yet saw a horse *bullied* into submission in the United States.

ending, Evans drew his revolver and shot her, and the calf for which she had fought so blindly lamented her piteously. She rushed at me several times mad with rage, but these trained cattle horses keep perfectly cool, and, nearly without will on my part, mine jumped aside at the right moment, and foiled the assailant. Just at dusk we reached the corral—an acre of grass enclosed by stout post-and-rail fences seven feet high—and by much patience and some subtlety lodged the whole herd within its shelter, without a blow, a shout, or even a crack of a whip, wild as the cattle were. It was fearfully cold. We galloped the last mile and a half in four and a half minutes, reached the cabin just as the snow began to fall, and found strong, hot tea ready.

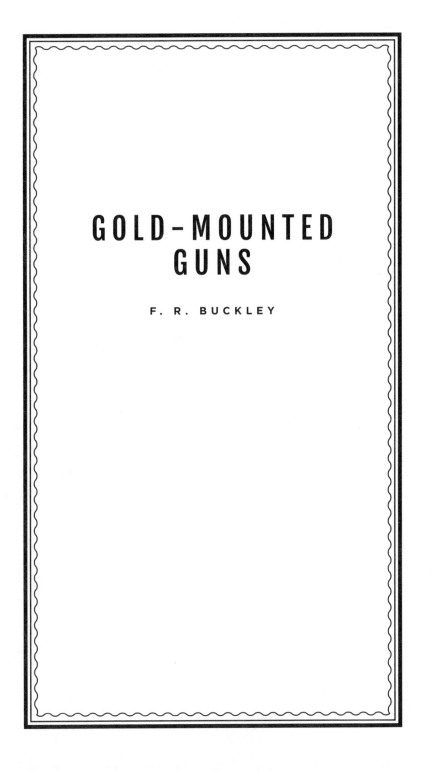

# GOLD–MOUNTED GUNS

F. R. BUCKLEY

Evening had fallen on Longhorn City, and already, to the south, an eager star was twinkling in the velvet sky, when a spare, hard-faced man slouched down the main street and selected a pony from the dozen hitched beside Tim Geogehan's general store. The town, which in the daytime suffered from an excess of eye-searing light in its open spaces, confined its efforts at artificial lighting to the one store, the one saloon, and its neighbour, the Temple of Chance; so it was from a dusky void that the hard-faced man heard himself called by name.

"Tommy!" a subdued voice accosted him.

The hard-faced man made, it seemed, a very slight movement—a mere flick of the hand at his low-slung belt; but it was a movement perfectly appraised by the man in the shadows.

"Wait a minute!" the voice pleaded.

A moment later, his hands upraised, his pony's bridle-reins caught in the crook of one arm, a young man moved into the zone of light that shone bravely out through Tim Geogehan's back window.

"Don't shoot," he said, trying to control his nervousness before the weapon unwaveringly trained on him. "I'm—a friend."

For perhaps fifteen seconds the newcomer and the hard-faced man examined each other with the unwinking scrutiny of those who take chances of life and death. The younger, with that lightning draw fresh in his mind, noted the sinister droop of a gray moustache over a hidden mouth, and shivered a little as his gaze met that of a pair of steel-blue eyes. The man with the gun saw before him a rather handsome face, marred, even in this moment of submission, by a certain desperation.

"What do you want?" he asked, tersely.

"Can I put my hands down?" countered the other.

The lean man considered.

"All things bein' equal," he said, "I think I'd rather you'd first tell me how you got round to callin' me Tommy. Been askin' people in the street?"

"No," said the boy. "I only got into town this afternoon, an' I ain't a fool anyway. I seen you ride in this afternoon, and the way folks backed away from you made me wonder who you was. Then I seen them gold-mounted guns of yourn, an' of course I knew. Nobody ever had guns like them but Pecos Tommy. I could ha' shot you while you was gettin' your horse, if I'd been that way inclined."

The lean man bit his moustache.

"Put 'em down. What do you want?"

"I want to join you."

"You want to *what?*"

"Yeah, I know it sounds foolish to you, mebbe," said the young man. "But, listen—your side-kicker's in jail down in Rosewell. I figured I could take his place—anyway, till he got out. I know I ain't got any record, but I can ride, an' I can shoot the pips out of a ten-spot at ten paces, an'—I got a little job to bring into the firm, to start with."

The lean man's gaze narrowed.

"Have, eh?" he asked, softly.

"It ain't anythin' like you go in for as a rule," said the boy, apologetically, "but it's a roll of cash an'—I guess it'll show you I'm straight. I only got on to it this afternoon. Kind of providential I should meet you right now."

The lean man chewed his moustache. His eyes did not shift.

"Yeah," he said, slowly. "What you quittin' punchin' for?"

"Sick of it."

"Figurin' robbin' trains is easier money?"

"No," said the young man, "I ain't. But I like a little spice in life. They ain't none in punchin'."

"Got a girl?" asked the lean man.

The boy shook his head. The hard-faced man nodded reflectively.

"Well, what's the job?" he asked.

The light from Geogehan's window was cut off by the body of a man who, cupping his hands about his eyes, stared out into the night, as if to locate the buzz of voices at the back of the store.

"If you're goin' to take me on," said the young man, "I can tell you while we're ridin' toward it. If you ain't—why, there's no need to go no further."

The elder slipped back into its holster the gold-mounted gun he had drawn, glanced once at the obscured window and again, piercingly, at the boy whose face now showed white in the light of the rising moon. Then he turned his pony and mounted.

"Come on," he commanded.

Five minutes later the two had passed the limits of the town, heading for the low range of hills which encircled it to the south—and Will Arblaster had given the details of his job to the unemotional man at his side.

"How do you know the old guy's got the money?" came a level question.

"I saw him come out of the bank this afternoon, grinnin' all over his face an' stuffin' it into his pants-pocket," said the boy. "An' when he was gone, I kind of inquired who he was. His name's Sanderson, an' he lives in this yer cabin right ahead a mile. Looked kind of a soft old geezer—kind that'd give up without any trouble. Must ha' been quite some cash there, judgin' by the size of the roll. But I guess when *you* ask him for it, he won't mind lettin' it go."

"I ain't goin' to ask him," said the lean man. "This is your job."

The boy hesitated.

"Well, if I do it right," he asked, with a trace of tremor in his voice, "will you take me along with you sure?"

"Yeah—I'll take you along."

The two ponies rounded a shoulder of the hill: before the riders were loomed, in the moonlight, the dark shape of a cabin, its windows unlighted. The lean man chuckled.

"He's out."

Will Arblaster swung off his horse.

"Maybe," he said, "but likely the money ain't. He started off home, an' if he's had to go out again, likely he's hid the money some place. Folks know *you're* about. I'm goin' to see."

Stealthily he crept toward the house. The moon went behind a cloud-bank, and the darkness swallowed him. The lean man, sitting his horse, motionless, heard the rap of knuckles on the door—then a pause, the rattle of the latch. A moment later there came the heavy thud of a shoulder against wood—a cracking sound, and a crash as the door went down. The lean man's lips tightened. From within the cabin came the noise of one stumbling over furniture, then the fitful fire of a match illumined the windows. In the quiet, out there in the night, the man on the horse, twenty yards away, could hear the clumping of the other's boots on the rough board floor, and every rustle of the papers that he fumbled in his search. Another match scratched and sputtered, and then, with a hoarse cry of triumph, was flung down. Running feet padded across the short grass and Will Arblaster drew up, panting.

"Got it!" he gasped. "The old fool! Put it in a tea-canister right on the mantelshelf. Enough to choke a horse! Feel it!"

The lean man, unemotional as ever, reached down and took the roll of money.

"Got another match?" he asked.

Willie struck one, and panting, watched while his companion, moistening a thumb, ruffled through the bills.

"Fifty-tens," said the lean man. "Five hundred dollars. Guess I'll carry it."

His cold blue eyes turned downward, and focused again with piercing attention on the younger man's upturned face. The bills were stowed in a pocket of the belt right next one of those gold-mounted guns which, earlier in the evening, had covered Willie Arblaster's heart. For a moment, the lean man's hand seemed to hesitate over its butt; then, as Willie smiled and nodded, it moved away. The match burned out.

"Let's get out of here," the younger urged; whereupon the hand which had hovered over the gun-butt grasped Will Arblaster's shoulder.

"No, not yet," he said quietly, "not just yet. Get on your hawss, an' set still awhile."

The young man mounted. "What's the idea?"

"Why!" said the level voice at his right. "This is a kind of novelty to me. Robbin' trains, you ain't got any chance to see results, like: this here's different. Figure this old guy'll be back pretty soon. I'd like to see what he does when he finds his wad's gone. Ought to be amusin'!"

Arblaster chuckled uncertainly.

"Ain't he liable to——"

"He can't see us," said the lean man with a certain new cheerfulness in his tone. "An' besides, he'll think we'd naturally be miles away; an' besides that, we're mounted, all ready."

"What's that?" whispered the young man, laying a hand on his companion's arm.

The other listened.

"Probably him," he said. "Now stay still."

There were two riders—by their voices, a man and a girl: they were laughing as they approached the rear of the house, where, roughly made of old boards, stood Pa Sanderson's substitute for a stable. They put up the horses; then their words came clearer to the ears of the listeners, as they turned the corner of the building, walking toward the front door.

"I feel mean about it, anyhow," said the girl's voice. "You going on living here, Daddy, while——"

"Tut-tut-tut!" said the old man. "What's five hundred to me? I ain't never had that much in a lump, an' shouldn't know what to do with it if I had. 'Sides, your Aunt Elviry didn't give it you for nothin'. 'If she wants to go to college,' says she, 'let her prove it by workin'. I'll pay half, but she's got to pay t'other half.' Well, you worked, an'—— Where on earth did I put that key?"

There was a silence, broken by the grunts of the old man as he contorted himself in the search of his pockets: and then the girl spoke: the tone of her voice was the more terrible for the restraint she was putting on it.

"Daddy—the—the—did you leave the money in the house?"

"Yes. What is it?" cried the old man.

"Daddy—the door's broken down, and——"

There was a hoarse cry: boot-heels stumbled across the boards, and again a match flared. Its pale light showed a girl standing in the doorway of the cabin, her hands clasped on her bosom—while beyond the wreckage of the door a bent figure with silver hair tottered away from the mantelshelf. In one hand Pa Sanderson held the flickering match, in the other a tin box.

"Gone!" he cried in his cracked voice. "Gone!"

Willie Arblaster drew a breath through his teeth and moved uneasily in his saddle. Instantly, a lean, strong hand, with a grip like steel, fell on his wrist and grasped it. The man behind the hand chuckled.

"Listen!" he said.

"Daddy—Daddy—don't take on so—please don't," came the girl's voice, itself trembling with repressed tears. There was a scrape of chairlegs on the floor as she forced the old man into his seat by the fireplace. He hunched there, his face in his hands, while she struck a match and laid the flame to the wick of the lamp on the table. As it burned up she went back to her father, knelt by him, and threw her arms about his neck.

"Now, now, now!" she pleaded. "Now, Daddy, it's all right. Don't take on so. It's all right."

But he would not be comforted.

"I can't replace it!" cried Pa Sanderson, dropping trembling hands from his face. "It's gone! Two years you've been away from me; two years you've slaved in a store; and now I've——"

"Hush, hush!" the girl begged. "Now, Daddy—it's all right. I can go on working, and——"

With a convulsive effort, the old man got to his feet. "Two years more slavery, while some skunk drinks your money, gambles it—throws it away!" he cried. "Curse him! Whoever it is, curse him! Where's God's justice? What's a man goin' to believe when years of scrapin' like your aunt done, an' years of slavin' like yours in Laredo there, an' all our happiness to-day can be wiped out by a damned thief in a minute?"

The girl put her little hand over her father's mouth.

"Don't, Daddy," she choked. "It only makes it worse. Come and lie down on your bed, and I'll make you some coffee. Don't cry, Daddy darling. Please."

Gently, like a mother with a little child, she led the heart-broken old man out of the watchers' line of vision, out of the circle of lamp-light. More faintly, but still with heartrending distinctness, the listeners could hear the sounds of weeping.

The lean man sniffed, chuckled, and pulled his bridle.

"Some circus!" he said appreciatively. "C'mon, boy."

His horse moved a few paces, but Will Arblaster's did not. The lean man turned in his saddle.

"Ain't you comin'?" he asked.

For ten seconds, perhaps, the boy made no answer. Then he urged his pony forward until it stood side by side with his companion's.

"No," he said. "An'—an I ain't goin' to take that money, neither."

"Huh?"

The voice was slow and meditative.

"Don't know as ever I figured what this game meant," he said. "Always seemed to me that all the hardships was on the stick-up man's side—gettin' shot at an' chased and so on. Kind of fun, at that. Never thought 'bout—old men cryin'."

"That ain't my fault," said the lean man.

"No," said Will Arblaster, still very slowly. "But I'm goin' to take that money back. You didn't have no trouble gettin' it, so you don't lose nothin'."

"Suppose I say I won't let go of it?" suggested the lean man with a sneer.

"Then," snarled Arblaster, "I'll blow your damned head off an' take it! Don't you move, you! I've got you covered. I'll take the money out myself."

His revolver muzzle under his companion's nose, he snapped open the pocket of the belt and extracted the roll of bills. Then, regardless of a possible shot in the back, he swung off his horse and shambled, with the mincing gait of the born horseman, into the lighted doorway of the cabin. The lean man, unemotional as ever, sat perfectly still, looking alternately at the cloud-dappled sky and at the cabin, from which now came a murmur of voices harmonizing with a strange effect of joy, to the half-heard bass of the night-wind.

It was a full ten minutes before Will Arblaster reappeared in the doorway alone, and made, while silhouetted against the light, a quick movement of his hand across his eyes, then stumbled forward through the darkness toward his horse.

"I'm—sorry," said the boy as he mounted. "But——"

"I ain't," said the lean man quietly. "What do you think I made you stay an' watch for, you young fool?"

The boy made no reply. Suddenly the hair prickled on the back of his neck and his jaw fell.

"Say," he demanded hoarsely at last. "Ain't you Pecos Tommy?"

The lean man's answer was a short laugh.

"But you got his guns, an' the people in Longhorn all kind of fell back!" the boy cried. "If you ain't him, who are you?"

The moon had drifted from behind a cloud and flung a ray of light across the face of the lean man as he turned it, narrow-eyed, toward Arblaster. The pallid light picked out with terrible distinctness the grim lines of that face—emphasized the cluster of sun-wrinkles about the corners of the piercing eyes and marked as if with underscoring black lines the long sweep of the fighting jaw.

"Why," said the lean man dryly, "I'm the sheriff that killed him yesterday. Let's be ridin' back."

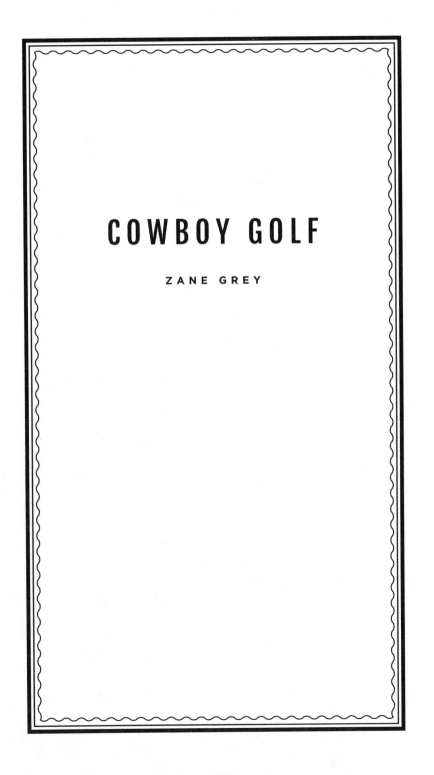

# COWBOY GOLF

ZANE GREY

In the whirl of the succeeding days it was a mooted question whether Madeline's guests or her cowboys or herself got the keenest enjoyment out of the flying time. Considering the sameness of the cowboys' ordinary life, she was inclined to think they made the most of the present. Stillwell and Stewart, however, had found the situation trying. The work of the ranch had to go on, and some of it got sadly neglected. Stillwell could not resist the ladies any more than he could resist the fun in the extraordinary goings-on of the cowboys. Stewart alone kept the business of cattle-raising from a serious setback. Early and late he was in the saddle, driving the lazy Mexicans whom he had hired to relieve the cowboys.

One morning in June Madeline was sitting on the porch with her merry friends when Stillwell appeared on the corral path. He had not come to consult Madeline for several days—an omission so unusual as to be remarked.

"Here comes Bill—in trouble," laughed Florence.

Indeed, he bore some faint resemblance to a thundercloud as he approached the porch; but the greetings he got from Madeline's party, especially from Helen and Dorothy, chased away the blackness from his face and brought the wonderful wrinkling smile.

"Miss Majesty, sure I'm a sad demoralized old cattleman," he said, presently. "An' I'm in need of a heap of help."

"What's wrong now?" asked Madeline, with her encouraging smile.

"Wal, it's so amazin' strange what cowboys will do. I jest am about to give up. Why, you might say my cowboys were all on strike for vacations. What do you think of that? We've changed the shifts, shortened hours, let one an' another off duty, hired Greasers, an', in fact, done everythin' that could be thought of. But this vacation idee growed worse. When Stewart set his foot down, then the boys begin to get sick. Never in my born days as a cattleman have I heerd of so many diseases. An' you ought to see how lame an' crippled an' weak many of the boys have got all of a sudden. The idee of a cowboy comin' to me with a sore finger an' askin' to be let off for a day! There's Booly. Now I've knowed a hoss to fall all over him, an' onct he rolled down a cañon. Never bothered him at all. He's got a blister on his heel, a ridin' blister, an' he says it's goin' to blood-poisonin' if he doesn't rest. There's Jim Bell. He's developed what he says is spinal mengalootis, or some such like. There's Frankie Slade. He swore he had scarlet fever because his face burnt so red, I guess, an' when I hollered that scarlet fever was contagious an' he must be put away somewhere, he up an' says he guessed it wasn't that. But he was sure awful sick an' needed to loaf around an' be amused. Why, even Nels doesn't want to work these days. If it wasn't for Stewart, who's had Greasers with the cattle, I don't know what I'd do."

"Why all this sudden illness and idleness?" asked Madeline.

"Wal, you see, the truth is every blamed cowboy on the range except Stewart thinks it's his bounden duty to entertain the ladies."

"I think that is just fine!" exclaimed Dorothy Coombs; and she joined in the general laugh.

"Stewart, then, doesn't care to help entertain us?" inquired Helen, in curious interest.

"Wal, Miss Helen, Stewart is sure different from the other cowboys," replied Stillwell. "Yet he used to be like them. There never was a cowboy fuller of the devil than Gene. But he's changed. He's foreman here, an' that must be it. All the responsibility rests on him. He sure has no time for amusin' the ladies."

"I imagine that is our loss," said Edith Wayne, in her earnest way. "I admire him."

"Stillwell, you need not be so distressed with what is only gallantry in the boys, even it if does make a temporary confusion in the work," said Madeline.

"Miss Majesty, all I said is not the half, nor the quarter, nor nuthin' of what's troublin' me," answered he, sadly.

"Very well; unburden yourself."

"Wal, the cowboys, exceptin' Gene, have gone plumb batty, jest plain crazy over this heah game of gol-lof."

A merry peal of mirth greeted Stillwell's solemn assertion.

"Oh, Stillwell, you are in fun," replied Madeline.

"I hope to die if I'm not in daid earnest," declared the cattleman. "It's an amazin' strange fact. Ask Flo. She'll tell you. She knows cowboys, an' how if they ever start on somethin' they ride it as they ride a hoss."

Florence being appealed to, and evidently feeling all eyes upon her, modestly replied that Stillwell had scarcely misstated the situation.

"Cowboys play like they work or fight," she added. "They give their whole souls to it. They are great big simple boys."

"Indeed they are," said Madeline. "Oh, I'm glad if they like the game of golf. They have so little play."

"Wal, somethin's got to be did if we're to go on raisin' cattle at Her Majesty's Rancho," replied Stillwell. He appeared both deliberate and resigned.

Madeline remembered that despite Stillwell's simplicity he was as deep as any of his cowboys, and there was absolutely no gaging him where possibilities of fun were concerned. Madeline fancied that his exaggerated talk about the cowboys' sudden craze for golf was in line with certain other remarkable tales that had lately emanated from him. Some very strange things had occurred of late, and it was impossible to tell whether or not there were accidents, mere coincidents, or deep-laid, skillfully worked-out designs of the fun-loving cowboys. Certainly there had been great fun, and at the expense of her guests, particularly Castleton. So Madeline was at a loss to know what to think about Stillwell's latest elaboration. From mere force of habit she sympathized with him and found difficulty in doubting his apparent sincerity.

"To go back a ways," went on Stillwell, as Madeline looked up expectantly, "you recollect what pride the boys took in fixin' up that gol-lof course out on the mesa? Wal, they worked on that job, an' though I never seen any other course, I'll gamble yours can't be beat. The boys was sure curious about that game. You recollect also how they all wanted to see you an' your brother play, an' be caddies for you? Wal, whenever you'd quit they'd go to work tryin' to play the game. Monty Price, he was the leadin' spirit. Old as I am, Miss Majesty, an' used as I am to cowboy excentrikities, I nearly dropped daid when I heered that little hobble-footed, burned-up Montana cowpuncher say there wasn't any game too swell for him, an' gol-lof was just his speed. Serious as a preacher, mind you, he was. An' he was always practisin'. When Stewart gave him charge of the course an' the club-house an' all them funny sticks, why, Monty was tickled to death. You see, Monty is sensitive that he ain't much good any more for cowboy work. He was glad to have a job that he didn't feel he was hangin' to by kindness. Wal, he practised the game, an' he read the books in the club-house, an' he got the boys to doin' the same. That wasn't very hard, I reckon. They played early an' late an' in the moonlight. For a while Monty was coach, an' the boys stood it. But pretty soon Frankie Slade got puffed on his game, an' he had to have it out with Monty. Wal, Monty beat him bad. Then one after another the other boys tackled Monty. He beat them all. After that they split up an' begin to play matches, two on a side. For a spell this worked fine. But cowboys can't never be satisfied long unless they win all the time. Monty an' Link Stevens, both cripples, you might say, joined forces an' elected to beat all comers. Wal, they did, an' that's the trouble. Long an' patient the other cowboys tried to beat them two game legs, an' hevn't done it. Mebbe if Monty an' Link was perfectly sound in their legs like the other cowboys there wouldn't hev been such a holler. But no sound cowboys'll ever stand for a disgrace like that. Why, down at the bunks in the evenin's it's some mortifyin' the way Monty an' Link crow over the rest of the outfit. They've taken on superior airs. You couldn't reach up to Monty with a trimmed spruce pole. An' Link— wal, he's just amazin' scornful.

"'It's a swell game, ain't it?' says Link, powerful sarcastic. 'Wal, what's hurtin' you low-down common cowmen? You keep harpin' on Monty's game leg an' on my game leg. If we hed good legs we'd beat you all the wuss. It's brains that wins in gol-lof. Brains an' airstoocratik blood, which of the same you fellers sure hev little.'

"An' then Monty he blows smoke powerful careless an' superior, an' he says:

"'Sure it's a swell game. You cow-headed gents think beef an' brawn ought to hev the call over skill an' gray matter. You'll all hev to back up an' get down. Go out an' learn the game. You don't know a baffy from a Chinee sandwich. All you can do is waggle with a club an' fozzle the ball.'

"Whenever Monty gets to usin' them queer names the boys go round kind of dotty. Monty an' Link hev got the books an' directions of the game, an' they won't let the other boys see them. They show the rules, but that's all. An', of course, every game ends in a row almost before it's started. The boys are all terrible in earnest about this gol-lof. An' I want to say, for the good of ranchin', not to mention a possible fight, that Monty an' Link hev got to be beat. There'll be no peace round this ranch till that's done."

Madeline's guests were much amused. As for herself, in spite of her scarcely considered doubt, Stillwell's tale of woe occasioned her anxiety. However, she could hardly control her mirth.

"What in the world can *I* do?"

"Wal, I reckon I couldn't say. I only come to you for advice. It seems that a queer kind of game has locoed my cowboys, an' for the time bein' ranchin' is at a stand-still. Sounds ridiculous, I know, but cowboys are as strange as wild cattle. All I'm sure of is that the conceit has got to be taken out of Monty an' Link. Onct, just onct, will square it, an' then we can resoome our work."

"Stillwell, listen," said Madeline, brightly. "We'll arrange a match game, a foursome, between Monty and Link and your best picked team. Castleton, who is an expert golfer, will umpire. My sister, and friends, and I will take turns as caddies for your team. That will be fair, considering yours is the weaker. Caddies may coach, and perhaps expert advice is all that is necessary for your team to defeat Monty's."

"A grand idee," declared Stillwell, with instant decision. "When can we have this match game?"

"Why, to-day—this afternoon. We'll ride out to the links."

"Wal, I reckon I'll be some indebted to you, Miss Majesty, an' all your guests," replied Stillwell, warmly. He rose with sombrero in hand, and a twinkle in his eye that again prompted Madeline to wonder. "An' now I'll be goin' to fix up for the game of cowboy gol-lof. *Adios.*"

The idea was as enthusiastically received by Madeline's guests as it had been by Stillwell. They were highly amused and speculative to the point of taking sides and making wagers on their choice. Moreover, this situation so frankly revealed by Stillwell had completed their deep mystification. They were now absolutely nonplussed by the singular character of American cowboys. Madeline was pleased to note how seriously they had taken the old cattleman's story. She had a little throb of wild expectancy that made her both fear and delight in the afternoon's prospect.

The June days had set in warm; in fact, hot during the noon hours; and this had inculcated in her insatiable visitors a tendency to profit by the experience of those used to the Southwest. They indulged in the restful siesta during the heated term of the day.

Madeline was awakened by Majesty's well-known whistle and pounding on the gravel. Then she heard the other horses. When she went out she found her party assembled in gala golf attire, and with spirits to match their costumes. Castleton, especially, appeared resplendent in a golf coat that beggared description. Madeline had faint misgivings when she reflected on what Monty and Nels and Nick might do under the influence of that blazing garment.

"Oh, Majesty," cried Helen, as Madeline went up to her horse, "don't make him kneel! Try that flying mount. We all want to see it. It's so stunning."

"But that way, too, I must have him kneel," said Madeline, "or I can't reach the stirrup. He's so tremendously high."

Madeline had to yield to the laughing insistence of her friends, and after all of them except Florence were up she made Majesty go down on one knee. Then she stood on his left side, facing back, and took a good firm grip on the bridle and pommel and his mane. After she had slipped the toe of her boot firmly into the stirrup she called to Majesty. He jumped and swung her up into the saddle.

"Now just to see how it ought to be done watch Florence," said Madeline.

The Western girl was at her best in riding-habit and with her horse. It was beautiful to see the ease and grace with which she accomplished the cowboys' flying mount. Then she led the party down the slope and across the flat to climb the mesa.

Madeline never saw a group of her cowboys without looking them over, almost unconsciously, for her foreman, Gene Stewart. This afternoon, as usual, he was not present. However, she now had a sense—of which she was wholly conscious—that she was both disappointed and irritated. He had really not been attentive to her guests, and he, of all her cowboys, was the only one of whom they wanted most to see something. Helen, particularly, had asked to have him attend the match. But Stewart was with the cattle. Madeline thought of his faithfulness, and was ashamed of her momentary lapse into that old imperious habit of desiring things irrespective of reason.

Stewart, however, immediately slipped out of her mind as she surveyed the group of cowboys on the links. By actual count there were sixteen, not including Stillwell. And the same number of splendid horses, all shiny and clean, grazed on the rim in the care of Mexican lads. The cowboys were on dress-parade, looking very different in Madeline's eyes, at least, from the way cowboys usually appeared. But they were real and natural to her guests; and they were so picturesque that they might have been stage cowboys instead of real ones. Sombreros with silver buckles and horsehair bands were in evidence; and bright silk scarves, embroidered vests, fringed and ornamented chaps, huge swinging guns, and clinking silver spurs lent a festive appearance.

Madeline and her party were at once eagerly surrounded by the cowboys, and she found it difficult to repress a smile. If these cowboys were still remarkable to her, what must they be to her guests?

"Wal, you-all raced over, I seen," said Stillwell, taking Madeline's bridle. "Get down—get down. We're sure amazin' glad an' proud. An', Miss Majesty, I'm offerin' to beg pawdin for the way the boys are packin' guns. Mebbe it ain't polite. But it's Stewart's orders."

"Stewart's orders!" echoed Madeline. Her friends were suddenly silent.

"I reckon he won't take no chances on the boys bein' surprised sudden by raiders. An' there's raiders operatin' in from the Guadalupes. That's all. Nothin' to worry over. I was just explainin'."

Madeline, with several of her party, expressed relief, but Helen showed excitement and then disappointment.

"Oh, I want something to happen!" she cried.

Sixteen pairs of keen cowboy eyes fastened intently upon her pretty, petulant face; and Madeline divined, if Helen did not, that the desired consummation was not far off.

"So do I," said Dot Coombs. "It would be perfectly lovely to have a real adventure."

The gaze of the sixteen cowboys shifted and sought the demure face of this other discontented girl. Madeline laughed, and Stillwell wore his strange, moving smile.

"Wal, I reckon you ladies sure won't have to go home unhappy," he said. "Why, as boss of this heah outfit I'd feel myself disgraced forever if you didn't have your wish. Just wait. An' now, ladies, the matter on hand may not be amusin' or excitin' to you; but to this heah cowboy outfit it's powerful important. An' all the help you can give us will sure be thankfully received. Take a look across the links. Do you-all see them two apologies for human bein's prancin' like a couple of hobbled broncs? Wal, you're gazin' at Monty Price an' Link Stevens, who have of a sudden got too swell to associate with their old bunkies. They're practisin' for the toornament. They don't want my boys to see how they handle them crooked clubs."

"Have you picked your team?" inquired Madeline.

Stillwell mopped his red face with an immense bandana, and showed something of confusion and perplexity.

"I've sixteen boys, an' they all want to play," he replied. "Pickin' the team ain't goin' to be an easy job. Mebbe it won't be healthy, either. There's Nels and Nick. They just stated cheerful-like that if they didn't play we won't have any game at all. Nick never tried before, an' Nels, all he wants is to get a crack at Monty with one of them crooked clubs."

"I suggest you let all your boys drive from the tee and choose the two who drive the farthest," said Madeline.

Stillwell's perplexed face lighted up.

"Wal, that's a plumb good idee. The boys'll stand for that."

Wherewith he broke up the admiring circle of cowboys round the ladies.

"Grap a rope—I mean a club—all you cow-punchers, an' march over hyar an' take a swipe at this little white bean."

The cowboys obeyed with alacrity. There was considerable difficulty over the choice of clubs and who should try first. The latter question had to be adjusted by lot. However, after Frankie Slade made several ineffectual attempts to hit the ball from the teeing-ground, at last to send it only a few yards, the other players were not so eager to follow. Stillwell had to push Booly forward, and Booly executed a most miserable shot and retired to the laughing comments of his comrades. The efforts of several succeeding cowboys attested to the extreme difficulty of making a good drive.

"Wal, Nick, it's your turn," said Stillwell.

"Bill, I ain't so all-fired particular about playin'," replied Nick.

"Why? You was roarin' about it a little while ago. Afraid to show how bad you'll play?"

"Nope, jest plain consideration for my feller cow-punchers," answered Nick, with spirit. "I'm appreciatin' how bad they play, an' I'm not mean enough to show them up."

"Wal, you've got to show me," said Stillwell. "I know you never seen a gol-lof stick in your life. What's more, I'll bet you can't hit that little ball square—not in a dozen cracks at it."

"Bill, I'm also too much of a gent to take your money. But you know I'm from Missouri. Gimme a club."

Nick's angry confidence seemed to evaporate as one after another he took up and handled the clubs. It was plain that he had never before wielded one. But, also, it was plain that he was not the kind of man to give in. Finally he selected a driver, looked doubtfully at the small knob, and then stepped into position on the teeing-ground.

Nick Steele stood six feet four inches in height. He had the rider's wiry slenderness, yet he was broad of shoulder. His arms were long. Manifestly he was an exceedingly powerful man. He swung the driver aloft and whirled it down with a tremendous swing. Crack! The white ball disappeared, and from where it had been rose a tiny cloud of dust.

Madeline's quick sight caught the ball as it lined somewhat to the right. It was shooting low and level with the speed of a bullet. It went up and up in swift, beautiful flight, then lost its speed and began to sail, to curve, to drop; and it fell out of sight beyond the rim of the mesa. Madeline had never seen a drive that approached this one. It was magnificent, beyond belief except for actual evidence of her own eyes.

The yelling of the cowboys probably brought Nick Steele out of the astounding spell with which he beheld his shot. Then Nick, suddenly alive to the situation, recovered from his trance and, resting nonchalantly upon his club, he surveyed Stillwell and the boys. After their first surprised outburst they were dumb.

"You-all seen thet?" Nick grandly waved his hand. "Thought I was joshin', didn't you? Why, I used to go to St. Louis an' Kansas City to play this here game. There was some talk of the golf clubs takin' me down East to play the champions. But I never cared fer the game. Too easy fer me! Them fellers back in Missouri were a lot of cheap dubs, anyhow, always kickin' because whenever I hit a ball hard I *always lost it.* Why, I hed to hit sort of left-handed to let 'em stay in my class. Now you-all can go ahead an' play Monty an' Link. I could beat 'em both, playin' with one hand, if I wanted to. But I ain't interested. I jest hit thet ball off the mesa to show you. I sure wouldn't be seen playin' on your team."

With that Nick sauntered away toward the horses. Stillwell appeared crushed. And not a scornful word was hurled after Nick, which fact proved the nature of his victory. Then Nels strode into the limelight. As far as it was possible for this iron-faced cowboy to be so, he was bland and suave. He remarked to Stillwell and the other cowboys that sometimes it was painful for them to judge of the gifts of superior cowboys such as belonged to Nick and himself. He picked up the club Nick had used and called for a new ball. Stillwell carefully built up a little mound of sand and, placing the ball upon it, squared away to watch. He looked grim and expectant.

Nels was not so large a man as Nick, and did not look so formidable as he waved his club at the gaping cowboys. Still he was lithe, tough, strong. Briskly, with a debonair manner, he stepped up and then delivered a mighty swing at the ball. He missed. The power and momentum of his swing flung him off his feet, and he actually turned upside down and spun round on his head. The cowboys howled. Stillwell's stentorian laugh rolled across the mesa. Madeline and her guests found it impossible to restrain their mirth. And when Nels got up he cast a reproachful glance at Madeline. His feelings were hurt.

His second attempt, not by any means so violent, resulted in as clean a miss as the first, and brought jeers from the cowboys. Nels's red face flamed redder. Angrily he swung again. The mound of sand spread over the teeing-ground and the exasperating little ball rolled a few inches. This time he had to build up the sand mound and replace the ball himself. Stillwell stood scornfully by, and the boys addressed remarks to Nels.

"Take off them blinders," said one.

"Nels, your eyes are shore bad," said another.

"You don't hit where you look."

"Nels, your left eye has sprung a limp."

"Why, you dog-goned old fule, you cain't hit thet bawl."

Nels essayed again, only to meet ignominious failure. Then carefully he gathered himself together, gaged distance, balanced the club, swung cautiously. And the head of the club made a beautiful curve round the ball.

"Shore it's jest thet crooked club," he declared.

He changed clubs and made another signal failure. Rage suddenly possessing him, he began to swing wildly. Always, it appeared, the illusive little ball was not where he aimed. Stillwell hunched his huge bulk, leaned hands on knees, and roared his riotous mirth. The cowboys leaped up and down in glee.

"You cain't hit thet bawl," sang out one of the noisiest.

A few more whirling, desperate lunges on the part of Nels, all as futile as if the ball had been thin air, finally brought to the dogged cowboy a realization that golf was beyond him.

Stillwell bawled: "Oh, haw, haw, haw! Nels, you're—too old—eyes no good!"

Nels slammed down the club, and when he straightened up with the red leaving his face, then the real pride and fire of the man showed. Deliberately he stepped off ten paces and turned toward the little mound upon which rested the ball. His arm shot down, elbow crooked, hand like a claw.

"Aw, Nels, this is fun!" yelled Stillwell.

But swift as a gleam of light Nels flashed his gun, and the report came with the action. Chips flew from the golf-ball as it tumbled from the mound. Nels had hit it without raising the dust. Then he dropped the gun back in its sheath and faced the cowboys.

"Mebbe my eyes ain't so orful bad," he said, coolly, and started to walk off.

"But look ah-heah, Nels," yelled Stillwell, "we come out to play gol-lof! We can't let you knock the ball around with your gun. What'd you want to get mad for? It's only fun. Now you an' Nick hang round heah an' be sociable. We ain't depreciatin' your company none, nor your useful-ness on occasions. An' if you just hain't got inborn politeness sufficient to do the gallant before the ladies, why, remember Stewart's orders."

"Stewart's orders?" queried Nels, coming to a sudden halt.

"That's what I said," replied Stillwell, with asperity. "His orders. Are you forgettin' orders? Wal, you're a fine cowboy. You an' Nick an' Monty, 'specially, are to obey orders."

Nels took off his sombrero and scratched his head. "Bill, I reckon I'm some forgetful. But I was mad. I'd 'a' remembered pretty soon, an' mebbe my manners."

"Sure you would," replied Stillwell. "Wal, now, we don't seem to be proceedin' much with my gol-lof team. Next ambitious player step up."

In Ambrose, who showed some skill in driving, Stillwell found one of his team. The succeeding players, however, were so poor and so evenly matched that the earnest Stillwell was in despair. He lost his temper just as speedily as Nels had. Finally Ed Linton's wife appeared riding up with Ambrose's wife, and perhaps this helped, for Ed suddenly disclosed ability that made Stillwell single him out.

"Let me coach you a little," said Bill.

"Sure, if you like," replied Ed. "But I know more about this game than you do."

"Wal, then, let's see you hit a ball straight. Seems to me you got good all-fired quick. It's amazin' strange." Here Bill looked around to discover the two young wives modestly casting eyes of admiration upon their husbands. "Haw, haw! It ain't so darned strange. Mebbe that'll help some. Now, Ed, stand up and don't sling your club as if you was ropin' a steer. Come round easy-like an' hit straight."

Ed made several attempts which, although better than those of his predecessors, were rather discouraging to the exacting coach. Presently, after a particularly atrocious shot, Stillwell strode in distress here and there, and finally stopped a dozen paces or more in front of the teeing-ground. Ed, who for a cowboy was somewhat phlegmatic, calmly made ready for another attempt.

"Fore!" he called.

Stillwell stared.

"*Fore!*" yelled Ed.

"Why're you hollerin' that way at me?" demanded Bill.

"I mean for you to lope off the horizon. Get back from in front."

"Oh, that was one of them durned crazy words Monty is always hollerin'. Wal, I reckon I'm safe enough hyar. You couldn't hit me in a million years."

"Bill, ooze away," urged Ed.

"Didn't I say you couldn't hit me? What am I coachin' you for? It's because you hit crooked, ain't it? Wal, go ahaid an' break your back."

Ed Linton was a short, heavy man, and his stocky build gave evidence of considerable strength. His former strokes had not been made at the expense of exertion, but now he got ready for a supreme effort. A sudden silence clamped down upon the exuberant cowboys. It was one of those fateful moments when the air was charged with disaster. As Ed swung the club it fairly whistled.

Crack! Instantly came a thump. But no one saw the ball until it dropped from Stillwell's shrinking body. His big hands went spasmodically to the place that hurt, and a terrible groan rumbled from him.

Then the cowboys broke into a frenzy of mirth that seemed to find adequate expression only in dancing and rolling accompaniment to their howls. Stillwell recovered his dignity as soon as he caught his breath, and he advanced with a rueful face.

"Wal, boys, it's on Bill," he said. "I'm a livin' proof of the pig-headedness of mankind. You're captain of the team. You hit straight, an' if I hadn't been obstructin' the general atmosphere that ball would sure have gone clear to the Chiricahuas."

Then making a megaphone of his huge hands, he yelled a loud blast of defiance at Monty and Link.

"Hey, you swell gol-lofers! We're waitin'. Come on if you ain't scared."

Instantly Monty and Link quit practicing, and like two emperors came stalking across the links.

"Guess my bluff didn't work much," said Stillwell. Then he turned to Madeline and her friends. "Sure I hope, Miss Majesty, that you-all won't weaken an' go over to the enemy. Monty is some eloquent, an', besides, he has a way of gettin' people to agree with him. He'll be plump wild when he heahs what he an' Link are up against. But it's a square deal, because he wouldn't help us or lend the book that shows how to play. An', besides, it's policy for us to beat him. Now, if you'll elect who's to be caddies an' umpire I'll be powerful obliged."

Madeline's friends were hugely amused over the prospective match; but, except for Dorothy and Castleton, they disclaimed any ambition for active participation. Accordingly, Madeline appointed Castleton to judge the play, Dorothy to act as caddie for Ed Linton, and she herself to be caddie for Ambrose. While Stillwell beamingly announced this momentous news to his team and supporters Monty and Link were striding up.

Both were diminutive in size, bow-legged, lame in one foot, and altogether unprepossessing. Link was young, and Monty's years, more than twice Link's, had left their mark. But it would have been impos-. sible to tell Monty's age. As Stillwell said, Monty was burned to the color and hardness of a cinder. He never minded the heat, and always wore heavy sheepskin chaps with the wool outside. This made him look broader than he was long. Link, partial to leather, had, since he became Madeline's chauffeur, taken to leather altogether. He carried no weapon, but Monty wore a huge gun-sheath and gun. Link smoked a cigarette and looked coolly impudent. Monty was dark-faced, swaggering, for all the world like a barbarian chief.

"That Monty makes my flesh creep," said Helen, low-voiced. "Really, Mr. Stillwell, is he so bad—desperate—as I've heard? Did he ever kill anybody?"

"Sure. 'Most as many as Nels," replied Stillwell, cheerfully.

"Oh! And is that nice Mr. Nels a desperado, too? I wouldn't have thought so. He's so kind and old-fashioned and soft-voiced."

"Nels is sure an example of the dooplicity of men, Miss Helen. Don't you listen to his soft voice. He's really as bad as a side-winder rattlesnake."

At this juncture Monty and Link reached the teeing-ground, and Stillwell went out to meet them. The other cowboys pressed forward to surround the trio. Madeline heard Stillwell's voice, and evidently he was explaining that his team was to have skilled advice during the play. Suddenly there came from the center of the group a loud, angry roar that broke off as suddenly. Then followed excited voices all mingled together. Presently Monty appeared, breaking away from restraining hands, and he strode toward Madeline.

Monty Price was a type of cowboy who had never been known to speak to a woman unless he was first addressed, and then he answered in blunt, awkward shyness. Upon this great occasion, however, it appeared that he meant to protest or plead with Madeline, for he showed stress of emotion. Madeline had never gotten acquainted with Monty. She was a little in awe, if not in fear, of him, and now she found it imperative for her to keep in mind that more than any other of the wild fellows on her ranch this one should be dealt with as if he were a big boy.

Monty removed his sombrero—something he had never done before—and the single instant when it was off was long enough to show his head entirely bald. This was one of the hall-marks of that terrible Montana prairie fire through which he had fought to save the life of a child. Madeline did not forget it, and all at once she wanted to take Monty's side. Remembering Stillwell's wisdom, however, she forebore yielding to sentiment, and called upon her wits.

"Miss—Miss Hammond," began Monty, stammering, "I'm extendin' admirin' greetin's to you an' your friends. Link an' me are right down proud to play the match game with you watchin'. But Bill says you're goin' to caddie for his team an' coach 'em on the fine points. An' I want to ask, all respectful, if thet's fair an' square?"

"Monty, that is for you to say," replied Madeline. "It was my suggestion. But if you object in the least, of course we shall withdraw. It seems fair to me, because you have learned the game; you are expert, and I understand the other boys have no chance with you. Then you have coached Link. I think it would be sportsmanlike of you to accept the handicap."

"Aw, a handicap! Thet was what Bill was drivin' at. Why didn't he say so? Every time Bill comes to a word thet's pie to us old golfers he jest stumbles. Miss Majesty, you've made it all clear as print. An' I may say with becomin' modesty thet you wasn't mistaken none about me bein' sportsmanlike. Me an' Link was born thet way. An' we accept the handicap. Lackin' thet handicap, I reckon Link an' me would have no ambish to play our most be-ootiful game. An' thankin' you, Miss Majesty, an' all your friends, I want to add thet if Bill's outfit couldn't beat us before, they've got a swell chanct now, with you ladies a-watchin' me an' Link."

Monty had seemed to expand with pride as he delivered this speech, and at the end he bowed low and turned away. He joined the group round Stillwell. Once more there was animated discussion and argument and expostulation. One of the cowboys came for Castleton and led him away to exploit upon ground rules.

It seemed to Madeline that the game never would begin. She strolled on the rim of the mesa, arm in arm with Edith Wayne, and while Edith talked she looked out over the gray valley leading to the rugged black mountains and the vast red wastes. In the foreground on the gray slope she saw cattle in movement and cowboys riding to and fro. She thought of Stewart. Then Boyd Harvey came for them, saying all details had been arranged. Stillwell met them half-way, and this cool, dry, old cattleman, whose face and manner scarcely changed at the announcement of a cattle-raid, now showed extreme agitation.

"Wal, Miss Majesty, we've gone an' made a foozle right at the start," he said, dejectedly.

"A foozle? But the game has not yet begun," replied Madeline.

"A bad start, I mean. It's amazin' bad, an' we're licked already."

"What in the world is wrong?"

She wanted to laugh, but Stillwell's distress restrained her.

"Wal, it's this way. That darn Monty is as cute an' slick as a fox. After he got done declaimin' about the handicap he an' Link was so happy to take, he got Castleton over hyar an' drove us all dotty with his crazy gol-lof names. Then he borrowed Castleton's gol-lof coat. I reckon borrowed is some kind word. He just about took that blazin' coat off the Englishman. Though I ain't sayin' but that Castleton was agreeable when he tumbled to Monty's meanin'. Which was nothin' more 'n to break Ambrose's heart. That coat dazzles Ambrose. You know how vain Ambrose is. Why, he'd die to get to wear that English-man's gol-lof coat. An' Monty forestalled him. It's plumb pitiful to see the look in Ambrose's eyes. He won't be able to play much. Then what do you think? Monty fixed Ed Linton, all right. Usually Ed is easy-goin' an' cool. But now he's on the rampage. Wal, mebbe it's news to you to learn that Ed's wife is powerful, turrible jealous of him. Ed was somethin' of a devil with the wimmen. Monty goes over an' tells Beulah—that's Ed's wife—that Ed is goin' to have for caddie the lovely Miss Dorothy with the goo-goo eyes. I reckon this was some disre-spectful, but with all doo respect to Miss Dorothy she has got a pair of unbridled eyes. Mebbe it's just natural for her to look at a feller like that. Oh, it's all right; I'm not sayin' anythin'! I know it's all proper an' regular for girls back East to use their eyes. But out hyar it's bound to result disastrous. All the boys talk about among themselves is Miss Dot's eyes, an' all they brag about is which feller is the luckiest. Anyway, sure Ed's wife knows it. An' Monty up an' told her that it was fine for her to come out an' see how swell Ed was prancin' round under the light of Miss Dot's brown eyes. Beulah calls over Ed, figgertively speakin', ropes him for a minnit. Ed comes back huggin' a grouch as big as a hill. Oh, it was funny! He was goin' to punch Monty's haid off. An' Monty stands there an' laughs. Says Monty, sarcastic as alkali water: 'Ed, we-all knowed you was a heap married man, but you're some locoed to give yourself away.' That settled Ed. He's some touchy about the way Beulah henpecks him. He lost his spirit. An' now he couldn't play marbles, let alone gol-lof. Nope, Monty was too smart. An' I reckon he was right about brains bein' what wins."

The game began. At first Madeline and Dorothy essayed to direct the endeavors of their respective players. But all they said and did only made their team play the worse. At the third hole they were far behind and hopelessly bewildered. What with Monty's borrowed coat, with its dazzling effect upon Ambrose, and Link's oft-repeated allusion to Ed's matrimonial state, and Stillwell's vociferated disgust, and the clamoring good intention and pursuit of the cowboy supporters, and the embarrassing presence of the ladies, Ambrose and Ed wore through all manner of strange play until it became ridiculous.

"Hey, Link," came Monty's voice booming over the links, "our esteemed rivals are playin' shinny."

Madeline and Dorothy gave up, presently, when the game became a rout, and they sat down with their followers to watch the fun. Whether by hook or crook, Ed and Ambrose forged ahead to come close upon

Monty and Link. Castleton disappeared in a mass of gesticulating, shouting cowboys. When that compact mass disintegrated Castleton came forth rather hurriedly, it appeared, to stalk back toward his hostess and friends.

"Look!" exclaimed Helen, in delight. "Castleton is actually excited. Whatever did they do to him? Oh, this is immense."

Castleton was excited, indeed, and also somewhat disheveled.

"By Jove! that was a rum go," he said, as he came up. "Never saw such blooming golf! I resigned my office as umpire."

Only upon considerable pressure did he reveal the reason.

"It was like this, don't you know. They were all together over there, watching each other. Monty Price's ball dropped into a hazard, and he moved it to improve the lie. By Jove! They've all been doing that. But over there the game was waxing hot. Stillwell and his cowboys saw Monty move the ball, and there was a row. They appealed to me. I corrected the play, showed the rules. Monty agreed he was in the wrong. However, when it came to moving his ball back to its former lie in the hazard there was more blooming trouble. Monty placed the ball to suit him, and then he transfixed me with an evil eye.

"'Dook,' he said. I wish the bloody cowboy would not call me that. 'Dook, mebbe this game ain't as important as international politics or some other things relatin', but there's some health an' peace dependin' on it. Savvy? For some space our opponents have been dead to honor an' sportsmanlike conduct. I calculate the game depends on my next drive. I'm placin' my ball as near to where it was as human eyesight could. You seen where it was same as I seen it. You're the umpire, an', Dook, I take you as a honorable man. Moreover, never in my born days has my word been doubted without sorrow. So I'm askin' you, wasn't my ball layin' just about here?'

"The bloody little desperado smiled cheerfully, and he dropped his right hand down to the butt of his gun. By Jove, he did! Then I had to tell a blooming lie!"

Castleton even caught the tone of Monty's voice, but it was plain that he had not the least conception that Monty had been fooling. Madeline and her friends divined it, however; and, there being no need of reserve, they let loose the fountains of mirth.

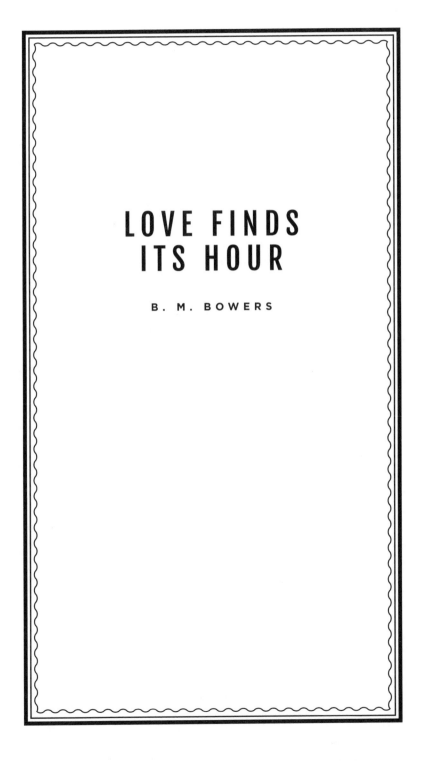

# LOVE FINDS ITS HOUR

B. M. BOWERS

"Bay Denver's broke out uh the little pasture," announced the Old Man, putting his head in at the door of the blacksmith shop where Chip was hammering gayly upon a bent branding iron, for want of a better way to kill time and give vent to his surplus energy. "I wish you'd saddle up an' go after him, Chip, if yuh can. I just seen him takin' down the coulee trail like a scared coyote."

"Sure, I'll go. Darn that old villain, he'd jump a fence forty feet high if he took a notion that way." Chip threw down the hammer and reached for his coat.

"I guess the fence must be down som'ers. I'll go take a look. Say! Dell ain't come back from Denson's yit. Yuh want t' watch out Denver don't meet her—he'd scare the liver out uh her."

Chip was well aware that the Little Doctor had not returned from Denson's, where she had been summoned to attend one of the children, who had run a rusty nail into her foot. She had gone alone, for Dr. Cecil was learning to make bread, and had refused to budge from the kitchen till her first batch was safely baked.

Chip limped hurriedly to the corral, and two minutes later was clattering down the coulee upon Blazes, after the runaway.

Denver was a beautiful bay stallion, the pride and terror of the ranch. He was noted for his speed and his vindictive hatred of the more plebeian horses, scarcely one of which but had, at some time, felt his teeth in their flesh—and he was hated and feared by them all.

He stopped at the place where the trail forked, tossed his crinkly mane triumphantly and looked back. Freedom was sweet to him—sweet as it was rare. His world was a roomy box stall with a small, high corral adjoining it for exercise, with an occasional day in the little pasture as a great treat. Two miles was a long, long way from home, it seemed to him. He watched the hill behind a moment, threw up his head and trotted off up the trail to Denson's.

Chip, galloping madly, caught a glimpse of the fugitive a mile away, set his teeth together, and swung Blazes sharply off the trail into a bypath which intersected the road further on. He hoped the Little Doctor was safe at Denson's, but at that very moment he saw her ride slowly over a distant ridge.

Now there was a race; Denver, cantering gleefully down the trail, Chip spurring desperately across the prairie.

The Little Doctor had disappeared into a hollow with Concho pacing slowly, half asleep, the reins drooping low on his neck. The Little Doctor loved to dream along the road, and Concho had learned to do likewise—and to enjoy it very much.

At the crest of the next hill she looked up, saw herself the apex of a rapidly shortening triangle, and grasped instantly the situation; she had peeped admiringly and fearsomely between the stout rails of the little, round corral too often not to know Denver when she saw him, and in a panic turned from the trail toward Chip. Concho was rudely awakened by a stinging blow from her whip—a blow which filled him with astonishment and reproach. He laid back his ears and galloped angrily—not in the path—the Little Doctor was too frightened for that—but straight as a hawk would fly. Denver, marking Concho for his prey and not to be easily cheated, turned and followed.

Chip swore inwardly and kept straight ahead, leaving the path himself to do so. He knew a deep washout lay now between himself and the Little Doctor, and his only hope was to get within speaking distance before she was overtaken.

Concho fled to the very brink of the washout and stopped so suddenly that his forefeet plowed a furrow in the grass, and the Little Doctor came near going clean over his head. She recovered her balance, and cast a frightened glance over her shoulder; Denver was rushing down upon them like an express train.

"Get off—your—*h-o-r-s-e!*" shouted Chip, making a trumpet of his hands. "Fight Denver off—with—your whip!"

The last command the Little Doctor did not hear distinctly. The first she made haste to obey. Throwing herself from the saddle, she slid precipitately into the washout just as Denver thundered up, snorting a challenge. Concho, scared out of his wits, turned and tore off down the washout, whipped around the end of it and made for home, his enemy at his heels and Chip after the two of them, leaning low over his horse as Blazes, catching the excitement and urged by the spurs, ran like an antelope.

The Little Doctor, climbing the steep bank to level ground, gazed after the fleeing group with consternation. Here was she a long four miles from home—five, if she followed the windings of the trail—and it looked very much as if her two feet must take her there. The prospect was not an enlivening one, but she started off across the prairie very philosophically at first, very dejectedly later on, and very angrily at last. The sun was scorching, and it was dinner time, and she was hungry, and hot, and tired, and—"mad." She did not bless her rescuer; she heaped maledictions upon his head—mild ones at first, but growing perceptibly more forcible and less genteel as the way grew rougher, and her feet grew wearier, and her stomach emptier. Then, as if her troubles were all to come in a lump—as they have a way of doing—she stepped squarely into a bunch of "pincushion" cactus.

"I just *hate* Montana!" she burst out, vehemently, blinking back some tears. "I don't care if Cecil did just come day before yesterday—I shall pack up and go back home. She can stay if she wants to, but I won't live here another day. I hate Chip Bennett, too, and I'll tell him so if I ever get home. I don't see what J. G.'s thinking of, to live in such a God-forgotten hole, where there's nothing but miles upon miles of cactuses——" The downfall of Eastern up-bringing! To deliberately say "cactuses"—but the provocation was great, I admit. If any man doubts, let him tread thin-shod upon a healthy little "pincushion" and be convinced. I think he will confess that "cactuses" is an exceedingly conservative epithet, and all too mild for the occasion.

Half an hour later, Chip, leading Concho by the bridle rein, rode over the brow of a hill and came suddenly upon the Little Doctor, sitting disconsolately upon a rock. She had one shoe off, and was striving petulantly to extract a cactus thorn from the leather with a hat pin. Chip rode close and stopped, regarding her with satisfaction from the saddle. It was the first time he had succeeded in finding the Little Doctor alone since the arrival of Dr. Cecil Granthum—God bless her!

"Hello! What you trying to do?"

No answer. The Little Doctor refused even to lift her lashes, which were wet and clung together in little groups of two or three. Chip also observed that there were suggestive streaks upon her cheeks—and not a sign of a dimple anywhere. He lifted one leg over the horn of the saddle to ease his ankle, which still pained him a little after a ride, and watched her a moment.

"What's the matter, Doctor? Step on a cactus?"

"Oh, no," snapped the Doctor in a tone to take one's head off, "I didn't step on a cactus—I just walked all over acres and acres of them!"

There was a suspicious gurgle from somewhere. The Little Doctor looked up.

"Don't hesitate to laugh, Mr. Bennett, if you happen to feel that way!"

Mr. Bennett evidently felt that way. He rocked in the saddle, and shouted with laughter. The Little Doctor stood this for as much as a minute.

"Oh, no doubt it's very funny to set me afoot away off from every-where——" Her voice quivered and broke from self-pity; her head bent lower over her shoe.

Chip made haste to stifle his mirth, in fear that she was going to cry. He couldn't have endured that. He reached for his tobacco and began to make a cigarette.

"I didn't set you afoot," he said. "That was a bad break you made yourself. Why didn't you do as I told you—hang to the bridle and fight Denver off with your whip? You had one."

"Yes—and let him gnaw me!"

Chip gurgled again, and drew the tobacco sack shut with his teeth. "He wouldn't 'gnaw' you—he wouldn't have come near you. He's whip trained. And I'd have been there myself in another minute."

"I didn't want you there! And I don't pretend to be a horse-trainer, Mr. Bennett. There's several things about your old ranch life that I don't know—and don't want to know! I'm going back to Ohio tomorrow, so there!"

"Yes?" He drew a match sharply along his stamped saddle-skirt and applied it to the cigarette, pinched out the blaze with extreme care, and tossed the match-end facetiously against Concho's nose. He did not seem particularly alarmed at her threat—or, perhaps, he did not care. The Little Doctor prodded savagely at her shoe, too angry to see the thorn, and Chip drove another nail into his coffin with apparent relish, and watched her. After a little, he slid to the ground and limped over to her.

"Here, give me that shoe; you'll have it all picked to pieces and not get the thorn, either. Where is it?"

"It?" sniffed the Little Doctor, surrendering the shoe with hypocritical reluctance. "It? There's a dozen, at the very least!"

Chip emptied his lungs of smoke, and turned the shoe in his hands.

"Oh, I guess not—there isn't room in this little bit of leather for a dozen. Two would be crowded."

"I detest flattery above all things!" But, being a woman, the brow of the Little Doctor cleared perceptibly.

"Yes? You're just like me in that respect. I love the truth."

Thinking of Dr. Cecil, the Little Doctor grew guiltily red. But she had never said Cecil was a man, she reflected, with what comfort she could. The boys, like Dunk, had simply made the mistake of taking too much for granted.

Chip opened the smallest blade of his knife deliberately, sat down upon a neighboring rock and finished his cigarette, still turning the shoe reflectively—and caressingly—in his hand.

"I'd smile to see the Countess try to put that shoe on," he remarked, holding the cigarette in some mysterious manner on his lip. "I'll bet she couldn't get one toe in it."

"I don't see that it matters, whether she could or not," snapped the Little Doctor. "For goodness sake, hurry!"

"You're pretty mad, aren't you?" inquired he, shoving his hat back off his forehead, and looking at her as though he enjoyed doing so.

"Do I look mad?" asked she, tartly.

"I'd tell a man you do!"

"Well—my appearance doesn't half express the state of my mind!"

"Your mind must be in an awful state."

"It is."

Two minutes passed silently.

"Dr. Cecil's bread is done—she gave me a slice as big as your hat, with butter and jelly on it. It was out of sight."

The Little Doctor groaned, and rallied.

"Butter and jelly on my hat, did you say?"

"Not on your hat—on the bread. I ate it coming back down the coulee—and I sure had my hands full, leading Concho, too."

The Little Doctor held back the question trembling on her hungry, parched lips as long as she could, but it would come.

"Was it good?"

"I'd tell a man!" said Chip, briefly and eloquently.

The Little Doctor sighed.

"Dr. Cecil Granthum's a mighty good fellow—I'm stuck on him, myself—and if I haven't got the symptoms sized up wrong, the Old Man's *going* to be."

"That's all the good it will do him. Cecil and I are going somewhere and practice medicine together—and we aren't either of us going to get married, ever!"

"Have you got the papers for that?" grinned Chip, utterly unmoved.

"I have my license," said the Little Doctor, coldly.

"You're ahead of me there, for I haven't—yet. I can soon get one, though."

"I wish to goodness you'd hurry up with that shoe! I'm half starved."

"Well, show me a dimple and you can have it. My, you are cranky!"

The Little Doctor showed him two, and Chip laid the shoe in her lap—after he had surprised himself, and the doctor, by planting a daring little kiss upon the toe.

"The idea!" exclaimed she, with a feeble show of indignation, and slipped her foot hurriedly into its orthodox covering. Feeling his inscrutable, hazel eyes upon her, she blushed uncomfortably and fumbled the laces.

"You better let me lace that shoe—you won't have it done in a thousand years, at that gait."

"If you're in a hurry," said she, without looking at him, "you can ride on ahead. It would please me better if you did."

"Yes? You've been pleased all summer—at my expense. I'm going to please myself, this time. It's my deal, Little Doctor. Do you want to know what's trumps?"

"No, I don't!" Still without looking at him, she tied her shoelaces with an impatient twitch that came near breaking them, and walked haughtily to where Concho stood dutifully waiting. With an impulsive movement, she threw her arms around his neck, and hid her hot face against his scanty mane.

A pair of arms clad in pink-and-white striped sleeves went suddenly about her. Her clasp on Concho loosened and she threw back her head, startled—to be still more startled at the touch of lips that were curved and thin and masterful. The arms whirled her about and held her against a heart which her trained senses knew at once was beating very irregularly.

"You—you ought to be ashamed!" she asserted feebly, at last.

"I'm not, though." The arms tightened their clasp a little.

"You—you don't *seem* to be," admitted the Little Doctor, meekly.

For answer he kissed her hungrily—not once, but many times.

"Aren't you going to let me go?" she demanded, afterward, but very faintly.

"No," said he, boldly. "I'm going to keep you—always." There was conviction in the tone.

She stood silent a minute, listening to his heart and her own, and digesting this bit of news.

"Are you—quite sure about—that?" she asked at length.

"I'd tell a man! Unless"—he held her off and looked at her—"you don't like me. But you do, don't you?" His eyes were searching her face.

The Little Doctor struggled to release herself from the arms which held her unyieldingly and tenderly. Failing this, she raised her eyes to the white silk handkerchief knotted around his throat; to the chin; to the lips, wistful with their well defined curve; to the eyes, where they lingered shyly a moment, and then looked away to the horizon.

"Don't you like me? Say!" He gave her a gentle shake.

"Ye—er—it doesn't seem to matter, whether I do or not," she retorted with growing spirit—witness the dimple dodging into her cheek.

"Yes, it does—it matters a whole heap. You've dealt me misery ever since I first set eyes on you—and I believe, on my soul, you liked to watch me squirm! But you do like me, don't you?"

"I—I'd tell a man!" said she, and immediately hid a very red face from sight of him.

Concho turned his head and gazed wonderingly upon the two. What amazed him was to see Chip kissing his mistress again and again, and to hear the idolatrous tone in which he was saying "My Little Doctor!"

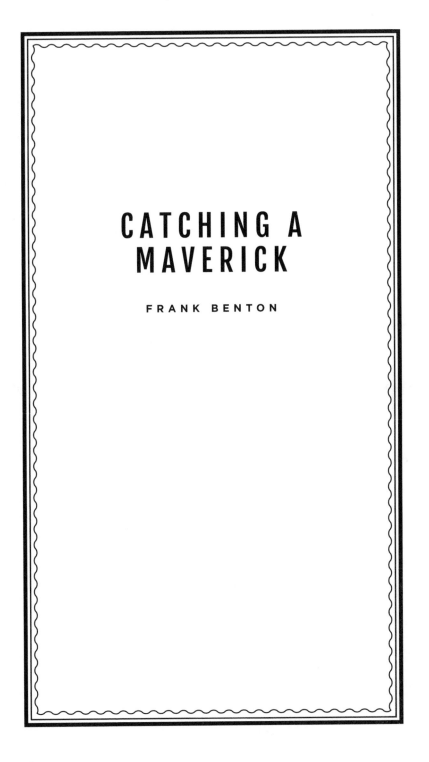

# CATCHING A MAVERICK

FRANK BENTON

One day while waiting for a gravel train going west, we all got to talking about catching mavericks. Eatumup Jake said he'd always been too honest to go out on the range and hunt mavericks; Dillbery Ike said he was too, but he wasn't so durned honest as to let a maverick chase him out of his own corral, and they asked me what I thought about branding mavericks. I told them that I thought it was a bad practice to hunt mavericks all the time, but whenever a maverick came around hunting me up, I generally built a fire and put a branding iron in to heat. But I told them I would always remember one maverick I had an adventure with, and after they had all promised me not to ever tell the story to any one, I told them the following:

One hot day in the spring of '84 I started across the hills from my ranch to town, fifteen miles away. I generally had a good riata on my saddle, but this day, for some reason, I didn't take anything but a piece of rope fifteen feet long. I didn't expect to meet any mavericks, as it was just after the spring roundup and there wasn't a chance in a hundred of seeing one. My way was across a high, broken country, without a house or a ranch the entire distance. There was bunches of cattle and horses everywhere eating the luxuriant grass, drinking out of the clear running streams of mountain water or lying down too full to eat or drink any more. I was riding one of my best hosses, as everybody did when they went to town; had my high-heeled boots blacked till you could see your face in them; was wearing a brand-new $12 Stetson hat that was made to order; had on a pair of new California pants—they were sort of a lavender color with checks an inch square, and I was more than proud of them. I had on a white silk shirt and a blue silk handkerchief round my neck, a red silk vest with black polka dots on it, but didn't have any coat to match this brilliant costume, so was in my shirt sleeves.

I rode along, setting kind of side ways, my hat cocked over my ear, a-looking down at myself from time to time, and I was about the most self-satisfied cowpuncher ever was, didn't envy a saloon-keeper in the territory, and saloon-keepers had as much influence in Wyoming them days as a sheepman does now, and that's saying all you can say, when it's known that the sheepmen to-day in Wyoming fill almost every office, elective and appointive.

Well I had got about half way to town and was a-studying 'bout a girl I bid goodbye to in the East fifteen years before, and sort a-wishing she could see me now, when all of a sudden I looked up and right there, not fifty feet away, was a big, fat, black bull maverick. He was about a year and a half old and would weigh 800 pounds. He was wild as an elk and had given a loud snuff on seeing me, which had called my attention to him. I immediately commenced making that short piece of rope into a lasso. There wasn't much more than enough for the loop, but I knew old Bill, the hoss I was riding, could catch him on any kind of ground, so throwed the spurs in and went sailing over the breaks and coolies after that wild bull maverick. I soon caught up with him, but found it almost impossible to throw the loop over his head with such a short rope, as he dodged to one side or the other every time I got in reach. However, I finally got it over his horns just as he went over a bank, but before I could take any dallys [*wrapping rope around the saddle horn*], he jerked the rope out of my hands and was gone with it.

Now I had got to pick up the rope, and as it only dragged five or six feet behind him, I would have to ride by him and grab the rope near his head as I went by; but he was still on the dodge, and I made several passes at it and missed. The bull was getting mad by this time, and lowering his head and elevating his tail he soon had me on the dodge. Whenever I wasn't chasing the bull, he was chasing me. Thus we had it up one gulch and down another. Many times I grabbed the rope only to have it jerked out of my fingers, but finally got a wrap around my saddle horn and a knot tied. It never had occurred to me I couldn't throw him with that short rope till I was tied hard and fast to him and riding down the gulch at breakneck speed with that black bull a close second.

We had been chasing each other now for over an hour and my hoss was getting tired, but Mr. Bull seemed to be fresher than ever. I had lost my new Stetson hat early in the game, and, as we had soused through a good many alkali mud-holes, I was spattered from head to foot with mud. My white silk shirt and lavender-colored pants were a total wreck. But something had got to be done, and watching the bull till he was veering a little to the left of my hoss I made a quick turn to the right, and stopping right quick, turned Mr. Bull over on his back. Before he could get up I was off and on top of him, had his tail between his hind legs, my knees in his flank, and, as every cowpuncher knows, I could hold him down. My hoss was pulling on the rope same as any well-trained cow hoss would, keeping the bull's head stretched out, and there wasn't the least possible show of him getting up; but as I didn't have any short foot ropes to tie his feet with, I just had to set in his flank and keep tight hold of his tail. Billy, my hoss, had got hot and excited during the race and kept surging on the rope more than necessary. I kept saying, "Whoa, Bill," but directly he give an extra hard pull, the rope broke right at the bull's head, and despite my nice talk, Billy turned his back to me and started across the hills for home. In vain I hollered, "Whoa, Bill; come Billy," he never looked around but once, and that was just as he disappeared over the hill. He sort a-looked back for a moment, as much as to say, "Well you wanted that darn little black bull so bad, now you got him stay with him," and that's what I had to do. He was twice as hard to hold now without any rope on his head, but I knew if he ever got up, he would gore me to death, as there wasn't a tree or rock to get behind.

It was about noon. The hot sun was pouring down on my bare head and I was choking with thirst. No one ever traveled that way but me. Miles away to any habitation, there I would have to stay in that stooping position, holding on to that little black bull's tail. I was young and strong, but my back began to ache, my hand would cramp clasping that bull's tail so tightly, but still I held on somehow, for I knew certain death awaited me if I let go. A bunch of cattle came along and circled around me with wide-eyed astonishment, then trotted off; a couple of antelope came running over the hill, and catching sight of me in that ridiculous position, their curiosity overcame their timidity and they kept getting nearer and nearer, till only a few rods away, the old buck antelope stopped and snuffed very loudly and stamped with his fore feet, but, not being able to get any response out of the black bull and me, finally left. Then a silly jackrabbit came hopping up on three legs, and after standing up several times on his hind legs as high as possible and pulling his whiskers some, he shook his big ears as much as to say, "It's beyond me," and he, too, left.

Just then the bull took a new fit of struggling and I heard the loud buzz of a rattlesnake behind me. I almost dropped my holt on the bull's tail then, but I had acquired the habit of holding on to it by this time, so glanced over my shoulder to see how far the snake was from me. I discovered he was only about ten feet behind me, coiled up and mad about something. He was about four and a half feet long and big around as my wrist, and didn't seem to have any notion of going around, but just laid there coiled up, and every time the bull or me moved, would begin to rattle and draw his head back and forth, run out his tongue and act disagreeable. Several times he started to uncoil and crawl in my direction, but I stirred up the bull to floundering around and bluffed the snake out of coming any closer. Still he seemed to like our company, and finally went to sleep; but every time I and the bull got to threshing around, he would drowsily sound his rattle, as much as to say, "I am still here; don't crowd me any." It was now about two o'clock in the afternoon. I felt kind of a goneness in my stomach, but my thirst was something awful, and in my mind's eye I could see the boys in town setting in the card-room of the saloon around the poker tables behind stacks of red, white, and blue chips, drinking Scotch highballs, while I was out on that high mesa dying of thirst and holding down a little black bull maverick with nothing for company but that old fat rattlesnake who insisted on staying there to see how the bull and I come out.

I hoped against hope that when old Billy arrived at the ranch some one would start back with him to hunt me up, but I remembered that most everybody at the ranch had gone up in the mountains trout fishing and wouldn't be back till night, and then I wondered which would live the longest, me or the bull, and I thought about slipping away from him while he was quiet; but the moment I would loosen up on his tail he would commence threshing around trying to get up, still I kept fooling with him. I'd loosen up on his tail, and then when he tried to get up, throw him back; so pretty soon he didn't pay any attention when I loosened up, and I thought I would try a sneak. However, in order to make him think I still had hold of his tail, I tied the end of it into a hard knot.

I looked around for his snakeship, as I had got to sneak back towards him, but he was sound asleep, and as the bull was pretty quiet, I sized up the country back of me and spied a gulch with steep broken banks about one hundred and fifty yards away, and made up my mind that that was the place to get to. So slipping by the snake I made the star run of my life for that gulch.

I had run about fifty feet when that bull first realized some of his company was missing, and jumping to his feet looked around and caught sight of me, and giving a snuff that I can hear in my dreams to this day, he was after me. Talk about running. I remember a jackrabbit jumped up in front of me, but I hollered to him to get out of the way. The bull caught up before I quite got to the gulch, but hesitated for a moment where to put his horns, and sort a-throwed his head up and down for a time or two, like he was practicing—kind a-getting a swing like throwing a hammer. When he got his neck to working good, biff! he took me and I went sailing through the air, but when I come down it was on the bank of the gulch, and before he could pick me up again I was over and under that bank. It was about fifteen feet to the bottom and straight up and down, but there was a little shelf of hard dirt on the side, and I caught on there and was safe. He had gone clear over me into the gulch, but was up and bawling and jawing around in a minute. However, he couldn't get up to me, so looked around, found a trail leading out of the gulch, and went up on top, then come around and looked down at me. He was mad clear through; went and hunted up the old rattlesnake, and after pawing and bellowing around him, charged him and got bit on the nose. Then he saw my Stetson hat, and giving a roar, went after it, putting his horn through it, went off across the hills mad clear through, full of snake poison, with my Stetson hat on one horn, and that was the last I saw of the little black bull.

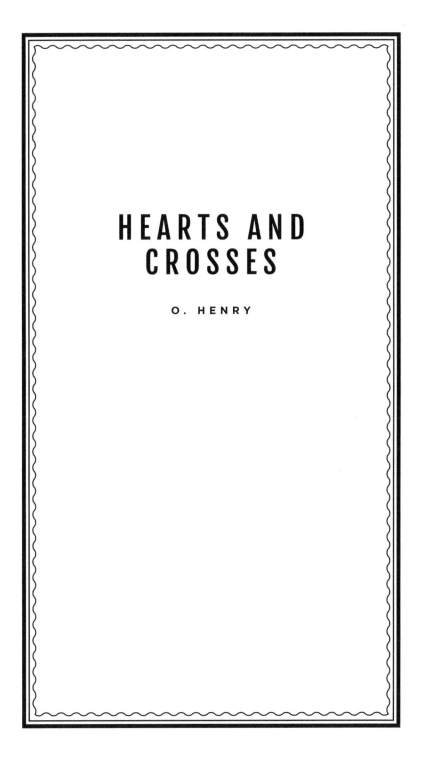

# HEARTS AND CROSSES

O. HENRY

Baldy Woods reached for the bottle, and got it. Whenever Baldy went for anything he usually—but this is not Baldy's story. He poured out a third drink that was larger by a finger than the first and second. Baldy was in consultation; and the consultee is worthy of his hire.

"I'd be king if I was you," said Baldy, so positively that his holster creaked and his spurs rattled.

Webb Yeager pushed back his flat-brimmed Stetson, and made further disorder in his straw-coloured hair. The tonsorial recourse being without avail, he followed the liquid example of the more resourceful Baldy.

"If a man marries a queen, it oughtn't to make him a two-spot," declared Webb, epitomising his grievances.

"Sure not," said Baldy, sympathetic, still thirsty, and genuinely solicitous concerning the relative value of the cards. "By rights you're a king. If I was you, I'd call for a new deal. The cards have been stacked on you—I'll tell you what you are, Webb Yeager."

"What?" asked Webb, with a hopeful look in his pale-blue eyes.

"You're a prince-consort."

"Go easy," said Webb. "I never blackguarded you none."

"It's a title," explained Baldy, "up among the picture-cards; but it don't take no tricks. I'll tell you, Webb. It's a brand they're got for certain animals in Europe. Say that you or me or one of them Dutch dukes marries in a royal family. Well, by and by our wife gets to be queen. Are we king? Not in a million years. At the coronation ceremonies we march between little casino and the Ninth Grand Custodian of the Royal Hall Bedchamber. The only use we are is to appear in photographs, and accept the responsibility for the heir-apparent. That ain't any square deal. Yes, sir, Webb, you're a prince-consort; and if I was you, I'd start a interregnum or a habeas corpus or somethin'; and I'd be king if I had to turn from the bottom of the deck."

Baldy emptied his glass to the ratification of his Warwick pose.

"Baldy," said Webb, solemnly, "me and you punched cows in the same outfit for years. We been runnin' on the same range, and ridin' the same trails since we was boys. I wouldn't talk about my family affairs to nobody but you. You was line-rider on the Nopalito Ranch when I married Santa McAllister. I was foreman then; but what am I now? I don't amount to a knot in a stake rope."

"When old McAllister was the cattle king of West Texas," continued Baldy with Satanic sweetness, "you was some tallow. You had as much to say on the ranch as he did."

"I did," admitted Webb, "up to the time he found out I was tryin' to get my rope over Santa's head. Then he kept me out on the range as far from the ranch-house as he could. When the old man died they commenced to call Santa the 'cattle queen.' I'm boss of the cattle—that's all. She 'tends to all the business; she handles all the money; I can't sell even a beef-steer to a party of campers, myself. Santa's the 'queen'; and I'm Mr. Nobody."

"I'd be king if I was you," repeated Baldy Woods, the royalist. "When a man marries a queen he ought to grade up with her—on the hoof—dressed—dried—corned—any old way from the chaparral to the packing-house. Lots of folks thinks it's funny, Webb, that you don't have the say-so on the Nopalito. I ain't reflectin' none on Miz Yeager—she's the finest little lady between the Rio Grande and next Christmas—but a man ought to be boss of his own camp."

The smooth, brown face of Yeager lengthened to a mask of wounded melancholy. With that expression, and his rumpled yellow hair and guileless blue eyes, he might have been likened to a school-boy whose leadership had been usurped by a youngster of superior strength. But his active and sinewy seventy-two inches, and his girded revolvers forbade the comparison.

"What was that you called me, Baldy?" he asked. "What kind of concert was it?"

"A 'consort,'" corrected Baldy—"a 'prince-consort.' It's a kind of short-card pseudonym. You come in sort of between Jack-high and a four-card flush."

Webb Yeager sighed, and gathered the strap of his Winchester scabbard from the floor.

"I'm ridin' back to the ranch to-day," he said half-heartedly. "I've got to start a bunch of beeves for San Antone in the morning."

"I'm your company as far as Dry Lake," announced Baldy. "I've got a round-up camp on the San Marcos cuttin' out two-year-olds."

The two *compañeros* mounted their ponies and trotted away from the little railroad settlement, where they had foregathered in the thirsty morning.

At Dry Lake, where their routes diverged, they reined up for a parting cigarette. For miles they had ridden in silence save for the soft drum of the ponies' hoofs on the matted mesquite grass, and the rattle of the chaparral against their wooden stirrups. But in Texas discourse is seldom continuous. You may fill in a mile, a meal, and a murder between your paragraphs without detriment to your thesis. So, without apology, Webb offered an addendum to the conversation that had begun ten miles away.

"You remember, yourself, Baldy, that there was a time when Santa wasn't quite so independent. You remember the days when old McAllister was keepin' us apart, and how she used to send me the sign that she wanted to see me? Old man Mac promised to make me look like a colander if I ever come in gun-shot of the ranch. You remember the sign she used to send, Baldy—the heart with a cross inside of it?"

"Me?" cried Baldy, with intoxicated archness.

"You old sugar-stealing coyote! Don't I remember! Why, you dad-blamed old long-horned turtle-dove, the boys in camp was all cognoscious about them hiroglyphs. The 'gizzard-and-crossbones' we used to call it. We used to see 'em on truck that was sent out from the ranch. They was marked in charcoal on the sacks of flour and in lead-pencil on the newspapers. I see one of 'em once chalked on the back of a new cook that old man McAllister sent out from the ranch—danged if I didn't."

"Santa's father," explained Webb gently, "got her to promise that she wouldn't write to me or send me any word. That heart-and-cross sign was her scheme. Whenever she wanted to see me in particular she managed to put that mark on somethin' at the ranch that she knew I'd see. And I never laid eyes on it but what I burnt the wind for the ranch the same night. I used to see her in that coma mott back of the little horse-corral."

"We knowed it," chanted Baldy; "but we never let on. We was all for you. We knowed why you always kept that fast paint in camp. And when we see that gizzard-and-crossbones figured out on the truck from the ranch we knowed old Pinto was goin' to eat up miles that night instead of grass. You remember Scurry—that educated horse-wrangler we had—the college fellow that tangle-foot drove to the range? Whenever Scurry saw that come-meet-your-honey brand on anything from the ranch, he'd wave his hand like that, and say, 'Our friend Lee Andrews will again swim the Hell's point to-night.' "

"The last time Santa sent me the sign," said Webb, "was once when she was sick. I noticed it as soon as I hit camp, and I galloped Pinto forty mile that night. She wasn't at the coma mott. I went to the house; and old McAllister met me at the door. 'Did you come here to get killed?' says he; 'I'll disoblige you for once. I just started a Mexican to bring you. Santa wants you. Go in that room and see her. And then come out here and see me.'

"Santa was lyin' in bed pretty sick. But she gives out a kind of smile, and her hand and mine lock horns, and I sets down by the bed—mud and spurs and chaps and all. 'I've heard you ridin' across the grass for hours, Webb,' she says. 'I was sure you'd come. You saw the sign?' she whispers. 'The minute I hit camp,' says I. ' 'Twas marked on the bag of potatoes and onions.' 'They're always together,' says she, soft like—'always together in life.' 'They go well together,' I says, 'in a stew.' 'I mean hearts and crosses,' says Santa. 'Our sign—to love and to suffer—that's what they mean.'

"And there was old Doc Musgrove amusin' himself with whisky and a palm-leaf fan. And by and by Santa goes to sleep; and Doc feels her forehead; and he says to me: 'You're not such a bad febrifuge. But you'd better slide out now; for the diagnosis don't call for you in regular doses. The little lady'll be all right when she wakes up.'

"I seen old McAllister outside. 'She's asleep,' says I. 'And now you can start in with your colander-work. Take your time; for I left my gun on my saddle-horn.'

"Old Mac laughs, and he says to me: 'Pumpin' lead into the best ranch-boss in West Texas don't seem to me good business policy. I don't know where I could get as good a one. It's the son-in-law idea, Webb, that makes me admire for to use you as a target. You ain't my idea for a member of the family. But I can use you on the Nopalito if you'll keep outside of a radius with the ranch-house in the middle of it. You go upstairs and lay down on a cot, and when you get some sleep we'll talk it over.'"

Baldy Woods pulled down his hat, and uncurled his leg from his saddle-horn. Webb shortened his rein, and his pony danced, anxious to be off. The two men shook hands with Western ceremony.

"*Adios*, Baldy," said Webb, "I'm glad I seen you and had this talk."

With a pounding rush that sounded like the rise of a covey of quail, the riders sped away toward different points of the compass. A hundred yards on his route Baldy reined in on the top of a bare knoll, and emitted a yell. He swayed on his horse; had he been on foot, the earth would have risen and conquered him; but in the saddle he was a master of equilibrium, and laughed at whisky, and despised the centre of gravity.

Webb turned in his saddle at the signal.

"If I was you," came Baldy's strident and perverting tones, "I'd be king!"

At eight o'clock on the following morning Bud Turner rolled from his saddle in front of the Nopalito ranch-house, and stumbled with whizzing rowels toward the gallery. Bud was in charge of the bunch of beef-cattle that was to strike the trail that morning for San Antonio. Mrs. Yeager was on the gallery watering a cluster of hyacinths growing in a red earthenware jar.

"King" McAllister had bequeathed to his daughter many of his strong characteristics—his resolution, his gay courage, his contumacious self-reliance, his pride as a reigning monarch of hoofs and horns.

*Allegro* and *fortissimo* had been McAllister's tempo and tone. In Santa they survived, transposed to the feminine key. Substantially, she preserved the image of the mother who had been summoned to wander in other and less finite green pastures long before the waxing herds of kine had conferred royalty upon the house. She had her mother's slim, strong figure and grave, soft prettiness that relieved in her the severity of the imperious McAllister eye and the McAllister air of royal independence.

Webb stood on one end of the gallery giving orders to two or three sub-bosses of various camps and outfits who had ridden in for instructions.

"'Morning," said Bud briefly. "Where do you want them beeves to go in town—to Barber's, as usual?"

Now, to answer that had been the prerogative of the queen. All the reins of business—buying, selling, and banking—had been held by her capable fingers. The handling of the cattle had been entrusted fully to her husband. In the days of "King" McAllister, Santa had been his secretary and helper; and she had continued her work with wisdom and profit. But before she could reply, the prince-consort spake up with calm decision:

"You drive that bunch to Zimmerman and Nesbit's pens. I spoke to Zimmerman about it some time ago."

Bud turned on his high boot-heels.

"Wait!" called Santa quickly. She looked at her husband with surprise in her steady grey eyes.

"Why, what do you mean, Webb?" she asked, with a small wrinkle gathering between her brows. "I never deal with Zimmerman and Nesbit. Barber has handled every head of stock from this ranch in that market for five years. I'm not going to take the business out of his hands." She faced Bud Turner. "Deliver those cattle to Barber," she concluded positively.

Bud gazed impartially at the water-jug hanging on the gallery, stood on his other leg, and chewed a mesquite-leaf.

"I want this bunch of beeves to go to Zimmerman and Nesbit," said Webb, with a frosty light in his blue eyes.

"Nonsense," said Santa impatiently. "You'd better start on, Bud, so as to noon at the Little Elm water-hole. Tell Barber we'll have another lot of culls ready in about a month."

Bud allowed a hesitating eye to steal upward and meet Webb's. Webb saw apology in his look, and fancied he saw commiseration.

"You deliver them cattle," he said grimly, "to—"

"Barber," finished Santa sharply. "Let that settle it. Is there anything else you are waiting for, Bud?"

"No, m'm," said Bud. But before going he lingered while a cow's tail could have switched thrice; for man is man's ally; and even the Philistines must have blushed when they took Samson in the way they did.

"You hear your boss!" cried Webb sardonically. He took off his hat, and bowed until it touched the floor before his wife.

"Webb," said Santa rebukingly, "you're acting mighty foolish to-day."

"Court fool, your Majesty," said Webb, in his slow tones, which had changed their quality. "What else can you expect? Let me tell you. I was a man before I married a cattle-queen. What am I now? The laughing-stock of the camps. I'll be a man again."

Santa looked at him closely.

"Don't be unreasonable, Webb," she said calmly. "You haven't been slighted in any way. Do I ever interfere in your management of the cattle? I know the business side of the ranch much better than you do. I learned it from Dad. Be sensible."

"Kingdoms and queendoms," said Webb, "don't suit me unless I am in the pictures, too. I punch the cattle and you wear the crown. All right. I'd rather be High Lord Chancellor of a cow-camp than the eight-spot in a queen-high flush. It's your ranch; and Barber gets the beeves."

Webb's horse was tied to the rack. He walked into the house and brought out his roll of blankets that he never took with him except on long rides, and his "slicker," and his longest stake-rope of plaited rawhide. These he began to tie deliberately upon his saddle. Santa, a little pale, followed him.

Webb swung up into the saddle. His serious, smooth face was without expression except for a stubborn light that smouldered in his eyes.

"There's a herd of cows and calves," said he, "near the Hondo Water-hole on the Frio that ought to be moved away from timber. Lobos have killed three of the calves. I forgot to leave orders. You'd better tell Simms to attend to it."

"Santa laid a hand on the horse's bridle, and looked her husband in the eye.

"Are you going to leave me, Webb?" she asked quietly.

"I am going to be a man again," he answered.

"I wish you success in a praiseworthy attempt," she said, with a sudden coldness. She turned and walked directly into the house.

Webb Yeager rode to the southeast as straight as the topography of West Texas permitted. And when he reached the horizon he might have ridden on into blue space as far as knowledge of him on the Nopalito went. And the days, with Sundays at their head, formed into hebdomadal squads; and the weeks, captained by the full moon, closed ranks into menstrual companies carrying "Tempus fugit" on their banners; and the months marched on toward the vast camp-ground of the years; but Webb Yeager came no more to the dominions of his queen.

One day a being named Bartholomew, a sheep-man—and therefore of little account—from the lower Rio Grande country, rode in sight of the Nopalito ranch-house, and felt hunger assail him. *Ex consuetudine* he was soon seated at the mid-day dining-table of that hospitable kingdom. Talk like water gushed from him: he might have been smitten with Aaron's rod—that is your gentle shepherd when an audience is vouchsafed him whose ears are not overgrown with wool.

"Missis Yeager," he babbled, "I see a man the other day on the Rancho Seco down in Hidalgo County by your name—Webb Yeager was his. He'd just been engaged as a manager. He was a tall, light-haired man, not saying much. Maybe he was some kin of yours, do you think?"

"A husband," said Santa cordially. "The Seco has done well. Mr. Yeager is one of the best stockmen in the West."

The dropping out of a prince-consort rarely disorganises a monarchy. Queen Santa had appointed as *mayordomo* of the ranch a trusty subject, named Ramsay, who had been one of her father's faithful vassals. And there was scarcely a ripple on the Nopalito ranch save when the gulf-breeze created undulations in the grass of its wide acres.

For several years the Nopalito had been making experiments with an English breed of cattle that looked down with aristocratic contempt upon the Texas long-horns. The experiments were found satisfactory; and a pasture had been set apart for the blue-bloods. The fame of them had gone forth into the chaparral and pear as far as men ride in saddles. Other ranches woke up, rubbed their eyes, and looked with new dissatisfaction upon the long-horns.

As a consequence, one day a sunburned, capable, silk-kerchiefed nonchalant youth, garnished with revolvers, and attended by three Mexican *vaqueros*, alighted at the Nopalito ranch and presented the following business-like epistle to the queen thereof:

Mrs. Yeager—The Nopalito Ranch:

DEAR MADAM:

I am instructed by the owners of the Rancho Seco to pur-
chase 100 head of two and three-year-old cows of the Sussex
breed owned by you. If you can fill the order please deliver the
cattle to the bearer; and a check will be forwarded to you at
once.

> Respectfully,
> WEBSTER YEAGER,
> Manager the Rancho Seco.

Business is business, even—very scantily did it escape being written
"especially"—in a kingdom.

That night the 100 head of cattle were driven up from the pasture
and penned in a corral near the ranch-house for delivery in the morning.

When night closed down and the house was still, did Santa Yeager
throw herself down, clasping that formal note to her bosom, weeping,
and calling out a name that pride (either in one or the other) had kept
from her lips many a day? Or did she file the letter, in her business way,
retaining her royal balance and strength?

Wonder, if you will; but royalty is sacred; and there is a veil. But this
much you shall learn:

At midnight Santa slipped softly out of the ranch-house, clothed
in something dark and plain. She paused for a moment under the live-
oak trees. The prairies were somewhat dim, and the moonlight was
pale orange, diluted with particles of an impalpable, flying mist. But
the mock-bird whistled on every bough of vantage; leagues of flowers
scented the air; and a kindergarten of little shadowy rabbits leaped and
played in an open space near by. Santa turned her face to the southeast
and threw kisses thitherward; for there was none to see.

Then she sped silently to the blacksmith-shop, fifty yards away; and what she did there can only be surmised. But the forge glowed red; and there was a faint hammering such as Cupid might make when he sharpens his arrow-points.

Later she came forth with a queer-shaped, handled thing in one hand, and a portable furnace, such as are seen in branding-camps, in the other. To the corral where the Sussex cattle were penned she sped with these things swiftly in the moonlight.

She opened the gate and slipped inside the corral. The Sussex cattle were mostly a dark red. But among this bunch was one that was milky white—notable among the others.

And now Santa shook from her shoulder something that we had not seen before—a rope lasso. She freed the loop of it, coiling the length in her left hand, and plunged into the thick of the cattle.

The white cow was her object. She swung the lasso, which caught one horn and slipped off. The next throw encircled the forefeet and the animal fell heavily. Santa made for it like a panther; but it scrambled up and dashed against her, knocking her over like a blade of grass.

Again she made the cast, while the aroused cattle milled around the four sides of the corral in a plunging mass. This throw was fair; the white cow came to earth again; and before it could rise Santa had made the lasso fast around a post of the corral with a swift and simple knot, and had leaped upon the cow again with the rawhide hobbles.

In one minute the feet of the animal were tied (no record-breaking deed) and Santa leaned against the corral for the same space of time, panting and lax.

And then she ran swiftly to her furnace at the gate and brought the branding-iron, queerly-shaped and white-hot.

The bellow of the outraged white cow, as the iron was applied, should have stirred the slumbering auricular nerves and consciences of the near-by subjects of the Nopalito, but it did not. And it was amid the deepest nocturnal silence that Santa ran like a lap-wing back to the ranch-house and there fell upon a cot and sobbed—sobbed as though queens had hearts as simple ranchmen's wives have, and as though she would gladly make kings of prince-consorts, should they ride back again from over the hills and far away.

In the morning the capable, revolvered youth and his *vaqueros* set forth, driving the bunch of Sussex cattle across the prairies to the Rancho Seco. Ninety miles it was; a six days' journey, grazing and watering the animals on the way.

The beasts arrived at Rancho Seco one evening at dusk; and were received and counted by the foreman of the ranch.

The next morning at eight o'clock a horseman loped out of the brush to the Nopalito ranch-house. He dismounted stiffly, and strode, with whizzing spurs, to the house. His horse gave a great sigh and swayed foam-streaked, with down-drooping head and closed eyes.

But waste not your pity upon Belshazzar, the flea-bitten sorrel. To-day, in Nopalito horse-pasture he survives, pampered, beloved, unridden, cherished record-holder of long-distance rides.

The horseman stumbled into the house. Two arms fell around his neck, and someone cried out in the voice of woman and queen alike: "Webb—oh, Webb!"

"I was a skunk," said Webb Yeager.

"Hush," said Santa, "did you see it?"

"I saw it," said Webb.

What they meant God knows; and you shall know, if you rightly read the primer of events.

"Be the cattle-queen," said Webb; "and overlook it if you can. I was a mangy, sheep-stealing coyote."

"Hush!" said Santa again, laying her fingers upon his mouth. "There's no queen here. Do you know who I am? I am Santa Yeager, First Lady of the Bedchamber. Come here."

She dragged him from the gallery into the room to the right. There stood a cradle with an infant in it—a red, ribald, unintelligible, babbling, beautiful infant, sputtering at life in an unseemly manner.

"There's no queen on this ranch," said Santa again. "Look at the king. He's got your eyes, Webb. Down on your knees and look at his Highness."

But jingling rowels sounded on the gallery, and Bud Turner stumbled there again with the same query that he had brought, lacking a few days, a year ago.

" 'Morning. Them beeves is just turned out on the trail. Shall I drive 'em to Barber's, or —"

He saw Webb and stopped, open-mouthed.

"Ba-ba-ba-ba-ba-ba!" shrieked the king in his cradle, beating the air with his fists.

"You hear your boss, Bud," said Webb Yeager, with a broad grin— just as he had said a year ago.

And that is all, except that when old man Quinn, owner of the Rancho Seco, went out to look over the herd of Sussex cattle that he had bought from the Nopalito ranch, he asked his new manager:

"What's the Nopalito ranch brand, Wilson?"

"X Bar Y," said Wilson.

"I thought so," said Quinn. "But look at that white heifer there; she's got another brand—a heart with a cross inside of it. What brand is that?"

# THE COW-BOY

BILL NYE

So much amusing talk is being made recently anent the blood-bedraggled cow-boy of the wild West, that I rise as one man to say a few things, not in a dictatorial style, but regarding this so-called or so esteemed dry land pirate who, mounted on a little cow-pony and under the black flag, sails out across the green surge of the plains to scatter the rocky shores of Time with the bones of his fellow-man.

A great many people wonder where the cow-boy, with his abnormal thirst for blood, originated. Where did this young Jesse James, with his gory record and his dauntless eye, come from? Was he born in a buffalo wallow at the foot of some rock-ribbed mountain, or did he first breathe the thin air along the brink of an alkali pond, where the horned toad and the centipede sang him to sleep, and the tarantula tickled him under the chin with its hairy legs?

Careful research and cold, hard statistics show that the cow-boy, as a general thing, was born in an unostentatious manner on the farm. I hate to sit down on a beautiful romance and squash the breath out of a romantic dream; but the cow-boy who gets too much moist damnation in his system, and rides on a gallop up and down Main Street shooting out the lights of the beautiful billiard palaces, would be just as unhappy if a mouse ran up his pantaloon-leg as you would, gentle reader. He is generally a youth who thinks he will not earn his twenty-five dollars per month if he does not yell, and whoop, and shoot, and scare little girls into St. Vitus's dance. I've known more cow-boys to injure themselves with their own revolvers than to injure anyone else. This is evidently because they are more familiar with the hoe than they are with the Smith & Wesson.

One night, while I had rooms in the business part of a Territorial city in the Rocky Mountain cattle country, I was awakened at about one o'clock A.M. by the most blood-curdling cry of "Murder" I ever heard. It was murder with a big "M." Across the street, in the bright light of a restaurant, a dozen cow-boys with broad sombreros and flashing silver braid, huge leather chaperajas, Mexican spurs and orange silk neckties, and with flashing revolvers, were standing. It seemed that a big, red-faced Captain Kidd of the band, with his skin full of valley tan, had marched into an ice-cream resort with a self-cocker in his hand, and ordered the vanilla coolness for the gang. There being a dozen young folks at the place, mostly male and female, from a neighboring hop, indulging in cream, the proprietor, a meek Norwegian with thin white hair, deemed it rude and outre to do so. He said something to that effect whereat the other eleven men of alcoholic courage let off a yell that froze the cream into a solid glacier, and shook two kerosene lamps out of their sockets in the chandeliers.

Thereupon the little Y.M.C.A. Norwegian said:

"Gentlemans, I kain't neffer like dot squealinks and dot kaind of a tings, and you fellers mit dot ledder pantses on and dot funny glose and such a tings like dot, better keep kaind of quiet, or I shall call up the policemen mit my delephone."

Then they laughed at him, and cried yet again with a loud voice.

This annoyed the ice-cream agriculturist, and he took the old axe-handle that he used to jam the ice down around the freezer with, and peeled a large area of scalp off the leader's dome of thought, and it hung down over his eyes, so that he could not see to shoot with any degree of accuracy.

After he had yelled "Murder!" three or four times, he fell under an ice-cream table, and the mild-eyed Scandinavian broke a silver-plated castor over the organ of self-esteem, and poured red pepper, and salt, and vinegar, and Halford sauce and other relishes, on the place where the scalp was loose.

This revived the brave but murderous cow-gentleman, and he begged that he might be allowed to go away.

The gentle Y.M.C.A. superintendent of the ten-stamp ice-cream freezers then took the revolvers away from the bold buccaneer, and kicked him out through a show-case, and saluted him with a bouquet of July oysters that suffered severely from malaria.

All cow-boys are not sanguinary; but out of twenty you will generally find one who is brave when he has his revolvers with him; but when he forgot and left his shooters at home on the piano, the most tropical violet-eyed dude can climb him with the butt-end of a sunflower, and beat his brains out and spatter them all over that school district.

In the wild, unfettered West, beware of the man who never carries arms, never gets drunk and always minds his own business. He don't go around shooting out the gas, or intimidating a kindergarten school; but when a brave frontiersman, with a revolver in each boot and a bowie down the back of his neck, insults a modest young lady, and needs to be thrown through a plate-glass window and then walked over by the populace, call on the silent man who dares to wear a clean shirt and human clothes.

# ON COWBOYS

STEWART EDWARD WHITE

Your cowboy is a species variously subdivided. If you happen to be traveled as to the wild countries, you will be able to recognize whence your chance acquaintance hails by the kind of saddle he rides, and the rigging of it; by the kind of rope he throws, and the method of the throwing; by the shape of hat he wears; by his twist of speech; even by the very manner of his riding. Your California "vaquero" from the Coast Ranges is as unlike as possible to your Texas cowman, and both differ from the Wyoming or South Dakota article. I should be puzzled to define exactly the habitat of the "typical" cowboy. No matter where you go, you will find your individual acquaintance varying from the type in respect to some of the minor details.

Certain characteristics run through the whole tribe, however. Of these some are so well known or have been so adequately done elsewhere that it hardly seems wise to elaborate on them here. Let us assume that you and I know what sort of human beings cowboys are—with all their taciturnity, their surface gravity, their keen sense of humor, their courage, their kindness, their freedom, their lawlessness, their foulness of mouth, and their supreme skill in the handling of horses and cattle. I shall try to tell you nothing of all that.

If one thinks down doggedly to the last analysis, he will find that the basic reason for the differences between a cowboy and other men rests finally on an individual liberty, a freedom from restraint either of society or convention, a lawlessness, an accepting of his own standard alone. He is absolutely self-poised and sufficient; and that self-poise and that sufficiency he takes pains to assure first of all. After their assurance he is willing to enter into human relations. His attitude toward everything in life is, not suspicious, but watchful. He is "gathered together," his elbows at his side.

This evidences itself most strikingly in his terseness of speech. A man dependent on himself naturally does not give himself away to the first comer. He is more interested in finding out what the other fellow is than in exploiting his own importance. A man who does much promiscuous talking he is likely to despise, arguing that man incautious, hence weak.

Yet when he does talk, he talks to the point and with a vivid and direct picturesqueness of phrase which is as refreshing as it is unexpected. The delightful remodeling of the English language in Mr. Alfred Lewis's "Wolfville" is exaggerated only in quantity, not in quality. No cowboy talks habitually in quite as original a manner as Mr. Lewis's Old Cattleman; but I have no doubt that in time he would be heard to say all the good things in that volume. I myself have notebooks full of just such gorgeous language, some of the best of which I have used elsewhere, and so will not repeat here.

This vividness manifests itself quite as often in the selection of the apt word as in the construction of elaborate phrases with a half-humorous intention. A cowboy once told me of the arrival of a tramp by saying, "He *sifted* into camp." Could any verb be more expressive? Does not it convey exactly the lazy, careless, out-at-heels shuffling gait of the hobo? Another in the course of description told of a saloon scene, "They all *bellied up to* the bar." Again, a range cook, objecting to purposeless idling about his fire, shouted: "If you fellows come *moping* around here any more, *I'll sure make you hard to catch!*" "Fish in the pond, son? Why, there's some fish in there big enough to rope," another advised me. "I quit shoveling," one explained the story of his life, "because I couldn't see nothing ahead of shoveling but dirt." The same man described ploughing as, "Looking at a mule's tail all day." And one of the most succinct epitomes of the motifs of fiction was offered by an old fellow who looked over my shoulder as I was reading a novel. "Well, son," said he, "what they doing now, *kissing or killing?*"

Nor are the complete phrases behind in aptness. I have space for only a few examples, but they will illustrate what I mean. Speaking of a companion who was "putting on too much dog," I was informed, "He walks like a man with a new suit of *wooden underwear!*" Or again, in answer to my inquiry as to a mutual acquaintance, "Jim? Or, poor old Jim! For the last week or so he's been nothing but an insignificant atom of humanity hitched to a boil."

But to observe the riot of imagination turned loose with the bridle off, you must assist at a burst of anger on the part of one of these men. It is mostly unprintable, but you will get an entirely new idea of what profanity means. Also you will come to the conclusion that you, with your trifling *damns*, and the like, have been a very good boy indeed. The remotest, most obscure, and unheard of conceptions are dragged forth from earth, heaven, and hell, and linked together in a sequence so original, so gaudy, and so utterly blasphemous, that you gasp and are stricken with the most devoted admiration. It is genius.

Of course I can give you no idea here of what these truly magnificent oaths are like. It is a pity, for it would liberalize your education. Occasionally, like a trickle of clear water into an alkali torrent, a straight English sentence will drop into the flood. It is refreshing by contrast, but weak.

"If your brains were all made of dynamite, you couldn't blow the top of your head off."

"I wouldn't speak to him if I met him in hell carrying a lump of ice in his hand."

"That little horse'll throw you so high the blackbirds will build nests in your hair before you come down."

These are ingenious and amusing, but need the blazing settings from which I have ravished them to give them their due force.

In Arizona a number of us were sitting around the feeble camp-fire the desert scarcity of fuel permits, smoking our pipes. We were all contemplative and comfortably silent with the exception of one very youthful person who had a lot to say. It was mainly about himself. After he had bragged awhile without molestation, one of the older cow-punchers grew very tired of it. He removed his pipe deliberately, and spat in the fire.

"Say, son," he drawled, "if you want to say something big, why don't you say 'elephant'?"

The young fellow subsided. We went on smoking our pipes.

Down near the Chiracahua Range in southeastern Arizona, there is a butte, and halfway up that butte is a cave, and in front of that cave is a ramshackle porch-roof or shed. This latter makes the cave into a dwelling-house. It is inhabited by an old "alkali" and half a dozen bear dogs. I sat with the old fellow one day for nearly an hour. It was a sociable visit, but economical of the English language. He made one remark, outside our initial greeting. It was enough, for in terseness, accuracy, and compression, I have never heard a better or more comprehensive description of the arid countries.

"Son," said he, "in this country thar is more cows and less butter, more rivers and less water, and you kin see farther and see less than in any other country in the world."

Now this peculiar directness of phrase means but one thing,— freedom from the influence of convention. The cowboy respects neither the dictionary nor usage. He employs his words in the manner that best suits him, and arranges them in the sequence that best expresses his idea, untrammeled by tradition. It is a phase of the same lawlessness, the same reliance on self, that makes for his taciturnity and watchfulness.

In essence, his dress is an adaptation to the necessities of his calling; as a matter of fact, it is an elaboration on that. The broad heavy felt hat he has found by experience to be more effective in turning heat than a lighter straw; he further runs to variety in the shape of the crown and in the nature of the band. He wears a silk handkerchief about his neck to turn the sun and keep out the dust, but indulges in astonishing gaudiness of color. His gauntlets save his hands from the rope; he adds a fringe and a silver star. The heavy wide "chaps" of leather about his legs are necessary to him when he is riding fast through brush; he indulges in such frivolities as stamped leather, angora hair, and the like. High heels to his boots prevent his foot from slipping through his wide stirrup, and are useful to dig into the ground when he is roping in the corral. Even his six-shooter is more a tool of his trade than a weapon of defense. With it he frightens cattle from the heavy brush; he slaughters old or diseased steers; he "turns the herd" in a stampede or when rounding it in; and especially is it handy and loose to his hip in case his horse should fall and commence to drag him.

So the details of his appearance spring from the practical, but in the wearing of them and the using of them he shows again that fine disregard for the way other people do it or think it.

Now in civilization you and I entertain a double respect for firearms and the law. Firearms are dangerous, and it is against the law to use them promiscuously. If we shoot them off in unexpected places, we first of all alarm unduly our families and neighbors, and in due course attract the notice of the police. By the time we are grown up we look on shooting a revolver as something to be accomplished after an especial trip for the purpose.

But to the cowboy shooting a gun is merely what lighting a match would be to us. We take reasonable care not to scratch that match on the wall nor to throw it where it will do harm. Likewise the cowboy takes reasonable care that his bullets do not land in someone's anatomy nor in too expensive bric-a-brac. Otherwise any time or place will do.

The picture comes to me of a bunk-house on an Arizona range. The time was evening. A half-dozen cowboys were sprawled out on the beds smoking, and three more were playing poker with the Chinese cook. A misguided rat darted out from under one of the beds and made for the empty fireplace. He finished his journey in smoke. Then the four who had shot slipped their guns back into their holsters and resumed their cigarettes and drawling low-toned conversation.

On another occasion I stopped for noon at the Circle I ranch. While waiting for dinner, I lay on my back in the bunk-room and counted three hundred and sixty-two bullet-holes in the ceiling. They came to be there because the festive cowboys used to while away the time while lying as I was lying, waiting for supper, in shooting the flies that crawled about the plaster.

This beautiful familiarity with the pistol as a parlor toy accounts in great part for a cowboy's propensity to "shoot up the town" and his indignation when arrested therefor.

The average cowboy is only a fair target-shot with the revolver. But he is chain lightning at getting his gun off in a hurry. There are exceptions to this, however, especially among the older men. Some can handle the Colts 45 and its heavy recoil with almost uncanny accuracy. I have seen individuals who could from their saddles nip lizards darting across the road; and one who was able to perforate twice before it hit the ground a tomato-can tossed into the air. The cowboy is prejudiced against the double-action gun, for some reason or other. He manipulates his single-action weapon fast enough, however.

His sense of humor takes the same unexpected slants, not because his mental processes differ from those of other men, but because he is unshackled by the subtle and unnoticed nothingnesses of precedent which deflect our action toward the common uniformity of our neighbors. It must be confessed that his sense of humor possesses also a certain robustness.

The J. H. outfit had been engaged for ten days in busting broncos. This the Chinese cook, Sang, a newcomer in the territory, found vastly amusing. He liked to throw the ropes off the prostrate broncos, when all was ready; to slap them on the flanks; to yell shrill Chinese yells; and to dance in celestial delight when the terrified animal arose and scattered out of there. But one day the range men drove up a little bunch of full-grown cattle that had been bought from a smaller owner. It was necessary to change the brands. Therefore a little fire was built, the stamp-brand put in to heat, and two of the men on horseback caught a cow by the horns and one hind leg, and promptly upset her. The old brand was obliterated, the new one burnt in. This irritated the cow. Promptly the branding-men, who were of course afoot, climbed to the top of the corral to be out of the way. At this moment, before the horsemen could flip loose their ropes, Sang appeared.

"Hol' on!" he babbled. "I take him off;" and he scrambled over the fence and approached the cow.

Now cattle of any sort rush at the first object they see after getting to their feet. But whereas a steer makes a blind run and so can be avoided, a cow keeps her eyes open. Sang approached that wild-eyed cow, a bland smile on his countenance.

A dead silence fell. Looking about at my companions' faces I could not discern even in the depths of their eyes a single faint flicker of human interest.

Sang loosened the rope from the hind leg, he threw it from the horns, he slapped the cow with his hat, and uttered the shrill Chinese yell. So far all was according to programme.

The cow staggered to her feet, her eyes blazing fire. She took one good look, and then started for Sang.

What followed occurred with all the briskness of a tune from a circus band. Sang darted for the corral fence. Now, three sides of the corral were railed, and so climbable, but the fourth was a solid adobe wall. Of course Sang went for the wall. There, finding his nails would not stick, he fled down the length of it, his queue streaming, his eyes popping, his talons curved toward an ideal of safety, gibbering strange monkey talk, pursued a scant arm's length behind by that infuriated cow. Did any one help him? Not any. Every man of that crew was hanging weak from laughter to the horn of his saddle or the top of the fence. The preternatural solemnity had broken to little bits. Men came running from the bunk-house, only to go into spasms outside, to roll over and over on the ground, clutching handfuls of herbage in the agony of their delight.

At the end of the corral was a narrow chute. Into this Sang escaped as into a burrow. The cow came too. Sang, in desperation, seized a pole, but the cow dashed such a feeble weapon aside. Sang caught sight of a little opening, too small for cows, back into the main corral. He squeezed through. The cow crashed through after him, smashing the boards. At the crucial moment Sang tripped and fell on his face. The cow missed him by so close a margin that for a moment we thought she had hit. But she had not, and before she could turn, Sang had topped the fence and was halfway to the kitchen. Tom Waters always maintained that he spread his Chinese sleeves and flew. Shortly after a tremendous smoke arose from the kitchen chimney. Sang had gone back to cooking.

Now that Mongolian was really in great danger, but no one of the outfit thought for a moment of any but the humorous aspect of the affair. Analogously, in a certain small cow-town I happened to be transient when the postmaster shot a Mexican. Nothing was done about it. The man went right on being postmaster, but he had to set up the drinks because he had hit the Mexican in the stomach. That was considered a poor place to hit a man.

The entire town of Willcox knocked off work for nearly a day to while away the tedium of an enforced wait there on my part. They wanted me to go fishing. One man offered a team, the other a saddle-horse. All expended much eloquence in directing me accurately, so that I should be sure to find exactly the spot where I could hang my feet over a bank beneath which there were "a plumb plenty of fish." Somehow or other they raked out miscellaneous tackle. But they were a little too eager. I excused myself and hunted up a map. Sure enough the lake was there, but it had been dry since a previous geological period. The fish were undoubtedly there too, but they were fossil fish. I borrowed a pickaxe and shovel and announced myself as ready to start.

Outside the principal saloon in one town hung a gong. When a stranger was observed to enter the saloon, that gong was sounded. Then it behooved him to treat those who came in answer to the summons.

But when it comes to a case of real hospitality or helpfulness, your cowboy is there every time. You are welcome to food and shelter without price, whether he is at home or not. Only it is etiquette to leave your name and thanks pinned somewhere about the place. Otherwise your intrusion may be considered in the light of a theft, and you may be pursued accordingly.

Contrary to general opinion, the cowboy is not a dangerous man to those not looking for trouble. There are occasional exceptions, of course, but they belong to the universal genus of bully, and can be found among any class. Attend to your own business, be cool and good-natured, and your skin is safe. Then when it is really "up to you," be a man; you will never lack for friends.

The Sierras, especially towards the south where the meadows are wide and numerous, are full of cattle in small bands. They come up from the desert about the first of June, and are driven back again to the arid countries as soon as the autumn storms begin. In the very high land they are few, and to be left to their own devices; but now we entered a new sort of country.

Below Farewell Gap and the volcanic regions one's surroundings change entirely. The meadows become high flat valleys, often miles in extent; the mountains—while registering big on the aneroid—are so little elevated above the plateaus that a few thousand feet is all of their apparent height; the passes are low, the slopes easy, the trails good, the rock outcrops few, the hills grown with forests to their very tops. Altogether it is a country easy to ride through, rich in grazing, cool and green, with its eight thousand feet of elevation. Consequently during the hot months thousands of desert cattle are pastured here; and with them come many of the desert men.

Our first intimation of these things was in the volcanic region where swim the golden trout. From the advantage of a hill we looked far down to a hair-grass meadow through which twisted tortuously a brook, and by the side of the brook, belittled by distance, was a miniature man. We could see distinctly his every movement, as he approached cautiously the stream's edge, dropped his short line at the end of a stick over the bank, and then yanked bodily the fish from beneath. Behind him stood his pony. We could make out in the clear air the coil of his rawhide "rope," the glitter of his silver bit, the metal points on his saddle skirts, the polish of his six-shooter, the gleam of his fish, all the details of his costume. Yet he was fully a mile distant. After a time he picked up his string of fish, mounted, and jogged loosely away at the cow-pony's little Spanish trot toward the south. Over a week later, having caught golden trout and climbed Mount Whitney, we followed him and so came to the great central camp at Monache Meadows.

Imagine an island-dotted lake of grass four or five miles long by two or three wide to which slope regular shores of stony soil planted with trees. Imagine on the very edge of that lake an especially fine grove perhaps a quarter of a mile in length, beneath whose trees a dozen different outfits of cowboys are camped for the summer. You must place a herd of ponies in the foreground, a pine mountain at the back, an unbroken ridge across ahead, cattle dotted here and there, thousands of ravens wheeling and croaking and flapping everywhere, a marvelous clear sun and blue sky. The camps were mostly open, though a few possessed tents. They differed from the ordinary in that they had racks for saddles and equipments. Especially well laid out were the cooking arrangements. A dozen accommodating springs supplied fresh water with the conveniently regular spacing of faucets.

Towards evening the men jingled in. This summer camp was almost in the nature of a vacation to them after the hard work of the desert. All they had to do was to ride about the pleasant hills examining that the cattle did not stray nor get into trouble. It was fun for them, and they were in high spirits.

Our immediate neighbors were an old man of seventy-two and his grandson of twenty-five. At least the old man said he was seventy-two. I should have guessed fifty. He was as straight as an arrow, wiry, lean, clear-eyed, and had, without food, ridden twelve hours after some strayed cattle. On arriving he threw off his saddle, turned his horse loose, and set about the construction of supper. This consisted of boiled meat, strong tea, and an incredible number of flapjacks built of water, baking-powder, salt, and flour, warmed through—not cooked—in a frying-pan. He deluged these with molasses and devoured three plate-fuls. It would have killed an ostrich, but apparently did this decrepit veteran of seventy-two much good.

After supper he talked to us most interestingly in the dry cowboy manner, looking at us keenly from under the floppy brim of his hat. He confided to us that he had had to quit smoking, and it ground him—he'd smoked since he was five years old.

"Tobacco doesn't agree with you any more?" I hazarded.

"Oh, 't aint that," he replied; "only I'd ruther chew."

The dark fell, and all the little camp-fires under the trees twinkled bravely forth. Some of the men sang. One had an accordion. Figures, indistinct and formless, wandered here and there in the shadows, suddenly emerging from mystery into the clarity of firelight, there to disclose themselves as visitors. Out on the plain the cattle lowed, the horses nickered. The red firelight flashed from the metal of suspended equipment, crimsoned the bronze of men's faces, touched with pink the high lights on their gracefully recumbent forms. After a while we rolled up in our blankets and went to sleep, while a band of coyotes wailed like lost spirits from a spot where a steer had died.

# BRANSFORD MEETS AUGHINBAUGH

EUGENE MANLOVE RHODES

*I always thought they were fabulous monsters. Is it alive?*

—*The Unicorn*

Sun and wind of thirty-six out-of-door years had tanned Mr. Jeff Bransford's cheek to a rosy-brown, contrasting sharply with the whiteness of the upper part of his forehead, when exposed—as now—by the pushing up of his sombrero. These same suns and winds had drawn at the corners of his eyes a network of fine lines: but the brown eyes were undimmed, and his face had a light, sure look of unquenchable boyishness; sure mark of the unattached, and therefore carefree and irresponsible man, who, as the saying goes, "is at home wherever his hat is hung."

The hat in question was a soft gray one, the crown deeply creased down the middle, the wide brim of it joyously atilt, merging insensibly from one wavy curve into another and on to yet a third, like Hogarth's line of beauty.

Mr. Bransford's step was alert and springy: perhaps it had even a slight, unconscious approach to a swagger, as of one not unsatisfied with himself. He turned at the corner of Temple Street, skipped lightsome up a stairway and opened an office door, bearing on its glass front the inscription:

SIMON HIBLER

ATTORNEY-AT-LAW

"Is Mr. Hibler in?"

The only occupant of the room—a smooth-faced and frank-eyed young man—rose from his desk and came forward.

"Mr. Hibler is not in town."

"Dee-lightful! And when will he be back?" The rising inflection on the last word conveyed a resolute vivacity proof against small annoyances.

"To tell you the truth, I do not know. He is over in Arizona, near San Simon—for change and rest."

"H'm!" The tip of the visitor's nose twitched slightly, the brown eyes widened reflectively; the capable mouth under the brown mustache puckered as if to emit a gentle whistle. "He'll bring back the change. I'll take all bets on that. San Simon! H'm!" He shrugged his shoulders, one corner of his mouth pulled down in whimsical fashion, while the opposite eyebrow arched, so giving his face an appearance indescribably odd: the drooping side expressive of profound melancholy, while the rest of his face retained its habitual look of invincible cheerfulness. "San Simon! Dear, oh dear! And I may just nicely contemplate my two thumbs till he gets back with the change—and maybe so the rest!" He elevated the thumbs and cast vigilant glances at each in turn: half-chanting, dreamily:

"'O, she left her Tombstone home

For to dwell in San Simon,

And she run off with a prairie-navigator.'

—Ran off, I should say." His nose tweaked again.

The clerk was a newcomer in El Paso, hardly yet wonted to the freakish humor and high spirits that there flourish unrebuked—and indeed, unnoticed. But he entered into the spirit of the occasion. "Is there anything I can do?" he inquired. "I am Mr. Hibler's chief—and only—clerk."

"No-o," said the visitor doubtfully, letting his eyes wander from his thumbs to the view of the white-walled Juárez beyond the river. "No-o—That is, not unless you can sell me his Rainbow ranch and brand for less than they're worth. Such is my errand—on behalf of Pringle, Beebe, Ballinger and Bransford. I'm Bransford—me."

"Jeff Bransford? Mr. Hibler's foreman?" asked the young man eagerly.

"*Mr.* Jeff Bransford—foreman *for* Hibler—not of," amended Bransford gently. His thumbs were still upreared. Becoming suddenly aware of this, he fixed them with a startled gaze.

"Say! Take supper with me!" The young man blurted out the words. "Mr. Hibler's always talking about you and I want to get acquainted with you. Aughinbaugh's my name."

Bransford sat down heavily, thumbs still erect, elbows well out from his side, and transferred his gaze, with marked respect, to the clerk's boyish face, now very rosy indeed.

Jeff's eyes grew big and round; his lips were slightly parted; the thumbs drooped, the fingers spread wide apart in mutual dismay. Holding Aughinbaugh's eyes with his own, he pressed one outspread hand over his heart. Slowly, cautiously, the other hand fumbled in a vest pocket, produced notebook and pencil, spread the book stealthily on his knee and began to write. "'A good name,'" he murmured, "'is rather to be chosen than great riches.'"

But the owner of the good name was a lad of spirit, and had no mind to submit tamely to such hazing. "See here! What does a cowboy know about the Bible, anyway?" he demanded, glaring indignantly. "I believe you're a sheep in wolves' clothing! You don't talk like a cowboy—or look like a cowboy."

Jeff glanced down at his writing, and back to his questioner. Then he made an alteration, closed the book and looked up again. He had a merry eye.

"Exactly how does a cowboy look? And how does it talk?" he asked mildly. He glanced with much interest over as much of his own person as he could see; turning and twisting to aid the process. "I don't see anything wrong. Is my hair on straight?"

"Wrong!" echoed Aughinbaugh severely, shaking an accusing finger. "Why, you're *all* wrong. What the public expects—"

Mr. Bransford's interruption may be omitted. It was profane. Also, it was plagiarized from Commodore Vanderbilt.

"You a cowboy! Yah!" said Aughinbaugh in vigorous scorn. "With a silk necktie! Everybody knows that the typical cowboy wears a red cotton handkerchief."

"How long since you left New York?"

"Me? I'm from Kansas City."

"Same thing," said Bransford coldly. "I mean, how long since you came to El Paso? And have you been out of town since?"

"About eight months. And I confess that my duties—at first in the bank and afterwards here, have kept me pretty close, except for a trip or two to Juárez. But why?"

"Why enough!" returned Jeff. "Young man, young man! I see the finger of fate in this. It is no blind chance that brought me here while Hibler was away. It was predestined from the foundations of earth that I was to come here at this very now to explain to you about cowboys. I have the concentrated venom of about twenty-one years stored away to work off on somebody, and I feel it in my bones that you are the man. Come with me and I will do you good—as it says in mournful Numbers. You've been led astray. You shouldn't believe all you read and only half what you see.

"In the first place, take the typical cowboy. There positively ain't so sich person! Maybe so half of 'em's from Texas and the other half from anywhere and everywhere else. But they're all alike in just one thing—and that is that every last one of them is entirely different from all the others. Each one talks as he pleases, acts as he pleases and they all dress pretty much alike. Because, the things they wear there have been tried out and they've kept only the best of each kind—the best for that particular kind of work."

"They 'proved all things and held fast that which was good,'" suggested Aughinbaugh.

"Exactly. For instance, that handkerchief business. That isn't meant as a substitute for a necktie. Ever see a drought? If you did, you probably remember that it was some dusty. Well—there's been a steady drought out here for two hundred and eight million years come August. And when you drive two, three thousand head of cattle, with four feet apiece, to the round-up ground and chouse 'em 'round half a day, cutting out steers, the dust is so thick a horse can't fall down when he stumbles. Then mister cowboy folds his little hankie, like them other triangles that the ladies, God bless 'em with their usual perversity, call 'squares,' ties the ends, puts the knot at the back of his neck, pulls the wide part *over* his mouth and up over the bridge of his nose, *and breathes through it!* Got that? By heavens, it's a filter to keep the dust out of your lungs, and not an ornament! It's usually silk—not because silk is booful but because it's better to breathe through."

"Really, I never dreamed—" began Aughinbaugh. But Jeff waved him down.

"Don't speak to the man at the wheel, my son. And everything a cowboy uses, at work, from hats to boots, from saddle to bed, has just as good a reason for being exactly what it is as that handkerchief. Take the high-heeled boots, now—"

"Dad," said Aughinbaugh firmly. "I am faint. Break it to me easy. I was once an interior decorator of some promise, though not a professional. Let me lead you to a restaurant and show you a sample of my skill. Then come round to my rooms and tell me your troubles at leisure. Maybe you'll feel better. But before you explain your wardrobe I want to know why you don't say 'You all' and 'that-a-way,' 'plumb' and 'done gone,' and the rest of it."

"I do, my dear, when I want to," said Bransford affectionately. "Them's all useful words, easy and comfortable, like old clothes and old shoes. I like 'em. But they go with the old clothes. And now, as you see, I am—to use the metropolitan idiom—in my 'glad rags' and my speech naturally rises in dignity to meet the occasion. Besides, associating with Beebe—he's one of them siss-boom-ah! boys—has mitigated me a heap. Then I read the signs, and the brands on the freight cars. And I'll tell you one more thing, my son. A large proportion—I mean, of course, a right smart chance—of the cowboys are illiterate, and some of them are grand rascals, but they ain't none of 'em plumb imbeciles. They couldn't stay on the job. If their brains don't naturally work pretty spry, things happen to 'em—the chuckwagon bunts 'em or something. And they all have a chance at 'the education of a gentleman'—'to ride, to shoot and to speak the truth.' They have to ride and shoot—and speakin' the truth comes easier for them than for some folks, 'cause if speaking the aforesaid truth displeases anyone they mostly don't give a damn."

"Stop! Spare me!" cried Aughinbaugh. He collapsed in his chair, sliding together in an attitude of extreme dejection. "My spirits are very low, but—" He rose, tottered feebly to his desk and took therefrom a small bottle, which, with a glass, he handed to Bransford.

"Thanks. But you—you're a tee-totaler?" said Jeff.

"A—well—not exactly," stammered Aughinbaugh. "But I have to be very careful. I—I only take one drink at a time!" He fumbled out another glass.

"I stumble, I stumble!" said Bransford gravely. He poured out a small drink and passed the bottle. "'I fill this cup to one made up!'"— He held the glass up to the light.

"Well?" said Aughinbaugh, expectantly. "Go on!"

"That description can't be bettered," said Bransford.

"Never will I drink such a toast as that," cried Aughinbaugh, laughing. "Let me substitute, Here's to our better acquaintance!"

# WILD BILL HICKOK

EMERSON HOUGH

As has been shown in preceding chapters, the Western plains were passed over and left unsettled until the advent of the railroads, which began to cross the plains coincident with the arrival of the great cattle herds which came up from the South after a market. This market did not wait for the completion of the railroads, but met the railroads more than half way; indeed, followed them quite across the plains. The frontier sheriff now came upon the Western stage as he had never done before. The bad man also sprang into sudden popular recognition, the more so because he was now accessible to view and within reach of the tourist and tenderfoot investigator of the Western fauna. These were palmy days for the Wild West.

Unless it be a placer camp in the mountains, there is no harder collection of human beings to be found than that which gathers in tents and shanties at a temporary railway terminus of the frontier. Yet such were all the capitals of civilization in the earliest days. One town was like another. The history of Wichita and Newton and Fort Dodge was the history of Abilene and Ellsworth and Hays City and all the towns at the head of the advancing rails. The bad men and women of one moved on to the next, just as they did in the stampedes of placer days.

To recount the history of one after another of these wild towns would be endless and perhaps wearisome. But this history has one peculiar feature not yet noted in our investigations. All these cow camps meant to be real towns some day. They meant to take the social compact. There came to each of these camps men bent upon making homes, and these men began to establish a law and order spirit and to set up a government. Indeed, the regular system of American government was there as soon as the railroad was there, and this law was strong on its legislative and executive sides. The frontier sheriff or town marshal was there, the man for the place, as bold and hardy as the bold and hardy men he was to meet and subdue, as skilled with weapons, as willing to die; and upheld, moreover, with that sense of duty and of moral courage which is granted even to the most courageous of men when he feels that he has the sentiment of the majority of good people at his back.

To describe the life of one Western town marshal, himself the best and most picturesque of them all, is to cover all this field sufficiently. There is but one man who can thus be chosen, and that is Wild Bill Hickok, better known for a generation as "Wild Bill," and properly accorded an honorable place in American history.

The real name of Wild Bill was James Butler Hickok, and he was born in May, 1837, in La Salle county, Illinois. This brought his youth into the days of Western exploration and conquest, and the boy read of Carson and Frémont, then popular idols, with the result that he proposed a life of adventure for himself. He was eighteen years of age when he first saw the West as a fighting man under Jim Lane, of Free Soil fame, in the guerrilla days of Kansas before the civil war. He made his mark, and was elected a constable in that dangerous country before he was twenty years of age. He was then a tall, "gangling" youth, six feet one in height, with yellow hair and blue eyes. He later developed into as splendid looking a man as ever trod on leather, muscular and agile as he was powerful and enduring. His features were clean-cut and expressive, his carriage erect and dignified, and no one ever looked less the conventional part of the bad man assigned in popular imagination. He was not a quarrelsome man, although a dangerous one, and his voice was low and even, showing a nervous system like that of Daniel Boone—"not agitated." It might have been supposed that he would be a natural master of weapons, and such was the case. The use of rifle and revolver was born in him, and perhaps no man of the frontier ever surpassed him in quick and accurate use of the heavy six-shooter. The religion of the frontier was not to miss, and rarely ever did he shoot except he knew that he would not miss. The tale of his killings in single combat is the longest authentically assigned to any man in American history.

After many experiences with the pro-slavery folk from the border, Bill, or "Shanghai Bill," as he was then known—a nickname which clung for years—went stage driving for the Overland, and incidentally did some effective Indian fighting for his employers, finally, in the year 1861, settling down as station agent for the Overland at Rock Creek station, about fifty miles west of Topeka. He was really there as guard for the horse band, for all that region was full of horse thieves and cut-throats, and robberies and killings were common enough. It was here that there occurred his greatest fight, the greatest fight of one man against odds at close range that is mentioned in any history of any part of the world. There was never a battle like it known, nor is the West apt again to produce one matching it.

The borderland of Kansas was at that time, as may be remembered, ground debated by the anti-slavery and pro-slavery factions, who still waged bitter war against one another, killing, burning, and pillaging without mercy. The civil war was then raging, and Confederates from Missouri were frequent visitors in eastern Kansas under one pretext or another, of which horse lifting was the one most common, it being held legitimate to prey upon the enemy as opportunity offered. Two border outlaws by the name of the McCandlas boys led a gang of hard men in enterprises of this nature, and these intended to run off the stage company's horses when they found they could not seduce Bill to join their number. He told them to come and take the horses if they could; and on the afternoon of December 16, 1861, ten of them, led by the McCandlas brothers, rode up to his dugout to do so. Bill was alone, his stableman being away hunting. He retreated to the dark interior of his dugout and got ready his weapons, a rifle, two six-shooters, and a knife.

The assailants proceeded to batter in the door with a log, and as it fell in, Jim McCandlas, who must have been a brave man to undertake so foolhardy a thing against a man already known as a killer, sprang in at the opening. He, of course, was killed at once. This exhausted the rifle, and Bill picked up the six-shooters from the table and in three quick shots killed three more of the gang as they rushed in at the door. Four men were dead in less than that many seconds; but there were still six others left, all inside the dugout now, and all firing at him at a range of three feet. It was almost a miracle that, under such surroundings, the man was not killed. Bill now was crowded too much to use his firearms, and took to the bowie, thrusting at one man and another as best he might. It is known among knife-fighters that a man will stand up under a lot of flesh-cutting and blood-letting until the blade strikes a bone. Then he seems to drop quickly if it be a deep and severe thrust. In this chance medley, the knife wounds inflicted on each other by Bill and his swarming foes did not at first drop their men; so that it must have been several minutes that all seven of them were mixed in a mass of shooting, thrusting, panting, and gasping humanity. Then Jack McCandlas swung his rifle barrel and struck Bill over the head, springing upon him with his knife as well. Bill got his hand on a six-shooter and killed him just as he would have struck. After that no one knows what happened, not even Bill himself, who got his name then and there. "I just got sort of wild," he said, describing it. "I thought my heart was on fire. I went out to the pump then to get a drink, and I was all cut and shot to pieces."

They called him Wild Bill after that, and he had earned the name. There were six dead men on the floor of the dugout. He had fairly whipped the ten of them, and the four remaining had enough and fled from that awful hole in the ground. Two of these were badly wounded. Bill followed them to the door. His own weapons were exhausted or not at hand by this time, but his stableman came up just then with a rifle in his hands. Bill caught it from him, and, cut up as he was, fired and killed one of the wounded desperadoes as he tried to mount his horse. The other wounded man later died of his wounds. Eight men were killed by the one. The two who got to their horses and escaped were perhaps never in the dugout at all, for it was hardly large enough to hold another man had any wanted to get in.

There is no record of any fighting man to equal this. It took Bill a year to recover from his wounds. The life of the open air and hard work brought many Western men through injuries which would be fatal in the States. The pure air of the plains had much to do with this. Bill now took service as wagon-master under General Frémont and managed to get attacked by a force of Confederates while on his way to Sedalia, the war being now in full swing. He fled and was pursued; but, shooting back with six-shooters, killed four men. It will be seen that he had now in single fight killed twelve men, and he was very young. This tally did not cover Indians, of whom he had slain several. Although he did not enlist, he went into the army as an independent sharpshooter, just because the fighting was good, and his work at this was very deadly. In four hours at the Pea Ridge battle, where he lay behind a log, on a hill commanding the flat where the Confederates were formed, he is said to have killed thirty-five men, one of them the Confederate General McCullough. It was like shooting buffalo for him. He was charged by a company of the enemy, but was rescued by his own men.

Not yet enlisting, Bill went in as a spy for General Curtis, and took the dangerous work of going into "Pap" Price's lines, among the touch-and-go Missourians and Arkansans, in search of information useful to the Union forces. Bill enlisted for business purposes in a company of Price's mounted rangers, got the knowledge desired, and fled, killing a Confederate sergeant by name of Lawson in his escape. Curtis sent him back again, this time into the forces of Kirby Smith, then in Texas, but reported soon to move up into Arkansas. Bill enlisted again, and again showed his skill in the saddle, killing two men as he fled. Count up all his known victims to this time, and the tally would be at least sixty-two men; and Bill was then but twenty-five.

A third time Curtis sent Bill back into the Confederate lines, this time into another part of Price's army. Here he was detected and arrested as a spy. Bound hand and foot in his death watch, he killed his captor after he had torn his hands free, and once more escaped. After that, he dared not go back again, for he was too well known and too difficult to disguise. He could not keep out of the fighting, however, and went as a scout and free lance with General Davis, during Price's second invasion of Missouri. He was not an enlisted man, and seems to have done pretty much as he liked. One day he rode out on his own hook, and was stopped by three men, who ordered him to halt and dismount. All three men had their hands on their revolvers; but, to show the difference between average men and a specialist, Bill killed two of them and fatally shot the other before they could get into action. His tally was now sixty-six men at least.

Curtis now sent Bill out into Kansas to look into a report that some Indians were about to join the Confederate forces. Bill got the news, and also engaged in a knife duel with the Sioux, Conquering Bear, whom he accused of trying to ambush him. It was a fair and desperate fight, with knives, and although Bill finally killed his man, he himself was so badly cut up that he came near dying, his arm being ripped from shoulder to elbow, a wound which it took years to mend. It is doubtful if any man ever survived such injuries as he did, for by this time he was a mass of scars from pistol and knife wounds. He had probably been in danger of his life more than a hundred times in personal difficulties; for the man with a reputation as a bad man has a reputation which needs continual defending.

After the war, Bill lived from hand to mouth, like most frontier dwellers. It was at Springfield, Missouri, that another duel of his long list occurred, in which he killed Dave Tutt, a fine pistol shot and a man with social ambitions in badness. It was a fair fight in the town square by appointment. Bill killed his man and wheeled so quickly on Tutt's followers that Tutt had not had time to fall before Bill's six-shooter was turned the opposite way, and he was asking Tutt's friends if they wanted any of it themselves. They did not. This fight was forced on Bill, and his quiet attempts to avoid it and his stern way of accepting it, when inevitable, won him high estimation on the border. Indeed, he was now known all over the country, and his like has not since been seen. He was still a splendid looking man, and as cool and quiet and modest as ever he had been.

Bill now went to trapping in the less settled parts of Nebraska, and for a while he lived in peace, until he fell into a saloon row over some trivial matter and invited four of his opponents outside to fight him with pistols; the four were to fire at the word, and Bill to do the same— his pistol against their four. In this fight he killed one man at first fire, but he himself was shot through the shoulder and disabled in his right arm. He killed two more with his left hand and badly wounded the other. This was a fair fight also, and the only wonder is he was not killed; but he seemed never to consider odds, and literally he knew nothing but fight.

His score was now seventy-two men, not counting Indians. He himself never reported how many Indians he and Buffalo Bill killed as scouts in the Black Kettle campaign under Carr and Primrose, but the killing of Black Kettle himself was sometimes attributed to Wild Bill. The latter was badly wounded in the thigh with a lance, and it took a long time for this wound to heal. To give this hurt and others better opportunity for mending, Bill now took a trip back East to his home in Illinois. While East he found that he had a reputation, and he undertook to use it. He found no way of making a living, however, and he returned to the West, where he could better market his qualifications.

At that time Hays City, Kansas, was one of the hardest towns on the frontier. It had more than a hundred gambling dives and saloons to its two thousand population, and murder was an ordinary thing. Hays needed a town marshal, and one who could shoot. Wild Bill was unanimously selected, and in six weeks he was obliged to kill Jack Strawhan for trying to shoot him. This he did by reason of his superior quickness with the six-shooter, for Strawhan was drawing first. Another bad man, Mulvey, started to run Hays, in whose peace and dignity Bill now felt a personal ownership. Covered by Mulvey's two revolvers, Bill found room for the lightning flash of time, which is all that is needed by the real revolver genius, and killed Mulvey on the spot. His tally was now seventy-five men. He made it seventy-eight in a fight with a bunch of private soldiers, who called him a "long-hair"—a term very accurate, by the way, for Bill was proud of his long, blond hair, as was General Custer and many another man of the West at that time. In this fight,

Bill was struck by seven pistol balls and barely escaped alive by flight to a ranch on the prairie near by. He lay there three weeks, while General Phil Sheridan had details out with orders to get him dead or alive. He later escaped in a box-car to another town, and his days as marshal of Hays were over.

Bill now tried his hand at Wild West theatricals, seeing that already many Easterners were "daffy," as he called it, about the West; but he failed at this, and went back once more to the plains where he belonged. He was chosen marshal of Abilene, then the cow camp par excellence of the middle plains, and as tough a community as Hays had been.

The wild men from the lower plains, fighting men, mad from whiskey and contact with the settlements' possibilities of long-denied indulgence, swarmed in the streets and dives, mingling with despera-does and toughs from all parts of the frontier. Those who have never lived in such a community will never be able by any description to understand its phenomena. It seems almost unbelievable that sober, steady-going America ever knew such days; but there they were, and not so long ago, for this was only 1870.

Two days after Bill was elected marshal of Abilene, he killed a des-perado who was "whooping-up" the town in customary fashion. That same night, he was on the street, in a dim light, when all at once he saw a man whisk around a corner, and saw something shine, as he thought, with the gleam of a weapon. As showing how quick were the hand and eye of the typical gun-man of the day, it may be stated that Bill killed this man in a flash, only to find later that it was a friend, and one of his own deputies. The man was only pulling a handkerchief from his pocket. Bill knew that he was watched every moment by men who wanted to kill him. He had his life in his hands all the time. For instance, he had next to kill the friend of the desperado whom he had shot. By this time, Abilene respected its new marshal; indeed, was rather proud of him. The reign of the bad man of the plains was at its height, and the professional man-killer, the specialist with firearms, was a figure here and there over wide regions. Among all these none compared with this unique specimen. He was generous, too, as he was deadly, for even yet he was supporting a McCandlas widow, and he always furnished funerals for his corpses. He had one more to furnish soon. Enemies down the range among the cow men made up a purse of five thousand dollars, and hired eight men to kill the town marshal and bring his heart back South. Bill heard of it, and literally made all of them jump off the railroad train where he met them. One was killed in the jump. His list of homicides was now eighty-one. He had never yet been arrested for murder, and his killing was in fair open fight, his life usually against large odds. He was a strange favorite of fortune, who seemed certainly to shield him round-about.

Bill now went East for another try at theatricals, in which, happily, he was unsuccessful, and for which he felt a strong distaste. He was scared—on the stage; and when he saw what was expected of him he quit and went back once more to the West. He appeared at Cheyenne, in the Black Hills, wandering thus from one point to another after the fashion of the frontier, where a man did many things and in many places. He had a little brush with a band of Indians, and killed four of them with four shots from his six-shooter, bringing his list in red and white to eighty-five men. He got away alive from the Black Hills with difficulty; but in 1876 he was back again at Deadwood, married now, and, one would have thought, ready to settle down.

But the life of turbulence ends in turbulence. He who lives by the sword dies by the sword. Deadwood was as bad a place as any that could be found in the mining regions, and Bill was not an officer here, as he had been in Kansas towns. As marshal of Hays and Abilene and

United States marshal later at Hays City, he had been a national character. He was at Deadwood for the time only plain Wild Bill, handsome, quiet, but ready for anything.

Ready for anything but treachery! He himself had always fought fair and in the open. His men were shot in front. Not such was to be his fate. On the day of August 2, 1876, while he was sitting at a game of cards in a saloon, a hard citizen by name of Jack McCall slipped up behind him, placed a pistol to the back of his head, and shot him dead before he knew he had an enemy near. The ball passed through Bill's head and out at the cheek, lodging in the arm of a man across the table.

Bill had won a little money from McCall earlier in the day, and won it fairly, but the latter had a grudge, and was no doubt one of those disgruntled souls who "had it in" for all the rest of the world. He got away with the killing at the time, for a miners' court let him go. A few days later, he began to boast about his act, seeing what fame was his for ending so famous a life; but at Yankton they arrested him, tried him before a real court, convicted him, and hanged him promptly.

Wild Bill's body was buried at Deadwood, and his grave, surrounded by a neat railing and marked by a monument, long remained one of the features of Deadwood. The monument and fence were disfigured by vandals who sought some memento of the greatest bad man ever in all likelihood seen upon the earth. His tally of eight-five men seems large, but in fair probability it is not large enough. His main encounters are known historically. He killed a great many Indians at different times, but of these no accurate estimate can be claimed. Nor is his list of victims as a sharpshooter in the army legitimately to be added to his record. Cutting out all doubtful instances, however, there remains no doubt that he killed between twenty and thirty men in personal combat in the open, and that never once was he tried in any court on a charge even of manslaughter.

This record is not approached by that of any other known bad man Many of them are credited with twenty men, a dozen men, and so forth; but when the records are sifted the list dwindles. It is doubted whether any other bad man in America ever actually killed twenty men in fair personal combat. Bill was not killed in fair fight, nor could McCall have hurt him had Bill suspected his intent.

Hickok was about thirty-nine years old when killed, and he had averaged a little more than two men for each year of his entire life. He was well-known among army officers, and esteemed as a scout and a man, never regarded as a tough in any sense. He was a man of singular personal beauty. Of him General Custer, soon thereafter to fall a victim himself upon the plains, said: "He was a plainsman in every sense of the word, yet unlike any other of his class. Whether on foot or on horseback, he was one of the most perfect types of physical manhood I ever saw. His manner was entirely free from all bluster and bravado. He never spoke of himself unless requested to do so. His influence among the frontiersmen was unbounded; his word was law. Wild Bill was anything but a quarrelsome man, yet none but himself could enumerate the many conflicts in which he had been engaged."

These are the words of one fighting man about another, and both men are entitled to good rank in the annals of the West. The praise of an army general for a man of no rank or wealth leaves us feeling that, after all, it was a possible thing for a bad man to be a good man, and worthy of respect and admiration, utterly unmingled with maudlin sentiment or weak love for the melodramatic.

---

*[Editor's Note: Custer died in June of 1876, more than a month before Hickok's murder.]*

# LASSITER

### ZANE GREY

A sharp clip-clop of iron-shod hoofs deadened and died away, and clouds of yellow dust drifted from under the cottonwoods out over the sage.

Jane Withersteen gazed down the wide purple slope with dreamy and troubled eyes. A rider had just left her and it was his message that held her thoughtful and almost sad, awaiting the churchmen who were coming to resent and attack her right to befriend a Gentile.

She wondered if the unrest and strife that had lately come to the little village of Cottonwoods was to involve her. And then she sighed, remembering that her father had founded this remotest border settlement of southern Utah and that he had left it to her. She owned all the ground and many of the cottages. Withersteen House was hers, and the great ranch, with its thousands of cattle, and the swiftest horses of the sage. To her belonged Amber Spring, the water which gave verdure and beauty to the village and made living possible on that wild purple upland waste. She could not escape being involved by whatever befell Cottonwoods.

That year, 1871, had marked a change which had been gradually coming in the lives of the peace-loving Mormons of the border.

Glaze—Stone Bridge—Sterling, villages to the north, had risen against the invasion of Gentile settlers and the forays of rustlers. There had been opposition to the one and fighting with the other. And now Cottonwoods had begun to wake and bestir itself and grow hard.

Jane prayed that the tranquillity and sweetness of her life would not be permanently disrupted. She meant to do so much more for her people than she had done. She wanted the sleepy quiet pastoral days to last always. Trouble between the Mormons and the Gentiles of the community would make her unhappy. She was Mormon-born, and she was a friend to poor and unfortunate Gentiles. She wished only to go on doing good and being happy. And she thought of what that great ranch meant to her. She loved it all—the grove of cottonwoods, the old stone house, the amber-tinted water, and the droves of shaggy, dusty horses and mustangs, the sleek, clean-limbed, blooded racers, and the browsing herds of cattle and the lean, sun-browned riders of the sage.

While she waited there she forgot the prospect of untoward change. The bray of a lazy burro broke the afternoon quiet, and it was comfortingly suggestive of the drowsy farmyard, and the open corrals, and the green alfalfa fields. Her clear sight intensified the purple sage-slope as it rolled before her. Low swells of prairie-like ground sloped up to the west. Dark, lonely cedar-trees, few and far between, stood out strikingly, and at long distances ruins of red rocks. Farther on, up the gradual slope, rose a broken wall, a huge monument, looming dark purple and stretching its solitary, mystic way, a wavering line that faded in the north. Here to the westward was the light and color and beauty. Northward the slope descended to a dim line of cañons from which rose an up-flinging of the earth, not mountainous, but a vast heave of purple uplands, with ribbed and fan-shaped walls, castle-crowned cliffs, and gray escarpments. Over it all crept the lengthening, waning afternoon shadows.

The rapid beat of hoofs recalled Jane Withersteen to the question at hand. A group of riders cantered up the lane, dismounted, and threw their bridles. They were seven in number, and Tull, the leader, a tall, dark man, was an elder of Jane's church.

"Did you get my message?" he asked, curtly.

"Yes," replied Jane.

"I sent word I'd give that rider Venters half an hour to come down to the village. He didn't come."

"He knows nothing of it," said Jane. "I didn't tell him. I've been waiting here for you."

"Where is Venters?"

"I left him in the courtyard."

"Here, Jerry," called Tull, turning to his men, "take the gang and fetch Venters out here if you have to rope him."

The dusty-booted and long-spurred riders clanked noisily into the grove of cottonwoods and disappeared in the shade.

"Elder Tull, what do you mean by this?" demanded Jane. "If you must arrest Venters you might have the courtesy to wait till he leaves my home. And if you do arrest him it will be adding insult to injury. It's absurd to accuse Venters of being mixed up in that shooting fray in the village last night. He was with me at the time. Besides, he let me take charge of his guns. You're only using this as a pretext. What do you mean to do to Venters?"

"I'll tell you presently," replied Tull. "But first tell me why you defend this worthless rider?"

"Worthless!" exclaimed Jane, indignantly. "He's nothing of the kind. He was the best rider I ever had. There's not a reason why I shouldn't champion him and every reason why I should. It's no little shame to me, Elder Tull, that through my friendship he has roused the enmity of my people and become an outcast. Besides, I owe him eternal gratitude for saving the life of little Fay."

"I've heard of your love for Fay Larkin and that you intend to adopt her. But—Jane Withersteen, the child is a Gentile!"

"Yes. But, Elder, I don't love the Mormon children any less because I love a Gentile child. I shall adopt Fay if her mother will give her to me."

"I'm not so much against that. You can give the child Mormon teaching," said Tull. "But I'm sick of seeing this fellow Venters hang around you. I'm going to put a stop to it. You've so much love to throw away on these beggars of Gentiles that I've an idea you might love Venters."

Tull spoke with the arrogance of a Mormon whose power could not be brooked and with the passion of a man in whom jealously had kindled a consuming fire.

"Maybe I do love him," said Jane. She felt both fear and anger stir her heart. "I'd never thought of that. Poor fellow! he certainly needs some one to love him."

"This'll be a bad day for Venters unless you deny that," returned Tull, grimly.

Tull's men appeared under the cottonwoods and led a young man out into the lane. His ragged clothes were those of an outcast. But he stood tall and straight, his wide shoulders flung back, with the muscles of his bound arms rippling and a blue flame of defiance in the gaze he bent on Tull.

For the first time Jane Withersteen felt Venters's real spirit. She wondered if she would love this splendid youth. Then her emotion cooled to the sobering sense of the issue at stake.

"Venters, will you leave Cottonwoods at once and forever?" asked Tull, tensely.

"Why?" rejoined the rider.

"Because I order it."

Venters laughed in cool disdain.

The red leaped to Tull's dark cheek.

"If you don't go it means your ruin," he said, sharply.

"Ruin!" exclaimed Venters, passionately. "Haven't you already ruined me? What do you call ruin? A year ago I was a rider. I had horses and cattle of my own. I had a good name in Cottonwoods. And now when I come into the village to see this woman you set your men on me. You hound me. You trail me as if I were a rustler. I've no more to lose—except my life."

"Will you leave Utah?"

"Oh! I know," went on Venters, tauntingly, "it galls you, the idea of beautiful Jane Withersteen being friendly to a poor Gentile. You want her all yourself. You're a wiving Mormon. You have use for her—and Withersteen House and Amber Spring and seven thousand head of cattle!"

Tull's hard jaw protruded, and rioting blood corded the veins of his neck.

"Once more. Will you go?"

"*No!*"

"Then I'll have you whipped within an inch of your life," replied Tull, harshly. "I'll turn you out in the sage. And if you ever come back you'll get worse."

Venters's agitated face grew coldly set and the bronze changed to gray.

Jane impulsively stepped forward. "Oh! Elder Tull!" she cried. "You won't do that!"

Tull lifted a shaking finger toward her.

"That'll do from you. Understand, you'll not be allowed to hold this boy to a friendship that's offensive to your Bishop. Jane Withersteen, your father left you wealth and power. It has turned your head. You haven't yet come to see the place of Mormon women. We've reasoned with you, borned with you. We've patiently waited. We've let you have your fling, which is more than I ever saw granted to a Mormon woman. But you haven't come to your senses. Now, once for all, you can't have any further friendship with Venters. He's going to be whipped, and he's got to leave Utah!"

"Oh! Don't whip him! It would be dastardly!" implored Jane, with slow certainty of her failing courage.

Tull always blunted her spirit, and she grew conscious that she had feigned a boldness which she did not possess. He loomed up now in different guise, not as a jealous suitor, but embodying the mysterious despotism she had known from childhood—the power of her creed.

"Venters, will you take your whipping here or would you rather go out in the sage?" asked Tull. He smiled a flinty smile that was more than inhuman, yet seemed to give out of its dark aloofness a gleam of righteousness.

"I'll take it here—if I must," said Venters. "But by God!—Tull, you'd better kill me outright. That'll be a dear whipping for you and your praying Mormons. You'll make me another Lassiter!"

The strange glow, the austere light which radiated from Tull's face, might have been a holy joy at the spiritual conception of exalted duty. But there was something more in him, barely hidden, a something personal and sinister, a deep of himself, an engulfing abyss. As his religious mood was fanatical and inexorable, so would his physical hate be merciless.

"Elder, I—I repent my words," Jane faltered. The religion in her, the long habit of obedience, of humility, as well as agony of fear, spoke in her voice. "Spare the boy!" she whispered.

"You can't save him now," replied Tull, stridently.

Her head was bowing to the inevitable. She was grasping the truth, when suddenly there came, in inward constriction, a hardening of gentle forces within her breast. Like a steel bar it was, stiffening all that had been soft and weak in her. She felt a birth in her of something new and unintelligible. Once more her strained gaze sought the sage-slopes. Jane Withersteen loved that wild and purple wilderness. In times of sorrow it had been her strength, in happiness its beauty was her continual delight. In her extremity she found herself murmuring, "Whence cometh my help!" It was a prayer, as if forth from those lonely purple reaches and walls of red and clefts of blue might ride a fearless man, neither creed-bound nor creed-mad, who would hold up a restraining hand in the faces of her ruthless people.

The restless movements of Tull's men suddenly quieted down. Then followed a low whisper, a rustle, a sharp exclamation.

"Look!" said one, pointing to the west.

"A rider!"

Jane Withersteen wheeled and saw a horseman, silhouetted against the western sky, coming riding out of the sage. He had ridden down from the left, in the golden glare of the sun, and had been unobserved till close at hand. An answer to her prayer!

"Do you know him? Does any one know him?" questioned Tull, hurriedly.

His men looked and looked, and one by one shook their heads.

"He's come from far," said one.

"Thet's a fine hoss," said another.

"A strange rider."

"Huh! he wears black leather," added a fourth.

With a wave of his hand, enjoining silence, Tull stepped forward in such a way that he concealed Venters.

The rider reined in his mount, and with a lithe forward-slipping action appeared to reach the ground in one long step. It was a peculiar movement in its quickness and inasmuch that while performing it the rider did not swerve in the slightest from a square front to the group before him.

"Look!" hoarsely whispered one of Tull's companions. "He packs two black-butted guns—low down—they're hard to see—black agin them black chaps."

"A gun-man!" whispered another. "Fellers, careful now about movin' your hands."

The stranger's slow approach might have been a mere leisurely manner of gait or the cramped short steps of a rider unused to walking; yet, as well, it could have been the guarded advance of one who took no chances with men.

"Hello, stranger!" called Tull. No welcome was in this greeting, only a gruff curiosity.

The rider responded with a curt nod. The wide brim of a black sombrero cast a dark shade over his face. For a moment he closely regarded Tull and his comrades, and then, halting in his slow walk, he seemed to relax.

"Evenin', ma'am," he said to Jane, and removed his sombrero with quaint grace.

Jane, greeting him, looked up into a face that she trusted instinctively and which riveted her attention. It had all the characteristics of the range rider's—the leanness, the red burn of the sun, and the set changelessness that came from years of silence and solitude. But it was not these which held her; rather the intensity of his gaze, a strained weariness, a piercing wistfulness of keen, gray sight, as if the man was forever looking for that which he never found. Jane's subtle woman's intuition, even in that brief instant, felt a sadness, a hungering, a secret.

"Jane Withersteen, ma'am?" he inquired.

"Yes," she replied.

"The water here is yours?"

"Yes."

"May I water my horse?"

"Certainly. There's the trough."

"But mebbe if you knew who I was—" He hesitated, with his glance on the listening men. "Mebbe you wouldn't let me water him—though I ain't askin' none for myself."

"Stranger, it doesn't matter who you are. Water your horse. And if you are thirsty and hungry come into my house."

"Thanks, ma'am. I can't accept for myself—but for my tired horse—"

Trampling of hoofs interrupted the rider. More restless movements on the part of Tull's men broke up the little circle, exposing the prisoner Venters.

"Mebbe I've kind of hindered somethin'—for a few moments, perhaps?" inquired the rider.

"Yes," replied Jane Withersteen, with a throb in her voice.

She felt the drawing power of his eyes; and then she saw him look at the bound Venters, and at the men who held him, and their leader.

"In this here country all the rustlers an' thieves an' cut-throats an' gun-throwers an' all-round no-good men jest happen to be Gentiles. Ma'am, which of the no-good class does that young feller belong to?"

"He belongs to none of them. He's an honest boy."

"You *know* that, ma'am?"

"Yes—yes."

"Then what has he done to get tied up that way?"

His clear and distinct question, meant for Tull as well as for Jane Withersteen, stilled the restlessness and brought a momentary silence.

"Ask him," replied Jane, her voice rising high.

The rider stepped away from her, moving out with the same slow, measured stride in which he had approached, and the fact that his action placed her wholly to one side, and him no nearer to Tull and his men, had a penetrating significance.

"Young feller, speak up," he said to Venters.

"Here, stranger, this's none of your mix," began Tull. "Don't try any interference. You've been asked to drink and eat. That's more than you'd have got in any other village on the Utah border. Water your horse and be on your way."

"Easy—easy—I ain't interferin' yet," replied the rider. The tone of his voice had undergone a change. A different man had spoken. Where, in addressing Jane, he had been mild and gentle, now, with his first speech to Tull, he was dry, cool, biting. "I've jest stumbled onto a queer deal. Seven Mormons all packin' guns, an' a Gentile tied with a rope, an' a woman who swears by his honesty! Queer, ain't that?"

"Queer or not, it's none of your business," retorted Tull.

"Where I was raised a woman's word was law. I ain't quite outgrowed that yet."

Tull fumed between amaze and anger.

"Meddler, we have a law here something different from woman's whim—Mormon law! . . . Take care you don't transgress it."

"To hell with your Mormon law!"

The deliberate speech marked the rider's further change, this time from kindly interest to an awakening menace. It produced a transformation in Tull and his companions. The leader gasped and staggered backward at a blasphemous affront to an institution he held most sacred. The man Jerry, holding the horses, dropped the bridles and froze in his tracks. Like posts the other men stood, watchful-eyed, arms hanging rigid, all waiting.

"Speak up now, young man. What have you done to be roped that way?"

"It's a damned outrage!" burst out Venters. "I've done no wrong. I've offended this Mormon Elder by being a friend to that woman."

"Ma'am, is it true—what he says?" asked the rider of Jane; but his quiveringly alert eyes never left the little knot of quiet men.

"True? Yes, perfectly true," she answered.

"Well, young man, it seems to me that bein' a friend to such a woman would be what you wouldn't want to help an' couldn't help. . . . What's to be done to you for it?"

"They intend to whip me. You know what that means—in Utah!"

"I reckon," replied the rider, slowly.

With his gray glance cold on the Mormons, with the restive bit-champing of the horses, with Jane failing to repress her mounting agitation, with Venters standing pale and still, the tension of the moment tightened. Tull broke the spell with a laugh, a laugh without mirth, a laugh that was only a sound betraying fear.

"Come on, men!" he called.

Jane Withersteen turned again to the rider.

"Stranger, can you do nothing to save Venters?"

"Ma'am, you ask me to save him—from your own people?"

"Ask you? I beg of you!"

"But you don't dream who you're askin'."

"Oh, sir, I pray you—save him!"

"These are Mormons, an' I . . ."

"At—at any cost—save him. For I—I care for him!"

Tull snarled. "You love-sick fool! Tell your secrets. There'll be a way to teach you what you've never learned. . . . Come men, out of here!"

"Mormon, the young man stays," said the rider.

Like a shot his voice halted Tull.

"What!"

"He stays."

"Who'll keep him? He's my prisoner!" cried Tull, hotly. "Stranger, again I tell you—don't mix here. You've meddled enough. Go your way now or—"

"Listen! . . . He stays."

Absolute certainty, beyond any shadow of doubt breathed in the rider's low voice.

"Who are you? We are seven here."

The rider dropped his sombrero and made a rapid movement, singular in that it left him somewhat crouched, arms bent and stiff, with the big black gun-sheaths swung round to the fore.

"*Lassiter!*"

It was Venters's wondering, thrilling cry that bridged the fateful connection between the rider's singular position and the dreaded name.

Tull put out a groping hand. The life of his eyes dulled to the gloom with which men of his fear saw the approach of death. But death, while it hovered over him, did not descend, for the rider waited for the twitching fingers, the downward flash of hand that did not come. Tull, gathering himself together, turned to the horses, attended by his pale comrades.

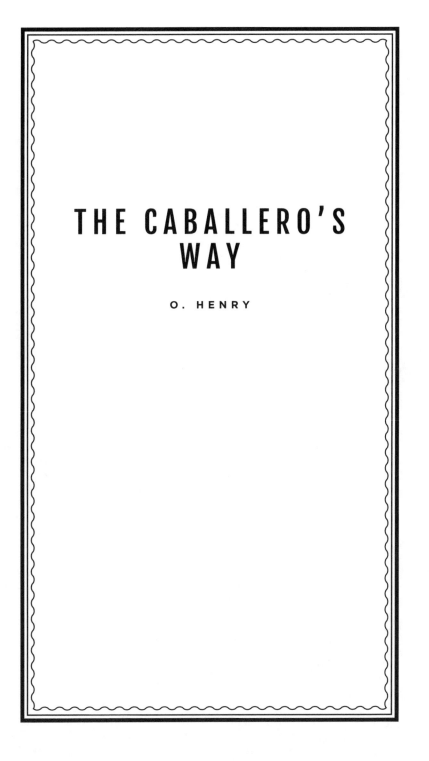

# THE CABALLERO'S WAY

O. HENRY

The Cisco Kid had killed six men in more or less fair scrimmages, had murdered twice as many (mostly Mexicans), and had winged a larger number whom he modestly forbore to count. Therefore a woman loved him.

The Kid was twenty-five, looked twenty; and a careful insurance company would have estimated the probable time of his demise at, say, twenty-six. His habitat was anywhere between the Frio and the Rio Grande. He killed for the love of it—because he was quick-tempered—to avoid arrest—for his own amusement—any reason that came to his mind would suffice. He had escaped capture because he could shoot five-sixths of a second sooner than any sheriff or ranger in the service, and because he rode a speckled roan horse that knew every cow-path in the mesquite and pear thickets from San Antonio to Matamoras.

Tonia Perez, the girl who loved the Cisco Kid, was half Carmen, half Madonna, and the rest—oh, yes, a woman who is half Carmen and half Madonna can always be something more—the rest, let us say, was humming-bird. She lived in a grass-roofed *jacal* near a little Mexican settlement at the Lone Wolf Crossing of the Frio. With her lived a father or grandfather, a lineal Aztec, somewhat less than a thousand years old, who herded a hundred goats and lived in a continuous drunken dream from drinking *mescal*. Back of the *jacal* a tremendous forest of bristling pear, twenty feet high at its worst, crowded almost to its door. It was along the bewildering maze of this spinous thicket that the speckled roan would bring the Kid to see his girl. And once, clinging like a lizard to the ridge-pole, high up under the peaked grass roof, he had heard Tonia, with her Madonna face and Carmen beauty and humming-bird soul, parley with the sheriff's posse, denying knowledge of her man in her soft *mélange* of Spanish and English.

One day the adjutant-general of the State, who is, *ex officio*, commander of the ranger forces, wrote some sarcastic lines to Captain Duval of Company X, stationed at Laredo, relative to the serene and undisturbed existence led by murderers and desperadoes in the said captain's territory.

The captain turned the colour of brick dust under his tan, and forwarded the letter, after adding a few comments, per ranger Private Bill Adamson, to ranger Lieutenant Sandridge, camped at a water hole on the Nueces with a squad of five men in preservation of law and order.

Lieutenant Sandridge turned a beautiful *couleur de rose* through his ordinary strawberry complexion, tucked the letter in his hip pocket, and chewed off the end of his gamboge moustache.

The next morning he saddled his horse and rode alone to the Mexican settlement at the Lone Wolf Crossing of the Frio, twenty miles away.

Six feet two, blond as a Viking, quiet as a deacon, dangerous as a machine gun, Sandridge moved among the *jacales*, patiently seeking news of the Cisco Kid.

Far more than the law, the Mexicans dreaded the cold and certain vengeance of the lone rider that the ranger sought. It had been one of the Kid's pastimes to shoot Mexicans "to see them kick": if he demanded from them moribund Terpsichorean feats, simply that he might be entertained, what terrible and extreme penalties would be certain to follow should they anger him! One and all they lounged with upturned palms and shrugging shoulders, filling the air with "*quien sabes*" and denials of the Kid's acquaintance.

But there was a man named Fink who kept a store at the Crossing— a man of many nationalities, tongues, interests, and ways of thinking.

"No use to ask them Mexicans," he said to Sandridge. "They're afraid to tell. This *hombre* they call the Kid—Goodall is his name, ain't it?—he's been in my store once or twice. I have an idea you might run across him at—but I guess I don't keer to say, myself. I'm two seconds later in pulling a gun than I used to be, and the difference is worth thinking about. But this Kid's got a half-Mexican girl at the Crossing that he comes to see. She lives in that *jacal* a hundred yards down the arroyo at the edge of the pear. Maybe she—no, I don't suppose she would, but that *jacal* would be a good place to watch, anyway."

Sandridge rode down to the *jacal* of Perez. The sun was low, and the broad shade of the great pear thicket already covered the grass-thatched hut. The goats were enclosed for the night in a brush corral near by. A few kids walked the top of it, nibbling the chaparral leaves. The old Mexican lay upon a blanket on the grass, already in a stupor from his mescal, and dreaming, perhaps, of the nights when he and Pizarro touched glasses to their New World fortunes—so old his wrinkled face seemed to proclaim him to be. And in the door of the *jacal* stood Tonia. And Lieutenant Sandridge sat in his saddle staring at her like a gannet agape at a sailorman.

The Cisco Kid was a vain person, as all eminent and successful assassins are, and his bosom would have been ruffled had he known that at a simple exchange of glances two persons, in whose minds he had been looming large, suddenly abandoned (at least for the time) all thought of him.

Never before had Tonia seen such a man as this. He seemed to be made of sunshine and blood-red tissue and clear weather. He seemed to illuminate the shadow of the pear when he smiled, as though the sun were rising again. The men she had known had been small and dark. Even the Kid, in spite of his achievements, was a stripling no larger than herself, with black, straight hair and a cold, marble face that chilled the noonday.

As for Tonia, though she sends description to the poorhouse, let her make a millionaire of your fancy. Her blue-black hair, smoothly divided in the middle and bound close to her head, and her large eyes full of the Latin melancholy, gave her the Madonna touch. Her motions and air spoke of the concealed fire and the desire to charm that she had inherited from the *gitanas* of the Basque province. As for the humming-bird part of her, that dwelt in her heart; you could not perceive it unless her bright red skirt and dark blue blouse gave you a symbolic hint of the vagarious bird.

The newly lighted sun-god asked for a drink of water. Tonia brought it from the red jar hanging under the brush shelter. Sandridge considered it necessary to dismount so as to lessen the trouble of her ministrations.

I play no spy; nor do I assume to master the thoughts of any human heart; but I assert, by the chronicler's right, that before a quarter of an hour had sped, Sandridge was teaching her how to plait a six-strand rawhide stake-rope, and Tonia had explained to him that were it not for her little English book that the peripatetic *padre* had given her and the little crippled *chivo*, that she fed from a bottle, she would be very, very lonely indeed.

Which leads to a suspicion that the Kid's fences needed repairing, and that the adjutant-general's sarcasm had fallen upon unproductive soil.

In his camp by the water hole Lieutenant Sandridge announced and reiterated his intention of either causing the Cisco Kid to nibble the black loam of the Frio country prairies or of haling him before a judge and jury. That sounded business-like. Twice a week he rode over to the Lone Wolf Crossing of the Frio, and directed Tonia's slim, slightly lemon-tinted fingers among the intricacies of the slowly growing lariata. A six-strand plait is hard to learn and easy to teach.

The ranger knew that he might find the Kid there at any visit. He kept his armament ready, and had a frequent eye for the pear thicket at the rear of the *jacal*. Thus he might bring down the kite and the humming-bird with one stone.

While the sunny-haired ornithologist was pursuing his studies the Cisco Kid was also attending to his professional duties. He moodily shot up a saloon in a small cow village on Quintana Creek, killed the town marshal (plugging him neatly in the centre of his tin badge), and then rode away, morose and unsatisfied. No true artist is uplifted by shooting an aged man carrying an old-style .38 bulldog.

On his way the Kid suddenly experienced the yearning that all men feel when wrong-doing loses its keen edge of delight. He yearned for the woman he loved to reassure him that she was his in spite of it. He wanted her to call his bloodthirstiness bravery and his cruelty devotion. He wanted Tonia to bring him water from the red jug under the brush shelter, and tell him how the *chivo* was thriving on the bottle.

The Kid turned the speckled roan's head up the ten-mile pear flat that stretches along the Arroyo Hondo until it ends at the Lone Wolf Crossing of the Frio. The roan whickered; for he had a sense of locality and direction equal to that of a belt-line street-car horse; and he knew he would soon be nibbling the rich mesquite grass at the end of a forty-foot stake rope while Ulysses rested his head in Circe's straw-roofed hut.

More weird and lonesome than the journey of an Amazonian explorer is the ride of one through a Texas pear flat. With dismal monotony and startling variety the uncanny and multiform shapes of the cacti lift their twisted trunks and fat, bristly hands to encumber the way. The demon plant, appearing to live without soil or rain, seems to taunt the parched traveller with its lush gray greenness. It warps itself a thousand times about what look to be open and inviting paths, only to lure the rider into blind and impassable spine-defended "bottoms of the bag," leaving him to retreat, if he can, with the points of the compass whirling in his head.

To be lost in the pear is to die almost the death of the thief on the cross, pierced by nails and with grotesque shapes of all the fiends hovering about.

But it was not so with the Kid and his mount. Winding, twisting, circling, tracing the most fantastic and bewildering trail ever picked out, the good roan lessened the distance to the Lone Wolf Crossing with every coil and turn that he made.

While they fared the Kid sang. He knew but one tune and he sang it, as he knew but one code and lived it, and but one girl and loved her. He was a single-minded man of conventional ideas. He had a voice like a coyote with bronchitis, but whenever he chose to sing his song he sang it. It was a conventional song of the camps and trail, running at its beginning as near as may be to these words:

> Don't you monkey with my Lulu girl
> Or I'll tell you what I'll do—

and so on. The roan was inured to it, and did not mind.

But even the poorest singer will, after a certain time, gain his own consent to refrain from contributing to the world's noises. So the Kid, by the time he was within a mile or two of Tonia's *jacal*, had reluctantly allowed his song to die away—not because his vocal performance had become less charming to his own ears, but because his laryngeal muscles were aweary.

As though he were in a circus ring the speckled roan wheeled and danced through the labyrinth of pear until at length his rider knew by certain landmarks that the Lone Wolf Crossing was close at hand. Then, where the pear was thinner, he caught sight of the grass roof of the *jacal* and the hackberry tree on the edge of the arroyo. A few yards farther the Kid stopped the roan and gazed intently through the prickly openings. Then he dismounted, dropped the roan's reins, and proceeded on foot, stooping and silent, like an Indian. The roan, knowing his part, stood still, making no sound.

The Kid crept noiselessly to the very edge of the pear thicket and reconnoitered between the leaves of a clump of cactus.

Ten yards from his hiding-place, in the shade of the *jacal*, sat his Tonia calmly plaiting a rawhide lariat. So far she might surely escape condemnation; women have been known, from time to time, to engage in more mischievous occupations. But if all must be told, there is to be added that her head reposed against the broad and comfortable chest of a tall red-and-yellow man, and that his arm was about her, guiding her nimble small fingers that required so many lessons at the intricate six-strand plait.

Sandridge glanced quickly at the dark mass of pear when he heard a slight squeaking sound that was not altogether unfamiliar. A gun-scabbard will make that sound when one grasps the handle of a six-shooter suddenly. But the sound was not repeated; and Tonia's fingers needed close attention.

And then, in the shadow of death, they began to talk of their love; and in the still July afternoon every word they uttered reached the ears of the Kid.

"Remember, then," said Tonia, "you must not come again until I send for you. Soon he will be here. A *vaquero* at the *tienda* said to-day he saw him on the Guadalupe three days ago. When he is that near he always comes. If he comes and finds you here he will kill you. So, for my sake, you must come no more until I send you the word."

"All right," said the ranger. "And then what?"

"And then," said the girl, "you must bring your men here and kill him. If not, he will kill you."

"He ain't a man to surrender, that's sure," said Sandridge. "It's kill or be killed for the officer that goes up against Mr. Cisco Kid."

"He must die," said the girl. "Otherwise there will not be any peace in the world for thee and me. He has killed many. Let him so die. Bring your men, and give him no chance to escape."

"You used to think right much of him," said Sandridge.

Tonia dropped the lariat, twisted herself around, and curved a lemon-tinted arm over the ranger's shoulder.

"But then," she murmured in liquid Spanish, "I had not beheld thee, thou great, red mountain of a man! And thou art kind and good, as well as strong. Could one choose him, knowing thee? Let him die; for then I will not be filled with fear by day and night lest he hurt thee or me."

"How can I know when he comes?" asked Sandridge.

"When he comes," said Tonia, "he remains two days, sometimes three. Gregorio, the small son of old Luisa, the *lavandera*, has a swift pony. I will write a letter to thee and send it by him, saying how it will be best to come upon him. By Gregorio will the letter come. And bring many men with thee, and have much care, oh, dear red one, for the rattlesnake is not quicker to strike than is 'El Chivato,' as they call him, to send a ball from his *pistola*."

"The Kid's handy with his gun, sure enough," admitted Sandridge, "but when I come for him I shall come alone. I'll get him by myself or not at all. The Cap wrote one or two things to me that make me want to do the trick without any help. You let me know when Mr. Kid arrives, and I'll do the rest."

"I will send you the message by the boy Gregorio," said the girl. "I knew you were braver than that small slayer of men who never smiles. How could I ever have thought I cared for him?"

It was time for the ranger to ride back to his camp on the water hole. Before he mounted his horse he raised the slight form of Tonia with one arm high from the earth for a parting salute. The drowsy stillness of the torpid summer air still lay thick upon the dreaming afternoon. The smoke from the fire in the *jacal*, where the *frijoles* blubbered in the iron pot, rose straight as a plumb-line above the clay-daubed chimney. No sound or movement disturbed the serenity of the dense pear thicket ten yards away.

When the form of Sandridge had disappeared, loping his big dun down the steep banks of the Frio crossing, the Kid crept back to his own horse, mounted him, and rode back along the tortuous trail he had come.

But not far. He stopped and waited in the silent depths of the pear until half an hour had passed. And then Tonia heard the high, untrue notes of his un-musical singing coming nearer and nearer; and she ran to the edge of the pear to meet him.

The Kid seldom smiled; but he smiled and waved his hat when he saw her. He dismounted, and his girl sprang into his arms. The Kid looked at her fondly. His thick, black hair clung to his head like a wrinkled mat. The meeting brought a slight ripple of some undercurrent of feeling to his smooth, dark face that was usually as motionless as a clay mask.

"How's my girl?" he asked, holding her close.

"Sick of waiting so long for you, dear one," she answered. "My eyes are dim with always gazing into that devil's pincushion through which you come. And I can see into it such a little way, too. But you are here, beloved one, and I will not scold. *Qué mal muchacho!* not to come to see your *alma* more often. Go in and rest, and let me water your horse and stake him with the long rope. There is cool water in the jar for you."

The Kid kissed her affectionately.

"Not if the court knows itself do I let a lady stake my horse for me," said he. "But if you'll run in, *chica*, and throw a pot of coffee together while I attend to the *caballo*, I'll be a good deal obliged."

Besides his marksmanship the Kid had another attribute for which he admired himself greatly. He was *muy caballero*, as the Mexicans express it, where the ladies were concerned. For them he had always gentle words and consideration. He could not have spoken a harsh word to a woman. He might ruthlessly slay their husbands and brothers, but he could not have laid the weight of a finger in anger upon a woman. Wherefore many of that interesting division of humanity who had come under the spell of his politeness declared their disbelief in the stories circulated about Mr. Kid. One shouldn't believe everything one heard, they said. When confronted by their indignant men folk with proof of the *caballero's* deeds of infamy, they said maybe he had been driven to it, and that he knew how to treat a lady, anyhow.

Considering this extremely courteous idiosyncrasy of the Kid and the pride that he took in it, one can perceive that the solution of the problem that was presented to him by what he saw and heard from his hiding-place in the pear that afternoon (at least as to one of the actors) must have been obscured by difficulties. And yet one could not think of the Kid overlooking little matters of that kind.

At the end of the short twilight they gathered around a supper of *frijoles*, goat steaks, canned peaches, and coffee, by the light of a lantern in the *jacal*. Afterward, the ancestor, his flock corralled, smoked a cigarette and became a mummy in a gray blanket. Tonia washed the few dishes while the Kid dried them with the flour-sacking towel. Her eyes shone; she chatted volubly of the inconsequent happenings of her small world since the Kid's last visit; it was as all his other homecomings had been.

Then outside Tonia swung in a grass hammock with her guitar and sang sad *canciones de amor*.

"Do you love me just the same, old girl?" asked the Kid, hunting for his cigarette papers.

"Always the same, little one," said Tonia, her dark eyes lingering upon him.

"I must go over to Fink's," said the Kid, rising, "for some tobacco. I thought I had another sack in my coat. I'll be back in a quarter of an hour."

"Hasten," said Tonia, "and tell me—how long shall I call you my own this time? Will you be gone again to-morrow, leaving me to grieve, or will you be longer with your Tonia?"

"Oh, I might stay two or three days this trip," said the Kid, yawning. "I've been on the dodge for a month, and I'd like to rest up."

He was gone half an hour for his tobacco. When he returned Tonia was still lying in the hammock.

"It's funny," said the Kid, "how I feel. I feel like there was somebody lying behind every bush and tree waiting to shoot me. I never had mullygrubs like them before. Maybe it's one of them presumptions. I've got half a notion to light out in the morning before day. The Guadalupe country is burning up about that old Dutchman I plugged down there."

"You are not afraid—no one could make my brave little one fear."

"Well, I haven't been usually regarded as a jack-rabbit when it comes to scrapping; but I don't want a posse smoking me out when I'm in your *jacal*. Somebody might get hurt that oughtn't to."

"Remain with your Tonia; no one will find you here."

The Kid looked keenly into the shadows up and down the arroyo and toward the dim lights of the Mexican village.

"I'll see how it looks later on," was his decision.

~~~~~~~~~~~~~~~~~~~~~~~~~~~~~~~~~~~~~~~~~~~~~

At midnight a horseman rode into the rangers' camp, blazing his way by noisy "halloes" to indicate a pacific mission. Sandridge and one or two others turned out to investigate the row. The rider announced himself to be Domingo Sales, from the Lone Wolf Crossing. He bore a letter for Señor Sandridge. Old Luisa, the *lavandera*, had persuaded him to bring it, he said, her son Gregorio being too ill of a fever to ride.

Sandridge lighted the camp lantern and read the letter. These were its words:

*Dear One*: He has come. Hardly had you ridden away when he came out of the pear. When he first talked he said he would stay three days or more. Then as it grew later he was like a wolf or a fox, and walked about without rest, looking and listening. Soon he said he must leave before daylight when it is dark and stillest. And then he seemed to suspect that I be not true to him. He looked at me so strange that I am frightened. I swear to him that I love him, his own Tonia. Last of all he said I must prove to him I am true. He thinks that even now men are waiting to kill him as he rides from my house. To escape he says he will dress in my clothes, my red skirt and the blue waist I wear and the brown mantilla over the head, and thus ride away. But before that he says that I must put on his clothes, his *pantalones* and *camisa* and hat, and ride away on his horse from the *jacal* as far as the big road beyond the crossing and back again. This before he goes, so he can tell if I am true and if men are hidden to shoot him. It is a terrible thing. An hour before daybreak this is to be. Come, my dear one, and kill this man and take me for your Tonia. Do not try to take hold of him alive, but kill him quickly. Knowing all, you should do that. You must come long before the time and hide yourself in the little shed near the *jacal* where the wagon and saddles are kept. It is dark in there. He will wear my red skirt and blue waist and brown mantilla. I send you a hundred kisses. Come surely and shoot quickly and straight.

THINE OWN TONIA.

Sandridge quickly explained to his men the official part of the missive. The rangers protested against his going alone.

"I'll get him easy enough," said the lieutenant. "The girl's got him trapped. And don't even think he'll get the drop on me."

Sandridge saddled his horse and rode to the Lone Wolf Crossing. He tied his big dun in a clump of brush on the arroyo, took his Winchester from its scabbard, and carefully approached the Perez *jacal*. There was only the half of a high moon drifted over by ragged, milk-white gulf clouds.

The wagon-shed was an excellent place for ambush; and the ranger got inside it safely. In the black shadow of the brush shelter in front of the *jacal* he could see a horse tied and hear him impatiently pawing the hard-trodden earth.

He waited almost an hour before two figures came out of the *jacal*. One, in man's clothes, quickly mounted the horse and galloped past the wagon-shed toward the crossing and village. And then the other figure, in skirt, waist, and mantilla over its head, stepped out into the faint moonlight, gazing after the rider. Sandridge thought he would take his chance then before Tonia rode back. He fancied she might not care to see it.

"Throw up your hands," he ordered loudly, stepping out of the wagon-shed with his Winchester at his shoulder.

There was a quick turn of the figure, but no movement to obey, so the ranger pumped in the bullets—one—two—three—and then twice more; for you never could be too sure of bringing down the Cisco Kid. There was no danger of missing at ten paces, even in that half moonlight.

The old ancestor, asleep on his blanket, was awakened by the shots. Listening further, he heard a great cry from some man in mortal distress or anguish, and rose up grumbling at the disturbing ways of moderns.

The tall, red ghost of a man burst into the *jacal*, reaching one hand, shaking like a *tule* reed, for the lantern hanging on its nail. The other spread a letter on the table.

"Look at this letter, Perez," cried the man. "Who wrote it?"

"*Ah, Dios!* it is Señor Sandridge," mumbled the old man, approaching. "*Pues, señor*, that letter was written by '*El Chivato*,' as he is called—by the man of Tonia. They say he is a bad man; I do not know. While Tonia slept he wrote the letter and sent it by this old hand of mine to Domingo Sales to be brought to you. Is there anything wrong in the letter? I am very old; and I did not know. *Valgame Dios!* it is a very foolish world; and there is nothing in the house to drink—nothing to drink."

Just then all that Sandridge could think of to do was to go outside and throw himself face downward in the dust by the side of his humming-bird, of whom not a feather fluttered. He was not a *caballero* by instinct, and he could not understand the niceties of revenge.

A mile away the rider who had ridden past the wagon-shed struck up a harsh, untuneful song, the words of which began:

> Don't you monkey with my Lulu girl
> Or I'll tell you what I'll do—

# IN SEARCH OF CHRISTMAS

OWEN WISTER

The Governor descended the steps of the Capitol slowly and with pauses, lifting a list frequently to his eyes. He had intermittently penciled it between the stages of the forenoon's public business, and his gait grew absent as he recurred now to his jottings in their accumulation, with a slight pain at their number, and the definite fear that they would be more in seasons to come. They were the names of his friends' children to whom his excellent heart moved him to give Christmas presents. He had put off this regenerating evil until the latest day, as was his custom, and now he was setting forth to do the whole thing at a blow, entirely planless among the guns and rocking-horses that would presently surround him. As he reached the highway he heard himself familiarly addressed from a distance, and, turning, saw four sons of the alkali jogging into town from the plain. One who had shouted to him galloped out from the others, rounded the Capitol's enclosure, and, approaching with radiant countenance, leaned to reach the hand of the Governor, and once again greeted him with a hilarious, "Hello, Doc!"

Governor Barker, M.D., seeing Lin McLean unexpectedly after several years, hailed the horseman with frank and lively pleasure, and, inquiring who might be the other riders behind, was told that they were Shorty, Chalkeye, and Dollar Bill, come for Christmas. "And dandies to hit town with," Mr. McLean added. "Red-hot."

"I am acquainted with them," assented his Excellency.

"We've been ridin' trail for twelve weeks," the cow-puncher continued, "makin' our beds down anywhere, and eatin' the same old chuck every day. So we've shook fried beef and heifer's delight, and we're goin' to feed high."

Then Mr. McLean overflowed with talk and pungent confidences, for the holidays already rioted in his spirit, and his tongue was loosed over their coming rites.

"We've soured on scenery," he finished, in his drastic idiom. "We're sick of moonlight and cow-dung, and we're heeled for a big time."

"Call on me," remarked the Governor, cheerily, "when you're ready for bromides and sulphates."

"I 'ain't box-headed no more," protested Mr. McLean; "I've got maturity, Doc, since I seen yu' at the rain-making, and I'm a heap older than them hospital days when I bust my leg on yu'. Three or four glasses and quit. That's my rule."

"That your rule, too?" inquired the Governor of Shorty, Chalkeye, and Dollar Bill. These gentlemen of the saddle were sitting quite expressionless upon their horses.

"We ain't talkin', we're waitin'," observed Chalkeye; and the three cynics smiled amiably.

"Well, Doc, see yu' again," said Mr. McLean. He turned to accompany his brother cow-punchers, but in that particular moment Fate descended or came up from whatever place she dwells in and entered the body of the unsuspecting Governor.

"What's your hurry?" said Fate, speaking in the official's hearty manner. "Come along with me."

"Can't do it. Where 're yu' goin'?"

"Christmasing," replied Fate.

"Well, I've got to feed my horse. Christmasing, yu' say?"

"Yes; I'm buying toys."

"Toys! You? What for?"

"Oh, some kids."

"Yourn?" screeched Lin, precipitately.

His Excellency the jovial Governor opened his teeth in pleasure at this, for he was a bachelor, and there were fifteen upon his list, which he held up for the edification of the hasty McLean. "Not mine, I'm happy to say. My friends keep marrying and settling, and their kids call me uncle, and climb around and bother, and I forget their names, and think it's a girl, and the mother gets mad. Why, if I didn't remember these little folks at Christmas they'd be wondering—not the kids, they just break your toys and don't notice; but the mother would wonder—'What's the matter with Dr. Barker? Has Governor Barker gone back on us?'—that's where the strain comes!" he broke off, facing Mr. McLean with another spacious laugh.

But the cow-puncher had ceased to smile, and now, while Barker ran on exuberantly, McLean's wide-open eyes rested on him, singular and intent, and in their hazel depths the last gleam of jocularity went out.

"That's where the strain comes, you see. Two sets of acqaintances. Grateful patients and loyal voters, and I've got to keep solid with both outfits, especially the wives and mothers. They're the people. So it's drums, and dolls, and sheep on wheels, and games, and monkeys on a stick, and the saleslady shows you a mechanical bear, and it costs too much, and you forget whether the Judge's second girl is Nellie or Susie, and—well, I'm just in for my annual circus this afternoon! You're in luck. Christmas don't trouble a chap fixed like you."

Lin McLean prolonged the sentence like a distant echo.

"A chap fixed like you!" The cow-puncher said it slowly to himself. "No, sure." He seemed to be watching Shorty, and Chalkeye, and Dollar Bill going down the road. "That's a new idea—Christmas," he murmured, for it was one of his oldest, and he was recalling the Christmas when he wore his first long trousers.

"Comes once a year pretty regular," remarked the prosperous Governor. "Seems often when you pay the bill."

"I haven't made a Christmas gift," pursued the cow-puncher, dreamily, "not for—for—Lord! it's a hundred years, I guess. I don't know anybody that has any right to look for such a thing from me." This was indeed a new idea, and it did not stop the chill that was spreading in his heart.

"Gee whiz!" said Barker, briskly, "there goes twelve o'clock. I've got to make a start. Sorry you can't come and help me. Good-bye!"

His Excellency left the rider sitting motionless, and forgot him at once in his own preoccupation. He hastened upon his journey to the shops with the list, not in his pocket, but held firmly, like a plank in the imminence of shipwreck. The Nellies and Susies pervaded his mind, and he struggled with the presentiment that in a day or two he would recall some omitted and wretchedly important child. Quick hoof-beats made him look up, and Mr. McLean passed like a wind. The Governor absently watched him go, and saw the pony hunch and stiffen in the check of his speed when Lin overtook his companions. Down there in the distance they took a side street, and Barker rejoicingly remembered one more name and wrote it as he walked. In a few minutes he had come to the shops, and met face to face with Mr. McLean.

"The boys are seein' after my horse," Lin rapidly began, "and I've got to meet 'em sharp at one. We're twelve weeks shy on a square meal, yu' see, and this first has been a date from 'way back. I'd like to—" Here Mr. McLean cleared his throat, and his speech went less smoothly. "Doc, I'd like just for a while to watch yu' gettin'—them monkeys, yu' know."

The Governor expressed his agreeable surprise at this change of mind, and was glad of McLean's company and judgment during the impending selections. A picture of a cow-puncher and himself discussing a couple of dolls rose nimbly in Barker's mental eye, and it was with an imperfect honesty that he said, "You'll help me a heap."

And Lin, quite sincere, replied, "Thank yu'."

So together these two went Christmasing in the throng. Wyoming's Chief Executive knocked elbows with the spurred and jingling waif, one man as good as another in that raw, hopeful, full-blooded cattle era, which now the sobered West remembers as the days of its fond youth. For one man has been as good as another in three places—paradise before the Fall; the Rocky Mountains before the wire fence; and the Declaration of Independence. And then this Governor, besides being young, almost as young as Lin McLean or the Chief Justice (who lately had celebrated his thirty-second birthday), had in his doctoring days at Drybone known the cow-puncher with that familiarity which lasts a lifetime without breeding contempt; accordingly he now laid a hand on Lin's tall shoulder and drew him among the petticoats and toys.

Christmas filled the windows and Christmas stirred in mankind. Cheyenne, not over-zealous in doctrines or litanies, and with the opinion that a world in the hand is worth two in the bush, nevertheless was flocking together, neighbor to think of neighbor, and everyone to remember the children; a sacred assembly, after all, gathered to rehearse unwittingly the articles of its belief, the Creed and Doctrine of the Child. Lin saw them hurry and smile among the paper fairies; they questioned and hesitated, crowded and made decisions, failed utterly to find the right thing, forgot and hastened back, suffered all the various desperations of the eleventh hour, and turned homeward, dropping their parcels with that undimmed good-will that once a year makes gracious the universal human face. This brotherhood swam and beamed before the cow-puncher's brooding eyes, and in his ears the greeting of the season sang. Children escaped from their mothers and ran chirping behind the counters to touch and meddle in places forbidden. Friends dashed against each other with rabbits and magic lanterns, greeted in haste, and were gone, amid the sound of musical boxes.

Through this tinkle and bleating of little machinery the murmur of the human heart drifted in and out of McLean's hearing; fragments of home talk, tendernesses, economies, intimate first names, and dinner hours; and whether it was joy or sadness, it was in common; the world seemed knit in a single skein of home ties. Two or three came by whose purses must have been slender, and whose purchases were humble and chosen after much nice adjustment; and when one plain man dropped a word about both ends meeting, and the woman with him laid a hand on his arm, saying that his children must not feel this year was different, Lin made a step toward them. There were hours and spots where he could readily have descended upon them at that, played the role of clinking affluence, waved thanks aside with competent blasphemy, and tossing off some infamous whiskey, cantered away in the full self-conscious strut of the frontier. But here was not the moment; the abashed cow-puncher could make no such parade in this place. The people brushed by him back and forth, busy upon their errands, and aware of him scarcely more than if he had been a spirit looking on from the helpless dead; and so, while these weaving needs and kindnesses of man were within arm's touch of him, he was locked outside with his impulses. Barker had, in the natural press of customers, long parted from him, to become immersed in choosing and rejecting; and now, with a fair part of his mission accomplished, he was ready to go on to the next place, and turned to beckon McLean. He found him obliterated in a corner beside a life-sized image of Santa Claus, standing as still as the frosty saint.

"He looks livelier than you do," said the hearty Governor. " 'Fraid it's been slow waiting."

"No," replied the cow-puncher, thoughtfully. "No, I guess not."

This uncertainty was expressed with such gentleness that Barker roared. "You never did lie to me," he said, "long as I've known you. Well, never mind. I've got some real advice to ask you now."

At this Mr. McLean's face grew more alert. "Say, Doc," said he, "what do yu' want for Christmas that nobody's likely to give yu'?"

"A big practice—big enough to interfere with my politics."

"What else? Things and truck, I mean."

"Oh—nothing I'll get. People don't give things much to fellows like me."

"Don't they? Don't they?"

"Why, you and Santa Claus weren't putting up any scheme on my stocking?"

"Well—"

"I believe you're in earnest!" cried his Excellency. "That's simply rich!" Here was a thing to relish! The Frontier comes to town "heeled for a big time," finds that presents are all the rage, and must immediately give somebody something. Oh, childlike, miscellaneous Frontier! So thought the good-hearted Governor; and it seems a venial misconception. "My dear fellow," he added, meaning as well as possible, "I don't want you to spend your money on me."

"I've got plenty all right," said Lin, shortly.

"Plenty's not the point. I'll take as many drinks as you please with you. You didn't expect anything from me?"

"That ain't—that don't—"

"There! Of course you didn't. Then, what are you getting proud about? Here's our shop." They stepped in from the street to new crowds and counters. "Now," pursued the Governor, "this is for a very particular friend of mine. Here they are. Now, which of those do you like best?"

They were sets of Tennyson in cases holding little volumes equal in number, but the binding various, and Mr. McLean reached his decision after one look. "That," said he, and laid a large muscular hand upon the Laureate. The young lady behind the counter spoke out acidly, and Lin pulled the abject hand away. His taste, however, happened to be sound, or, at least, it was at one with the Governor's; but now they learned that there was a distressing variance in the matter of price.

The Governor stared at the delicate article of his choice. "I know that Tennyson is what she—is what's wanted," he muttered; and, feeling himself nudged, looked around and saw Lin's extended fist. This gesture he took for a facetious sympathy, and, dolorously grasping the hand, found himself holding a lump of bills. Sheer amazement relaxed on him, and the cow-puncher's matted wealth tumbled on the floor in sight of all people. Barker picked it up and gave it back. "No, no, no!" he said, mirthful over his own inclination to be annoyed; "you can't do that. I'm just as much obliged, Lin," he added.

"Just as a loan, Doc—some of it. I'm grass-bellied with spot-cash."

A giggle behind the counter disturbed them both, but the sharp young lady was only dusting. The Governor at once paid haughtily for Tennyson's expensive works, and the cow-puncher pushed his discountenanced savings back into his clothes. Making haste to leave the book department of this shop, they regained a mutual ease, and the Governor became waggish over Lin's concern at being too rich. He suggested to him the list of delinquent taxpayers and the latest census from which to select indigent persons. He had patients, too, whose inveterate pennilessness he could swear cheerfully to—"since you want to bolt from your own money," he remarked.

"Yes, I'm a green horse," assented Mr. McLean, gallantly; "ain't used to the looks of a twenty-dollar bill, and I shy at 'em."

From his face—that jocular mask—one might have counted him the most serene and careless of vagrants, and in his words only the ordinary voice of banter spoke to the Governor. A good woman, it may well be, would have guessed before this the sensitive soul in the blundering body; but Barker saw just the familiar, whimsical, happy-go-lucky McLean of old days, and so he went gaily and innocently on, treading upon holy ground. "I've got it!" he exclaimed; "give your wife something."

The ruddy cow-puncher grinned. He had passed through the world of women with but few delays, rejoicing in informal and transient entanglements, and he welcomed the turn which the conversation seemed now to be taking. "If you'll give me her name and address," said he, with the future entirely in his mind.

"Why, Laramie!" and the Governor feigned surprise.

"Say, Doc," said Lin, uneasily, "none of 'em 'ain't married me since I saw yu' last."

"Then she hasn't written from Laramie," said the hilarious Governor; and Mr. McLean understood and winced in his spirit deep down. "Gee whiz!" went on Barker, "I'll never forget you and Lusk that day!"

But the mask fell now. "You're talking of his wife, not mine," said the cow-puncher very quietly, and smiling no more; "and, Doc, I'm going to say a word to yu' for I know yu've always been my good friend. I'll never forget that day myself—but I don't want to be reminded of it."

"I'm a fool, Lin," said the Governor, generous instantly. "I never supposed—"

"I know yu' didn't, Doc. It ain't you that's the fool. And in a way—in a way—" Lin's speech ended among his crowding memories, and Barker, seeing how wistful his face had turned, waited. "But I ain't quite the same fool I was before that happened to me," the cowpuncher resumed, "though maybe my actions don't show to be wiser. I know that there was better luck than a man like me had any call to look for."

The sobered Barker said, simply, "Yes, Lin." He was put to thinking by these words from the unsuspected inner man.

Out in the Bow Leg country Lin McLean had met a woman with thick, red cheeks, calling herself by a maiden name, and this was his whole knowledge of her when he put her one morning astride a Mexican saddle and took her 50 miles to a magistrate and made her his lawful wife to the best of his ability and belief. His sagebrush intimates were confident he would never have done it but for a rival. Racing the rival and beating him had swept Mr. McLean past his own intentions, and the marriage was an inadvertence. "He jest bumped into it before he could pull up," they explained, and this casualty, resulting from Mr. McLean's sporting blood, had entertained several hundred square miles of alkali.

For the new-made husband the joke soon died. In the immediate weeks that came upon him he tasted a bitterness worse than in all his life before, and learned also how deep the woman, when once she begins, can sink beneath the man in baseness. That was a knowledge of which he had lived innocent until this time. But he carried his outward self serenely, so that citizens in Cheyenne who saw the cowpuncher with his bride argued shrewdly that men of that sort liked women of that sort. And before the strain had broken his endurance, an unexpected first husband, named Lusk, had appeared one Sunday in the street, prosperous, forgiving, and exceedingly drunk. To the arms of

Lusk she went back in the public street, deserting McLean in the presence of Cheyenne. And when Cheyenne saw this, and learned how she had been Mrs. Lusk for eight long, if intermittent, years, Cheyenne laughed loudly.

Lin McLean laughed, too, and went about his business, ready to swagger at the necessary moment, and with the necessary kind of joke always ready to shield his hurt spirit. And soon, of course, the matter grew stale, seldom raked up in the Bow Leg country where Lin had been at work; so lately he had begun to remember other things besides the smoldering humiliation.

"Is she with him?" Lin now asked Barker, and musingly listened while Barker told him. The Governor had thought to make it a racy story, with the moral that the joke was now on Lusk; but that inner man had spoken and revealed the cow-puncher to him in a new and complicated light; hence he quieted the proposed lively cadence and vocabulary of his anecdote about the house of Lusk, but instead of narrating how Mrs. beat Mr. on Mondays, Wednesdays, and Fridays, and Mr. took his turn the odd days, thus getting one ahead of his lady, while the kid Lusk had outlined his opinion of the family by recently skipping to parts unknown, Barker detailed these incidents more gravely, adding that Laramie believed Mrs. Lusk addicted to opium.

"I don't guess I'll leave my card on 'em," said McLean grimly, "if I strike Laramie."

"You don't mind my saying I think you're well out of that scrape?" Barker ventured.

"Shucks, no! That's all right, Doc. Only—yu' see now. A man gets tired pretending—onced in a while."

Time had gone while they were in talk, and it was now half after one and Mr. McLean late for that long-plotted first square meal. So the friends shook hands, wishing each other Merry Christmas, and the cow-puncher hastened toward his chosen companions through the stirring cheerfulness of the season. His play-hour had made a dull beginning among the toys. He had come upon people engaged in a pleasant game, and waited, shy and well disposed, for some bidding to join, but they had gone on playing with one another and left him out. And now he went along in a sort of hurry to escape from that loneliness where his human promptings had been lodged with him useless. Here was Cheyenne, full of holiday for sale, and he with his pockets full of money to buy; and when he thought of Shorty, and Chalkeye, and Dollar Bill, those dandies to hit a town with, he stepped out with a brisk, false hope. It was with a mental hurrah and a foretaste of a good time coming that he put on his town clothes, after shaving and admiring himself, and sat down to the square meal. He ate away and drank with a robust imitation of enjoyment that took in even himself at first. But the sorrowful process of his spirit went on, for all he could do. As he groped for the contentment which he saw around him he began to receive the jokes with counterfeit mirth. Memories took the place of anticipation, and through their moody shiftings he began to feel a distaste for the company of his friends and a shrinking from their lively voices. He blamed them for this at once. He was surprised to think he had never recognized before how light a weight was Shorty; and here was Chalkeye, who knew better, talking religion after two glasses. Presently this attack of noticing his friends' shortcomings mastered him, and his mind, according to its wont, changed at a stroke. "I'm celebrating no Christmas with this crowd," said the inner man; and when they had next remembered Lin McLean in their hilarity he was gone.

Governor Barker, finishing his purchases at half-past three, went to meet a friend come from Evanston. Mr. McLean was at the railway station, buying a ticket for Denver.

"Denver!" exclaimed the amazed Governor.

"That's what I said," stated Mr. McLean, doggedly.

"Gee whiz!" went his Excellency. "What are you going to do there?"

"Get good and drunk."

"Can't you find enough whiskey in Cheyenne?"

"I'm drinking champagne this trip."

The cow-puncher went out on the platform and got aboard, and the train moved off. Barker had walked out too in his surprise, and as he stared after the last car, Mr. McLean waved his wide hat defiantly and went inside the door.

"And he says he's got maturity," Barker muttered. "I've known him since seventy-nine, and he's kept about eight years old right along." The Governor was cross, and sorry, and presently crosser. His jokes about Lin's marriage came back to him and put him in a rage with the departed fool. "Yes, about eight. Or six," said his Excellency, justifying himself by the past. For he had first known Lin, the boy of nineteen, supreme in length of limb and recklessness, breaking horses and feeling for an early mustache. Next, when the mustache was nearly accomplished, he had mended the boy's badly broken thigh at Drybone. His skill (and Lin's utter health) had wrought so swift a healing that the surgeon overflowed with the pride of science, and over the bandages would explain the human body technically to his wild-eyed and flattered patient. Thus young Lin heard all about tibia, and comminuted, and other glorious new words, and when sleepless would rehearse them. Then, with the bone so nearly knit that the patient might leave the ward on crutches to sit each morning in Barker's room as a privilege, the disobedient child of twenty-one had slipped out of the hospital and hobbled hastily to the hog ranch, where whiskey and variety waited for a languishing convalescent. Here he grew gay, and was soon carried back with the leg refractured. Yet Barker's surgical rage was disarmed, the patient was so forlorn over his doctor's professional chagrin.

"I suppose it ain't no better this morning, Doc?" he had said, humbly, after a new week of bed and weights.

"Your right leg's going to be shorter. That's all."

"Oh, gosh! I've been and spoiled your comminuted fee-mur! Ain't I a son-of-a-gun?"

You could not chide such a boy as this; and in time's due course he had walked jauntily out into the world with legs of equal length after all, and in his stride the slightest halt possible. And Doctor Barker had missed the child's conversation. To-day his mustache was a perfected thing, and he in the late end of his twenties.

"He'll wake up about noon to-morrow in a dive, without a cent," said Barker. "Then he'll come back on a freight and begin over again."

~~~~~~~~~~~~~~~~~~~~~~~~~~~~~~~~~~~~~~~~~~~~~~~~~~~~~~~~~

At the Denver station Lin McLean passed through the shoutings and omnibuses, and came to the beginning of Seventeenth Street, where is the first saloon. A customer was ordering Hot Scotch; and because he liked the smell and had not thought of the mixture for a number of years, Lin took Hot Scotch. Coming out upon the pavement, he looked across and saw a saloon opposite with brighter globes and windows more prosperous. That should have been his choice; lemon peel would undoubtedly be fresher over there; and over he went at once, to begin the whole thing properly. In such frozen weather no drink could be more timely, and he sat, to enjoy without haste its mellow fitness. Once again on the pavement, he looked along the street toward up-town beneath the crisp, cold electric lights, and three little bootblacks gathered where he stood and cried, "Shine? Shine?" at him. Remembering that you took the third turn to the right to get the best dinner in Denver, Lin hit on the skillful plan of stopping at all Hot Scotches between; but the next occurred within a few yards, and it was across the street. This one being attained and appreciated, he found that he must cross back again or skip number four. At this rate he would not be dining in time to see much of the theater, and he stopped to consider. It was a German place he had just quitted, and a huge light poured out on him from its window, which the proprietor's father-land sentiment had made into a show. Lights shone among a well-set pine forest, where beery, jovial gnomes sat on roots and reached upward to Santa Claus; he, grinning, fat, and Teutonic, held in his right hand forever a foaming glass, and forever in his left a string of sausages that dangled down among the gnomes. With his American back to this, the cow-puncher, wearing the same serious, absent face he had not changed since he ran away from himself at Cheyenne, considered carefully the Hot Scotch question, and which side of the road to take and stick to, while the little bootblacks found him once more and cried, "Shine? Shine?" monotonous as snow-birds. He settled to stay over here with the south-side Scotches, and the little one-note song reaching his attention, he suddenly shoved his foot at the nearest boy, who lightly sprang away.

"Dare you to touch him!" piped a snow-bird, dangerously. They were in short trousers, and the eldest enemy, it may be, was ten.

"Don't hit me," said Mr. McLean. "I'm innocent."

"Well, you leave him be," said one.

"What's he layin' to kick you for, Billy? 'Tain't yer pop, is it?"

"Naw!" said Billy in scorn. "Father never kicked me. Don't know who he is."

"He's a special!" shrilled the leading bird, sensationally. "He's got a badge, and he's goin' to arrest yer."

Two of them hopped instantly to the safe middle of the street, and scattered with practised strategy; but Billy stood his ground. "Dare you to arrest me!" said he.

"What'll you give me not to?" inquired Lin, and he put his hands in his pockets, arms akimbo.

"Nothing; I've done nothing," announced Billy, firmly. But even in the last syllable his voice suddenly failed, a terror filled his eyes, and he, too, sped into the middle of the street.

"What's he claim you lifted?" inquired the leader, with eagerness. "Tell him you haven't been inside a store to-day. We can prove it!" they screamed to the special officer.

"Say," said the slow-spoken Lin from the pavement, "you're poor judges of a badge, you fellows."

His tone pleased them where they stood, wide apart from each other.

Mr. McLean also remained stationary in the bluish illumination of the window. "Why, if any policeman was caught wearin' this here," said he, following his sprightly invention, "he'd get arrested himself."

This struck them extremely. They began to draw together, Billy lingering the last.

"If it's your idea," pursued Mr. McLean, alluringly, as the three took cautious steps nearer the curb, "that blue, clasped hands in a circle of red stars gives the bearer the right to put folks in the jug—why, I'll get somebody else to black my boots for a dollar."

The three made a swift rush, fell on simultaneous knees, and clattering their boxes down, began to spit in an industrious circle.

"Easy!" wheedled Mr. McLean, and they looked up at him, staring and fascinated. "Not having three feet," said the cow-puncher, always grave and slow, "I can only give two this here job."

"He's got a big pistol and a belt!" exulted the leader, who had precociously felt beneath Lin's coat.

"You're a smart boy," said Lin, considering him, "and yu' find a man out right away. Now you stand off and tell me all about myself while they fix the boots—and a dollar goes to the quickest through."

Young Billy and his tow-headed competitor flattened down, each to a boot, with all their might, while the leader ruefully contemplated Mr. McLean.

"That's a Colt .45 you've got," ventured he.

"Right again. Some day, maybe, you'll be wearing one of your own, if the angels don't pull yu' before you're ripe."

"I'm through!" sang out Towhead, rising in haste.

Small Billy, was struggling still but leaped at that, the two heads bobbing to a level together; and Mr. McLean, looking down, saw that the arrangement had not been a good one for the boots.

"Will you kindly referee," said he, forgivingly, to the leader, "and decide which of them smears is the awfulest?"

But the leader looked the other way and played upon a mouth-organ.

"Well, that saves me money," said Mr. McLean, jingling his pocket. "I guess you've both won." He handed each of them a dollar. "Now," he continued, "I just dassent show these boots uptown, so this time it's a dollar for the best shine."

The two went palpitating at their brushes again, and the leader played his mouth-organ with brilliant unconcern. Lin, tall and brooding, leaned against the jutting sill of the window, a figure somehow plainly strange in town, while through the bright plate-glass Santa Claus, holding out his beer and sausages, perpetually beamed.

Billy was laboring gallantly, but it was labor, the cow-puncher perceived, and Billy no seasoned expert. "See here," said Lin, stopping, "I'll show yu' how it's done. He's playin' that toon cross-eyed enough to steer anybody crooked. There. Keep your blacking soft, and work with a dry brush."

"Lemme," said Billy. "I've got to learn." So he finished the boot his own way with wiry determination, breathing and repolishing; and this event was also adjudged a dead heat, with results gratifying to both parties. So here was their work done, and more money in their pockets than from all the other boots and shoes of this day; and Towhead and Billy did not wish for further trade, but to spend this handsome fortune as soon as might be. Yet they delayed in the brightness of the window, drawn by curiosity near this new kind of man whose voice held them and whose remarks dropped them into constant uncertainty. Even the omitted leader had been unable to go away and nurse his pride alone.

"Is that a secret society?" inquired Towhead, lifting a finger at the badge.

Mr. McLean nodded. "Turrble," said he.

"You're a Wells & Fargo detective," asserted the leader.

"Play your harp," said Lin.

"Are you a—a desperaydo?" whispered Towhead.

"Oh, my!" observed Mr. McLean, sadly; "what has our Jack been readin'?"

"He's a cattle-man!" cried Billy. "I seen his heels."

"That's you!" said the discovered puncher, with approval. "You'll do. But I bet you can't tell me what the wearers of this badge have sworn to do this night."

At this they craned their necks and glared at him

"We—are—sworn—don't yu' jump, now, and give me away—sworn—to—blow off three bootblacks to a dinner."

"Ah, pshaw!" They backed away, bristling with distrust.

"That's the oath, fellows. Yu' may as well make your minds up—*for I have it to do!*"

"Dare you to! Ah!"

"And after dinner it's the Opera-house, to see 'The Children of Captain Grant'!"

They screamed shrilly at him, keeping off beyond the curb.

"I can't waste my time on such smart boys," said Mr. McLean, rising lazily to his full height from the window-sill. "I am goin' somewhere to find boys that ain't so turruble quick stampeded by a roast turkey."

He began to lounge slowly away, serious as he had been throughout, and they, stopping their noise short, swiftly picked up their boxes, and followed him. Some change in the current of electricity that fed the window disturbed its sparkling light, so that Santa Claus, with his arms stretched out behind the departing cow-puncher, seemed to be smiling more broadly from the midst of his flickering brilliance.

On their way to turkey, the host and his guests exchanged but few remarks. He was full of good-will, and threw off a comment or two that would have led to conversation under almost any circumstances save these; but the minds of the guests were too distracted by this whole state of things for them to be capable of more than keeping after Mr. McLean in silence, at a wary interval, and with their mouths, during most of the journey, open. The badge, the pistol, their patron's talk, and the unusual dollars, wakened wide their bent for the unexpected, their street affinity for the spur of the moment; they believed slimly in the turkey part of it, but what this man might do next, to be there when he did it, and not to be trapped, kept their wits jumping deliciously; so when they saw him stop, they stopped instantly, too, ten feet out of reach. This was Denver's most civilized restaurant—that one which Mr. McLean had remembered, with foreign dishes and private rooms, where he had promised himself, among other things, champagne. Mr. McLean had never been inside it, but heard a tale from a friend; and now he caught a sudden sight of people among geraniums, with plumes and white shirt-fronts, very elegant. It must have been several minutes that he stood contemplating the entrance and the luxurious couples who went in.

"Plumb French!" he observed at length; and then, "Shucks!" in a key less confident, while his guests ten feet away watched him narrowly. "They're eatin' patty de parley-voo in there," he muttered, and the three bootblacks came beside him. "Say, fellows," said Lin, confidingly, "I wasn't raised good enough for them dude dishes. What do yu' say? I'm after a place where yu' can mention oyster stoo without givin' anybody a fit. What do yu' say, boys?"

That lighted the divine spark of brotherhood!

"Ah, you come along with us—we'll take yer! You don't want to go in there. We'll show yer the boss place in Market Street. We won't lose yer." So, shouting together in their shrill little city trebles, they clustered about him, and one pulled at his coat to start him. He started obediently, and walked in their charge, they leading the way.

"Christmas is comin' now, sure," said Lin, grinning to himself. "It ain't exactly what I figured on." It was the first time he had laughed since Cheyenne, and he brushed a hand over his eyes, that were dim with the new warmth in his heart.

Believing at length in him and his turkey, the alert street faces, so suspicious of the unknown, looked at him with ready intimacy as they went along; and soon, in the friendly desire to make him acquainted with Denver, the three were patronizing him. Only Billy, perhaps, now and then stole at him a doubtful look.

The large Country Mouse listened solemnly to his three Town Mice, who presently introduced him to the place in Market Street. It was not boss, precisely, and Denver knows better neighborhoods; but the turkey and the oyster stew were there, with catsup and vegetables in season, and several choices of pie. Here the Country Mouse became again efficient; and to witness his liberal mastery of ordering and imagine his pocket and its wealth, which they had heard and partly seen, renewed in the guests a transient awe. As they dined, however, and found the host as frankly ravenous as themselves, this reticence evaporated, and they all grew fluent with oaths and opinions. At one or two words, indeed, Mr. McLean stared and had a slight sense of blushing.

"Have a cigarette?" said the leader, over his pie.

"Thank yu'," said Lin. "I won't smoke, if yu'll excuse me." He had devised a wholesome meal, with water to drink.

"Chewin's no good at meals," continued the boy. "Don't you use tobaccer?"

"Onced in a while."

The leader spat brightly. "He 'ain't learned yet," said he, slanting his elbows at Billy and sliding a match over his rump. "But beer, now—I never seen anything in it." He and Towhead soon left Billy and his callow conversation behind, and engaged in a town conversation that silenced him, and set him listening with all his admiring young might. Nor did Mr. McLean join in the talk, but sat embarrassed by this knowledge, which seemed about as much as he knew himself.

"I'll be goshed," he thought, "if I'd caught on to half that when I was streakin' around in short pants! Maybe they grow up quicker now." But now the Country Mouse perceived Billy's eager and attentive apprenticeship. "Hello, boys!" he said, "that theatre's got a big start on us."

They had all forgotten he had said anything about theatre; other topics left their impatient minds, while the Country Mouse paid the bill and asked to be guided to the Opera-house. "This man here will look out for your blackin' and truck, and let yu' have it in the morning."

They were very late. The spectacle had advanced far into passages of the highest thrill, and Denver's eyes were riveted upon a ship and some icebergs. The party found its seats during several beautiful lime-light effects, and that remarkable fly-buzzing of violins which is pronounced so helpful in times of peril and sentiment. The Children of

Captain Grant had been tracking their father all over the equator and other scenic spots, and now the north pole was about to impale them. The Captain's youngest child, perceiving a hummock rushing at them with a sudden motion, loudly shouted, "Sister, the ice is closing in!" and she replied, chastely, "Then let us pray." It was a superb tableau: the ice split, and the sun rose and joggled at once to the zenith. The act-drop fell, and male Denver, wrung to its religious deeps, went out to the rum-shop.

Of course Mr. McLean and his party did not do this. The party had applauded exceedingly the defeat of the elements, and the leader, with Towhead, discussed the probable chances of the ship's getting farther south in the next act. Until lately, Billy's doubt of the cow-puncher had lingered; but during this intermission whatever had been holding out in him seemed won, and in his eyes, that he turned stealthily upon his unconscious, quiet neighbor, shone the beginnings of hero-worship.

"Don't you think this is splendid?" said he.

"Splendid," Lin replied, a trifle remotely.

"Don't you like it when they all get balled up and get out that way?"

"Humming," said Lin.

"Don't you guess it's just the girls, though, that do that?"

"What, young fellow?"

"Why, all that prayer-saying an' stuff."

"I guess it must be."

"She said to do it when the ice scared her, an' of course a man had to do what she wanted him."

"Sure."

"Well, do you believe they'd a' done it if she hadn't been on that boat, an' clung around an' cried an' everything, an' made her friends feel bad?"

"I hardly expect they would," replied the honest Lin, and then, suddenly mindful of Billy, "except there wasn't nothing else they could think of," he added, wishing to speak favorably of the custom.

"Why, that chuck of ice weren't so awful big anyhow. I'd 'a' shoved her off with a pole. Wouldn't you?"

"Butted her like a ram," exclaimed Mr. McLean.

"Well, I don't say my prayers any more. I told Mr. Perkins I wasn't a-going to, an' he—I think he is a flubdub anyway."

"I'll bet he is!" said Lin, sympathetically. He was scarcely a prudent guardian.

"I told him straight, an' he looked at me an' down he flops on his knees, an' he made 'em all flop, but I told him I didn't care for them putting up any camp-meeting over me; an' he says, 'I'll lick you,' an' I says, 'Dare you to!' I told him mother kep' a-licking me for nothing an' I'd not pray for her, not in Sunday-school or anywheres else. Do you pray much?"

"No," replied Lin, uneasily.

"There! I told him a man didn't, an' he said then a man went to hell. 'You lie; father ain't going to hell,' I says, and you'd ought to heard the first-class laugh right out loud, girls an' boys. An' he was that mad! But I didn't care. I came here with fifty cents."

"You must have felt like a millionaire."

"Ah, I felt all right! I bought papers an' sold 'em, an' got more an' saved, an' got my box an' blacking outfit. I weren't going to be licked by her just because she felt like it, an' she feeling like it most any time. Lemme see your pistol."

"You wait," said Lin. "After this show is through I'll put it on you."

"Will you, honest? Belt an' everything? Did you ever shoot a bear?"

"Lord! Lots."

"Honest? Silver-tips?"

"Silver-tips, cinnamon, black; and I roped a cub onced."

"O-h! I never shot a bear."

"You'd ought to try it."

"I'm a-going to. I'm a-going to camp out in the mountains. I'd like to see you when you camp. I'd like to camp with you. Mightn't I some time?" Billy had drawn nearer to Lin, and was looking up at him adoringly.

"You bet!" said Lin; and though he did not, perhaps, entirely mean this, it was with a curiously softened face that he began to look at Billy. As with dogs and his horse, so always he played with what children he met—the few in his sage-brush world; but this was ceasing to be quite play for him, and his hand went to the boy's shoulder.

"Father took me camping with him once, the time mother was off. Father gets awful drunk, too. I've quit Laramie for good."

Lin sat up, and his hand gripped the boy. "Laramie!" said he, almost shouting it. "Yu'—yu'—is your name Lusk?"

But the boy had shrunk from him instantly. "You're not going to take me home?" he piteously wailed.

"Heaven and heavens!" murmured Lin McLean. "So you're her kid!"

~~~~~~~~~~~~~~~~~~~~~~~~~~~~~~~~~~~~~~~~~~~~~~~~~~~~~~~~~~~~~~~~

He relaxed again, down in his chair, his legs stretched their straight length below the chair in front. He was waked from his bewilderment by a brushing under him, and there was young Billy diving for escape to the aisle, like the cornered city mouse that he was. Lin nipped that poor little attempt and had the limp Billy seated inside again before the two in discussion beyond had seen anything. He had said not a word to the boy, and now watched his unhappy eyes seizing upon the various exits and dispositions of the theater; nor could he imagine anything to tell him that would restore the perished confidence. "Why did yu' lead him off?" he asked himself unexpectedly, and found that he did not seem to know; but as he watched the restless and estranged runaway he grew more and more sorrowful. "I just hate him to think that of me," he reflected. The curtain rose, and he saw Billy make up his mind to wait until they should all be going out in the crowd. While the children of Captain Grant grew hotter and hotter upon their father's geographic trail, Lin sat saying to himself a number of contradictions. "He's nothing to me; what's any of them to me?" Driven to bay by his bewilderment, he restated the facts of the past. "Why, she'd deserted him and Lusk before she'd ever laid eyes on me. I needn't to bother myself. He wasn't never even my step-kid." The past, however, brought no guidance. "Lord, what's the thing to do about this? If I had any home—This is a stinkin' world in some respects," said Mr. McLean, aloud, unknowingly. The lady in the chair beneath which the cow-puncher had his legs nudged her husband. They took it for emotion over the sad fortune of Captain Grant, and their backs shook. Presently each turned, and saw the singular man with untamed, wide-open eyes glowering at the stage, and both backs shook again.

Once more his hand was laid on Billy. "Say!"

The boy glanced at him, and quickly away.

"Look at me, and listen."

Billy swervingly obeyed.

"I ain't after yu', and never was. This here's your business, not mine. Are yu' listenin' good?"

The boy made a nod, and Lin proceeded, whispering: "You've got no call to believe what I say to yu'—yu've been lied to, I guess, pretty often. So I'll not stop you runnin' and hidin', and I'll never give it away I saw yu', but yu' keep doin' what yu' please. I'll just go now. I've saw all I want, but you and your friends stay with it till it quits. If yu' happen to wish to speak to me about that pistol or bears, yu'come around to Smith's Palace—that's the boss hotel here, ain't it?—and if yu' don't come too late I'll not be gone to bed. But this time of night I'm liable to get sleepy. Tell your friends good-bye for me, and be good to yourself. I've appreciated your company."

Mr. McLean entered Smith's Palace, and, engaging a room with two beds in it, did a little delicate lying by means of the truth. "It's a lost boy—a runaway," he told the clerk. "He'll not be extra clean, I expect, if he does come. Maybe he'll give me the slip, and I'll have a job cut out to-morrow. I'll thank yu' to put my money in your safe."

The clerk placed himself at the disposal of the secret service, and Lin walked up and down, looking at the railroad photographs for some ten minutes, when Master Billy peered in from the street.

"Hello!" said Mr. McLean, casually, and returned to a fine picture of Pike's Peak.

Billy observed him for a space, and, receiving no further attention, came stepping along. "I'm not a-going back to Laramie," he stated, warningly.

"I wouldn't," said Lin. "It ain't half the town Denver is. Well, good-night. Sorry yu' couldn't call sooner—I'm dead sleepy."

"O-h!" Billy stood blank. "I wish I'd shook the darned old show. Say, lemme black your boots in the morning?"

"Not sure my train don't go too early."

"I'm up! I'm up! I get around to all of 'em."

"Where do yu' sleep?"

"Sleeping with the engine-man now. Why can't you put that gun on me to-night?"

"Goin' up-stairs. This gentleman wouldn't let you go up-stairs."

But the earnestly petitioned clerk consented, and Billy was the first to hasten into the room. He stood rapturous while Lin buckled the belt round his scanty stomach, and ingeniously buttoned the suspenders outside the accoutrement to retard its immediate descent to earth.

"Did it ever kill a man?" asked Billy, touching the six-shooter.

"No. It 'ain't never had to do that, but I expect maybe it's stopped some killin' me."

"Oh, leave me wear it just a minute! Do you collect arrow-heads? I think they're bully. There's the finest one you ever seen." He brought out the relic, tightly wrapped in paper, several pieces. "I foun' it myself, camping with father. It was sticking in a crack right on top of a rock, but nobody'd seen it till I came along. Ain't it fine?"

Mr. McLean pronounced it a gem.

"Father an' me found a lot, an' they made mother mad laying around, an' she throwed 'em out. She takes stuff from Kelley's."

"Who's Kelley?"

"He keeps the drug-store at Laramie. Mother gets awful funny. That's how she was when I came home. For I told Mr. Perkins he lied, an' I ran then. An' I knowed well enough she'd lick me when she got through her spell—an' father can't stop her, an' I—ah, I was sick of it! She's lamed me up twice beating me—an' Perkins wanting me to say 'God bless my mother!' a-getting up and a-going to bed—he's a flubdub! An' so I cleared out. But I'd just as leaves said for God to bless father—an' you. I'll do it now if you say it's any sense."

Mr. McLean sat down in a chair. "Don't yu' do it now," said he.

"You wouldn't like mother," Billy continued. "You can keep that." He came to Lin and placed the arrow-head in his hands, standing beside him. "Do you like birds' eggs? I collect them. I got twenty-five kinds—sage-hen, an' blue grouse, an' willow-grouse, an' lots more kinds harder—but I couldn't bring all them from Laramie. I brought the magpie's, though. D'you care to see a magpie egg? Well, you stay to-morrow an' I'll show you that an' some other things I got, the engine-man lets me keep there, for there's boys that would steal an egg. An' I could take you where we could fire that pistol. Bet you don't know what that is!"

He brought out a small tin box shaped like a thimble, in which were things that rattled.

Mr. McLean gave it up.

"That's a kinni-kinnic seed. You can have that, for I got some more with the engine-man."

Lin received this second token also, and thanked the giver for it. His first feeling had been to prevent the boy's parting with his treasures, but something that came not from the polish of manners and experience made him know that he should take them. Billy talked away, laying bare his little soul; the street boy that was not quite come made place for the child that was not quite gone, and unimportant words and confidences dropped from him disjointed as he climbed to the knee of Mr. McLean, and inadvertently took that cow-puncher for some sort of parent he had not hitherto met. It lasted but a short while, however, for he went to sleep in the middle of a sentence, with his head upon Lin's breast. The man held him perfectly still, because he had not the faintest notion that Billy would be impossible to disturb. At length he spoke to him, suggesting that bed might prove more comfortable; and, finding how it was, rose and undressed the boy and laid him between the sheets. The arms and legs seemed aware of the moves required of them, and stirred conveniently; and directly the head was upon the pillow the whole small frame burrowed down, without the opening of an eye or a change in the breathing. Lin stood some time by the bedside, with his eyes on the long, curling lashes and the curly hair. Then he glanced craftily at the door of the room, and at himself in the looking-glass. He stooped and kissed Billy on the forehead, and, rising from that, gave himself a hangdog stare in the mirror, and soon in his own bed was sleeping the sound sleep of health.

He was faintly roused by the church bells, and lay still, lingering with his sleep, his eyes closed, and his thoughts unshaped. As he became slowly aware of the morning, the ringing and the light reached him, and he waked wholly, and, still lying quiet, considered the strange room filled with the bells and the sun of the winter's day. "Where have I struck now?" he inquired; and as last night returned abruptly upon his mind, he raised himself on his arm.

There sat Responsibility in a chair, washed clean and dressed, watching him.

"You're awful late," said Responsibility. "But I weren't a-going without telling you good-bye."

"Go!" exclaimed Lin. "Go where? Yu' surely ain't leavin' me to eat breakfast alone?" The cow-puncher made his voice very plaintive. Set Responsibility free after all his trouble to catch him? This was more than he could do!

"I've got to go. If I'd thought you'd want for me to stay—why, you said you was a-going by the early train!"

"But the durned thing's got away on me," said Lin, smiling sweetly from the bed.

"If I hadn't a-promised them—"

"Who?"

"Sidney Ellis and Pete Goode. Why, you know them; you grubbed with them."

"Shucks!"

"We're a-going to have fun to-day."

"Oh!"

"For it's Christmas, an' we've bought some good cigars, an' Pete says he'll learn me sure. O' course I've smoked some, you know. But

I'd just as leaves stayed with you if I'd only knowed sooner. I wish you lived here. Did you smoke whole big cigars when you was beginning?"

"Do you like flapjacks and maple syrup?" inquired the artful McLean. "That's what I'm figuring on inside twenty minutes."

"Twenty minutes! If they'd wait—"

"See here, Bill. They've quit expecting yu', don't yu' think? I ought to waked, yu' see, but I slep' and slep', and kep' yu' from meetin' your engagements, yu' see—for you couldn't go, of course. A man couldn't treat a man that way now, could he?"

"Course he couldn't," said Billy, brightening.

"And they wouldn't wait, yu' see. They wouldn't fool away Christmas, that only comes onced a year, kickin' their heels and sayin' 'Where's Billy?' They'd say, 'Bill has sure made other arrangements, which he'll explain to us at his leesyure.' And they'd skip with the cigars."

The advocate paused, effectively, and from his bolster regarded Billy with a convincing eye.

"That's so," said Billy.

"And where would yu' be then, Bill? In the street, out of friends, out of Christmas, and left both ways, no tobaccer and no flapjacks. Now, Bill, what do yu' say to us putting up a Christmas deal together? Just you and me?"

"I'd like that," said Billy. "Is it all day?"

"I was thinkin' of all day," said Lin. "I'll not make yu' do anything yu'd rather not."

"Ah, they can smoke without me," said Billy, with sudden acrimony. "I'll see 'em to-morro'."

"That's you!" cried Mr. McLean. "Now, Bill, you hustle down and tell them to keep a table for us. I'll get my clothes on and follow yu'."

The boy went, and Mr. McLean procured hot water and dressed himself, tying his scarf with great care. "Wished I'd a clean shirt," said he. "But I don't look very bad. Shavin' yesterday afternoon was a good move." He picked up the arrow-head and the kinni-kinnic, and was particular to store them in his safest pocket. "I ain't sure whether you're crazy or not," said he to the man in the looking-glass. "I 'ain't never been sure." And he slammed the door and went down-stairs.

He found young Bill on guard over a table for four, with all the chairs tilted against it as warning to strangers. No one sat at any other table or came into the room, for it was late, and the place quite emptied of breakfasters, and the several entertained waiters had gathered behind Billy's important-looking back. Lin provided a thorough meal, and Billy pronounced the flannel cakes superior to flapjacks, which were not upon the bill of fare.

"I'd like to see you often," said he. "I'll come and see you if you don't live too far."

"That's the trouble," said the cow-puncher. "I do. Awful far." He stared out of the window.

"Well, I might come some time. I wish you'd write me a letter. Can you write?"

"What's that? Can I write? Oh, yes."

"I can write, an' I can read, too. I've been to school in Sidney, Nebraska, an' Magaw, Kansas, an' Salt Lake—that's the finest town except Denver."

Billy fell into that cheerful strain of comment which, unreplied to, yet goes on contented and self-sustaining, while Mr. McLean gave amiable signs of assent, but chiefly looked out of the window; and when the now interested waiter said respectfully that he desired to close the room, they went out to the office, where the money was got out of the safe and the bill paid.

The streets were full of the bright sun, and seemingly at Denver's gates stood the mountains sparkling; an air crisp and pleasant wafted from their peaks; no smoke hung among the roofs, and the sky spread wide over the city without a stain; it was holiday up among the chimneys and tall buildings, and down among the quiet ground-stories below as well; and presently from their scattered pinnacles through the town the bells broke out against the jocund silence of the morning.

"Don't you like music?" inquired Billy.

"Yes," said Lin.

Ladies with their husbands and children were passing and meeting, orderly yet gayer than if it were only Sunday, and the salutations of Christmas came now and again to the cow-puncher's ears; but to-day, possessor of his own share in this, Lin looked at everyone with a sort of friendly challenge, and young Billy talked along beside him.

"Don't you think we could go in here?" Billy asked. A church door was open, and the rich organ sounded through to the pavement. "They've good music here, an' they keep it up without much talking between. I've been in lots of times."

They went in and sat to hear the music. Better than the organ, it seemed to them, were the harmonious voices raised from somewhere outside, like unexpected visitants; and the pair sat in their back seat, too deep in listening to the processional hymn to think of rising in decent imitation of those around them. The crystal melody of the refrain especially reached their understandings, and when for the fourth time "Shout the glad tidings, exultingly sing," pealed forth and ceased, both the delighted faces fell.

"Don't you wish there was more?" Billy whispered.

"Wish there was a hundred verses," answered Lin.

But canticles and responses followed, with so little talking between them they were held spell-bound, seldom thinking to rise or kneel. Lin's eyes roved over the church, dwelling upon the pillars in their evergreen, the flowers and leafy wreaths, the texts of white and gold. "Peace, good-will towards men," he read. "That's so. Peace and good-will. Yes, that's so. I expect they got that somewheres in the Bible. It's awful good, and you'd never think of it yourself."

There was a touch on his arm, and a woman handed a book to him. "This is the hymn we have now," she whispered, gently; and Lin, blushing scarlet, took it passively without a word. He and Billy stood up and held the book together, dutifully reading the words:

"It came upon the midnight clear,
    That glorious song of old,
From angels bending near the earth
    To touch their harps of gold;
Peace on the earth—"

This tune was more beautiful than all, and Lin lost himself in it, until he found Billy recalling him with a finger upon the words, the concluding ones:

"And the whole world sent back the song
    Which now the angels sing."

The music rose and descended to its lovely and simple end; and, for a second time in Denver, Lin brushed a hand across his eyes. He turned his face from his neighbor, frowning crossly; and since the heart has reasons which Reason does not know, he seemed to himself a fool; but when the service was over and he came out, he repeated again, "'Peace and good-will.' When I run on to the Bishop of Wyoming I'll tell him if he'll preach on them words I'll be there."

"Couldn't we shoot your pistol now?" asked Billy.

"Sure, boy. Ain't yų' hungry, though?"

"No. I wish we were away off up there. Don't you?"

"The mountains? They look pretty, so white! A heap better 'n houses. Why, we'll go there! There's trains to Golden. We'll shoot around among the foothills."

To Golden they immediately went, and after a meal there, wandered in the open country until the cartridges were gone, the sun was low, and Billy was walked off his young heels—a truth he learned complete in one horrid moment, and battled to conceal.

"Lame!" he echoed, angrily. "I ain't."

"Shucks! said Lin, after the next ten steps, "You are, and both feet."

"Tell you, there's stones here, an' I'm just a-skipping them."

Lin, briefly, took the boy in his arms and carried him to Golden. "I'm played out myself," he said, sitting in the hotel and looking lugubriously at Billy on a bed. "And I ain't fit to have charge of a hog." He came and put his hand on the boy's head.

"I'm not sick," said the cripple. "I tell you I'm bully. You wait an' see me eat dinner."

But Lin had hot water and cold water and salt, and was an hour upon his knees bathing the hot feet. And then Billy could not eat dinner!

There was a doctor in Golden; but in spite of his light prescription and most reasonable observations, Mr. McLean passed a foolish night of vigil, while Billy slept, quite well at first, and, as the hours passed, better and better. In the morning he was entirely brisk, though stiff.

"I couldn't work quick to-day," he said. "But I guess one day won't lose me my trade."

"How d' yu' mean?" asked Lin.

"Why, I've got regulars, you know. Sidney Ellis an' Pete Goode has theirs, an' we don't cut each other. I've got Mr. Daniels an' Mr. Fisher an' lots, an' if you lived in Denver, I'd shine your boots every day for nothing. I wished you lived in Denver."

"Shine my boots? Yu'l' never! And yu' don't black Daniels or Fisher, or any of the outfit."

"Why, I'm doing first-rate," said Billy, surprised at the swearing into which Mr. McLean now burst. "An' I ain't big enough to get to make money at any other job."

"I want to see that engine-man," muttered Lin. "I don't like your smokin' friend."

"Pete Goode? Why, he's awful smart. Don't you think he's smart?"

"Smart's nothin'," observed Mr. McLean.

"Pete has learned me and Sidney a lot," pursued Billy, engagingly.

"I'll bet he has!" growled the cow-puncher; and again Billy was taken aback at his language.

It was not so simple, this case. To the perturbed mind of Mr. McLean it grew less simple, during that day at Golden, while Billy recovered, and talked, and ate his innocent meals. The cow-puncher was far too wise to think for a single moment of restoring the runaway to his debauched and shiftless parents. Possessed of some imagination, he went through a scene in which he appeared at the Lusk threshold with Billy and forgiveness, and intruded upon a conjugal assault and battery. "Shucks!" said he. "The kid would be off again inside a week. And I don't want him there, anyway."

Denver, upon the following day, saw the little bootblack again at his corner, with his trade not lost; but near him stood a tall, singular man, with hazel eyes and a sulky expression. And citizens during that week noticed, as a new sight in the streets, the tall man and the little boy walking together. Sometimes they would be in shops. The boy seemed as happy as possible, talking constantly, while the man seldom said a word, and his face was serious.

Upon New Year's Eve Governor Barker was overtaken by Mr. McLean riding a horse up Hill Street, Cheyenne.

"Hello!" said Barker, staring humorously through his glasses. "Have a good drunk?"

"Changed my mind," said Lin, grinning. "Proves I've got one. Struck Christmas all right, though."

"Who's your friend?" inquired his Excellency.

"This is Mister Billy Lusk. Him and me have agreed that towns ain't nice to live in. If Judge Henry's foreman and his wife won't board him at Sunk Creek—why, I'll fix it somehow."

The cow-puncher and his Responsibility rode on together toward the open plain.

"Suffering Moses!" remarked his Excellency.

# SOURCES

"Em'ly," by Owen Wister. From *The Virginian: A Horseman of the Plains* (The Macmillan Co., 1911; Wister's revision of his 1902 original).

"Winter Weather," by Theodore Roosevelt. From *Ranch Life and the Hunting-Trail* (The Century Co., 1888).

"A Rescue," by William MacLeod Raine. From *Wyoming, A Story of the Outdoor West* (G.W. Dillingham Company, 1908).

"A Rodeo at Los Ojos," by Frederic Remington. From *Pony Tracks* (1895; University of Oklahoma Press, 1961).

"Buckskin," by Clarence E. Mulford. From *Bar-20* (1907).

"Estes Park, Colorado" by Isabella L. Bird. From *A Lady's Life in the Rocky Mountains* (G. P. Putnam's Sons, 1879).

"Gold-Mounted Guns," by F. R. Buckley. From *The Redbook Magazine* (1922).

"Cowboy Golf," by Zane Grey. From *The Light of Western Stars* (Harper & Brothers, 1914).

"Love Finds Its Hour" by B. M. Bower. From *Chip of the Flying U* (G.W. Dillingham,1906).

"Catching a Maverick," by Frank Benton. From *Cowboy Life on the Sidetrack* (Frank Benton, 1903).

"Hearts and Crosses," by O. Henry. From *Heart of the West* (Doubleday, Page & Company, 1904).

"The Cow-Boy," by Bill Nye. From *Remarks By Bill Nye* (M. W. Hazen Company, 1886).

"On Cowboys," by Stewart Edward White. From *The Mountains* (McClure, Phillips & Company, 1904).

"Bransford Meets Aughinbaugh," by Eugene Manlove Rhodes. From *Good Men and True*, Chapter 1 (Henry Holt, 1910).

"Wild Bill Hickok," by Emerson Hough. From *The Story of the Outlaw* (1906).

"Lassiter," by Zane Grey. From *Riders of the Purple Sage* (Harper & Brothers, 1912).

"The Caballero's Way," by O. Henry. From *Heart of the West* (Doubleday, Page & Company, 1904).

"In Search of Christmas," by Owen Wister. From *Lin McLean* (A. L. Burt Company, 1897).

# ABOUT THE EDITOR

**Michael McCoy** is a freelance writer and the managing editor of *Greater Yellowstone* magazine. A native of Wyoming—the Cowboy State—he is the author of ten books on travel and the outdoors, including *Journey to the Northern Rockies* and *Travel Historic America: The Wild West* (Globe Pequot). His travel and recreation pieces have appeared in numerous magazines and compilations by National Geographic, The Discovery Channel, and other publishers. He lives in the morning shadow of the Tetons, outside Victor, Idaho.